LISTENING IN THE CLASSROOM

TEACHING STUDENTS HOW TO LISTEN

MARNIE REED AND TAMARA JONES, EDITORS

tesol press

www.tesol.org/bookstore

TESOL International Association
1925 Ballenger Avenue
Alexandria, VA 22314 USA
www.tesol.org

Group Director, Content and Learning: Myrna Jacobs
Copy and Production Editor: Tomiko Breland
Manuscript Reviewers: Elsa Anderson, Hind Elyas, Patricia George, Neda Sahranavard, Sharon Tjaden-Glass
Cover Design: Citrine Sky Design
Design and Layout: Capitol Communications, LLC

Recommended citation:
Reed, M., & Jones, T. (Eds.). (2022). *Listening in the classroom: Teaching students how to listen.* TESOL Press.

ISBN 978-1-945351-90-7
ISBN (ebook) 978-1-945351-91-4
Library of Congress Control Number 2019956786

TABLE OF CONTENTS

FOREWORD

CHRISTINE C. M. GOH

When I was a doctoral student researching second language (L2) listening, the literature available was limited for both research and teaching. Twenty-five years on, it has clearly expanded. Many topics that Rubin (1994) identified as internal and external factors that affected listening are now extensively examined, discussed, and debated. These are positive signs that the field of L2 listening is maturing. We see more research articles in a wide array of academic journals. There is also more evidence about ways of teaching L2 listening that work or work in limited ways. Although we still need more research to draw conclusive findings about various aspects of L2 listening, the research and theoretical insights that we now have offer many promising avenues for researchers and practitioners to pursue.

This increase in interest in L2 listening is good news not only for teachers helping L2 learners to listen well, but also for all who are interested in language learners' overall L2 acquisition. Though good listening skills are necessary for oral interaction, L2 listening is intrinsically important because it can facilitate L2 acquisition. Through the processing of comprehensible input, learners can acquire new vocabulary and grammatical knowledge, all contributing to better proficiency in the language.

Language learners who listen well are able to control their listening sufficiently to obtain the information they need and arrive at adequate interpretations of what they hear. Listening well requires learners to listen flexibly using different skills according to their purpose for listening. For example, they can identify specific details when required, grasp key ideas and gist when only a broad understanding of a message is needed, and make inferences to draw meanings when these are missing or not explicitly stated. When there is a problem with comprehension, they are also able to apply strategies to improve their understanding of the message.

Teachers who want to develop learners' ability to listen well need to devote much effort and attention to the teaching process. Many teachers today would agree that we should teach students how to listen and not just have students do listening activities. In other words, listening instruction must move away from merely checking students' understanding (product of listening) to engaging students in learning how to listen (process of listening). The focus of a process-based approach to listening instruction is the learner. Though there is growing research on process-based instruction, the reality is that there is still a gap between research and theory published in academic journals and the day-to-day practice in the classroom (Graham, 2017). There is an urgent need to translate promising research findings and theory into practical teaching ideas.

This is where this book, *Listening in the Classroom*, makes a valuable contribution. The authors, all well-versed in research and solidly grounded in practice, offer pedagogical insights and practical ideas drawn from their knowledge of the field. The chapters are written in teacher-friendly language and focus on a variety of topics that include developing metacognitive awareness; noticing mistakes in listening; attending to phonological features in spoken utterances; segmenting and parsing speech; perceiving and recognizing words; applying metacognitive strategies, such as prediction; recognizing discourse features; taking academic notes; and listening beyond classroom listening tasks. Teachers can apply this wide array of ideas to provide learners with much needed scaffolding and guidance as they develop their listening competence.

In the early days of listening instruction in the 1950s, 60s, and even into the 70s, language learners were given little help and guidance on how to improve their comprehension. Instead of learning how to listen, they were tested for their comprehension of listening passages, many of which were written texts read aloud. When communicative language teaching became popular in the 70s and 80s, listening activities became more enjoyable and meaningful. Learners no longer listened to texts to answer comprehension questions. Instead, they engaged in oral communication activities where listening was task relevant and purposeful. Special listening activities were introduced for learners to practice their listening through a variety of individual or pair/group tasks, such as information completion, note-taking, jigsaw listening, and so on. Teachers also brought real-world or authentic texts into the classroom.

With the focus on listening for communicative purposes, scholars identified taxonomies and lists of listening skills deemed necessary for communication. These became valuable resources for curriculum developers, textbook writers, and teachers. Listening activities were reoriented from a focus on text comprehension to one that promoted listening as part of oral communication, resembling more real-world listening tasks. Teachers planned and carried out lessons with clear instructional objectives on developing specific enabling skills, such as listening for detail and listening for gist. This approach continues to be important today.

In spite of these new and interesting methods for teaching listening, many learners still had difficulty with their listening development. Encouraged by their teachers, many tried to improve by listening to more audio and video texts outside class. Many others, however, were quite literally left to their own devices, receiving little guidance on how to manage their listening. Some were asked to write summaries or reports of what they listen to, and so the listening practice outside class took on another disguised form of testing. Learners may also have experienced negative emotions, such as discouragement and anxiety, when they did not see success. What was needed was a reorientation from the tasks to the learners themselves. A learner-orientated approach for L2 listening began to emerge with the learner strategy movement in the 80s and early 90s. It focused on understanding what language learners could do themselves to have greater agency over their own language use and learning. Learners learnt strategies to facilitate their language learning and use. Strategy instruction continues to be an important area of focus in many language programmes today (Chamot & Harris, 2019).

Teaching learners how to learn was particularly urgent for L2 listening because of the transient nature of spoken input. Because listening occurs over a short duration of time, learners were often unaware of and had little control over their listening processes. A learner-oriented approach would help learners understand various processes of learning to listen and not be limited to learning to use strategies, important though these are. Just as learners who learn to write have to focus on the mechanics of writing, the language system, and their own thinking processes, learners who learn to listen must focus on different elements in their listening process. By breaking down the task of listening into smaller manageable parts, whether they are top-down (knowledge/schema-driven), bottom-up (text/sound-driven), or social-interactional processes, we enable learners to attend to and work on specific aspects of their listening. This approach also reduces learner anxiety and increases their confidence.

One way of framing such an approach is through the lens of learner metacognition, or learners thinking about their own thinking and learning. Metacognition is a psychological construct that can drive the learning of any skill or knowledge, including an L2 (Wenden, 1987). A metacognitive approach is not a top-down approach, as it is sometimes thought to be. Rather it is a way of framing learning and offering teachers a systematic way of organizing and planning learning activities that can develop learners' person knowledge, task knowledge, and strategy knowledge. A metacognitive approach to listening instruction enables learners to develop greater metacognitive awareness in three ways. These are (1) recognizing their own listening problems, strengths, and learning preferences (person knowledge); (2) understanding the nature and demands of L2 listening comprehension in top-down, bottom-up, and social processes (task knowledge); and (3) identifying and managing strategies to facilitate comprehension and listening development over time (Vandergrift & Goh, 2012).

Listening development is a long and gradual process. Even though studies may show a particular method works for a group of learners, we need to be patient in applying them in our own classroom. This is because we are dealing with students who each come with singular traits, backgrounds, and learning experiences, and because classroom environments are dynamic. When something does not seem to work, it does not mean it is a wrong or ineffective method. What does not work with one group of students may work well for another group, or work better when tried a second time with the same group. At the end of the day, what is important for teaching L2 listening is for teachers to develop our repertoire of teaching methods and techniques and to experiment with ways of delivering them. Not one method or technique is going to help our learners, but rather a combination of them. The various chapters in this book have offered us just such a variety of options.

I want to congratulate the editors, Marnie Reed and Tamara Jones, for putting together such a timely and valuable volume, and all contributors to this book for bringing their work to the larger TESOL community. I am confident that this book will be an important reference for not only teachers of English, but also L2 teachers of other languages. For our language learners, being able to listen well is key to their personal, academic, and professional success. We need everyone's effort and commitment to take the teaching of L2 listening to new heights for their sake.

Christine C. M. Goh
National Institute of Education
Nanyang Technological University, Singapore

References

Chamot, A. U., & Harris, V. (2019). *Learning strategy instruction in the language classroom: Issues and implementation.* Multilingual Matters.

Graham, S. (2017). Research into practice: Listening strategies in an instructed classroom setting. *Language Teaching, 50*(1), 107–119. https://doi.org/10.1017/S0261444816000306

Rubin, J. (1994). A review of second language listening comprehension research. *Modern Language Journal, 78*(2) 199–221. https://doi.org/10.2307/329010

Vandergrift, L., & Goh, C. C. M. (2012). *Teaching and learning second language listening: Metacognition in action.* Routledge.

Wenden, A. (1987). Metacognition: An expanded view of the cognitive abilities of L2 learners. *Language Learning, 37,* 573–594. https://doi.org/10.1111/j.1467-1770.1987.tb00585.x

CHRISTINE C. M. GOH is professor of education (Linguistics & Language Education) at the National Institute of Education, Nanyang Technological University, Singapore. A qualified English teacher, Christine is passionate about second language education, particularly in listening and speaking, learner metacognition, and language teacher cognition. She publishes extensively in these areas and is frequently invited to speak and lead workshops at conferences for second language researchers and practitioners.

ACKN@WLEDGEMENT

Enduring gratitude to Steven J. Molinsky for enduring mentoring and inspiration.

INTRODUCTION

TAMARA JONES

Why Do We Need to *Teach* Listening?

Listening as an Essential Skill

As a Russian student living in Moscow in the early 1990s, I quickly reached the conclusion that though listening was the most difficult skill for me to improve, it was also the most crucial. My reading and writing skills were very weak, but there was rarely that sense of immediacy which always accompanied listening. If it took me whole minutes to sound out a street address in my map, it usually didn't matter. Similarly, I could take as long as I needed to address an envelope or write a note to a friend. Speaking was trickier because it always happened in real time, so I couldn't pause a conversation for 5 minutes to formulate a sentence in my mind.

But, I was still in control of my speech. I could choose to speak, or, if I didn't know how to say what I was thinking, I could remain silent. I could steer the conversation toward topics that I had the vocabulary and grammar to talk about, and even when I could only string words together into grammatically fraught phrases, I usually got my point across. Listening, however, was different. I had no control over the vocabulary choices, syntactic complexity, or speed of the speaker. Conversations always seemed to progress at lightning speed, and I often found myself just getting the gist of a topic only to find that my friends had moved on to talk about something new. Until I was able to improve my listening skills, I felt like I wasn't able to fully participate in my exciting expat life.

Clearly, language learners need to develop listening skills. Quite simply, it is the skill learners use the most; according to Nunan (1998), students spend 50% of their second language (L2) time listening. In addition, listening facilitates the emergence of other skills. Comprehensible input can encourage noticing (Nation & Newton, 2009), and when English is the language of English instruction, as it often is, "common sense tells us that we can learn nothing from listening to a language unless we understand it" (Richards, 2005, p. 88). Likewise, students need strong listening proficiency to learn things in their mainstream classes, where "some information will be presented visually through course books and on the whiteboard; but most will be presented through the voice of the teacher" (Field, 2008a, p. 3), as well as in their workplaces and personal lives. Finally, a lack of listening strategies can lead to anxiety for our learners, which, in turn, negatively impacts their overall comprehension (Elkhafaifi, 2005; Mills et al., 2006).

Unfortunately, the importance of developing strong listening proficiency is undermined by the fact that it is a difficult skill to master. Speech comes at the listener in an unbroken stream and listeners must break the stream into groups of sounds; recognize the groups as words; attach meaning to the words; understand how the words are related to each other; and use knowledge of the language, the words, and the context to clear up any ambiguities. This complex process happens instantaneously, invisibly and, for proficient listeners, generally unconsciously. However, for weaker listeners, there are many opportunities for breakdown in this process. Further confounding the issue for English language teachers is that we can't see where the breakdown occurred or if there even was a breakdown. Students will frequently report understanding instructions even when they don't because in many cultures, asking your teacher to explain something again is insulting, as it implies the teacher did not explain it well the first time (Mendelsohn, 2002). As well, students may think they've understood and are often reluctant to abandon their guess (Broersma & Cutler, 2008; Field, 2008b). Therefore, it's important for teachers to remember that when they are listening to a text along with their students, their experience will be vastly different from what their students are experiencing (Cauldwell, 2018), so it can be difficult to know how to help or if help is even necessary.

The Default to a Product-Oriented Approach

Of all the skills, listening always felt most to me like the final frontier. I had strategies for teaching students vocabulary and grammar, I balanced fluency and accuracy instruction in speaking and writing class, and I felt confident teaching students bottom-up and top-down reading strategies. However, for many years, listening felt a bit mysterious. It all seemed to happen inside my students' heads, and they either got the comprehension questions right or wrong. It appeared to have very little to do with me, other than I was the person who pressed "play" on the tape recorder.

No matter what proficiency level my students were, from absolute beginner to advanced, whenever we encountered a listening activity in the textbook, we'd do the provided prelistening activities; we might even brainstorm some potential vocabulary associated with the listening topic. Then, I'd play the recording, and my students would do the textbook comprehension activity. We'd check the answers and then move on to the postlistening conversation questions. For years, I was pretty content with this product-oriented approach. Sure, my students occasionally got frustrated when they got a question wrong, but I'd play the recording again for them, pausing at their mistake, and assume that all confusion had been cleared up. Sadly, rather than providing my learners with instruction and practice that developed their listening skills, I had been really just testing their listening comprehension (Vandergrift, 2004). I simply didn't know there was any other way to "do" listening in a language learning context.

Unfortunately, many other English language educators may have had a similar experience. Very often "listening activities in many classrooms tend to focus on the outcome of listening; listeners are asked to record or repeat the details they have heard, or to explain the meaning of a passage they have heard" (Vandergrift & Goh, 2012, p. 4). Certainly, many of the authors in this volume describe employing a traditional approach to teaching listening until they realized that it wasn't working well for their students. Graham et al. (2014) found that teachers often implement a product-oriented approach to listening instruction, even though they believe that the teaching of listening is important. Moreover, Siegel (2014) revealed that the English as a foreign language teachers in his study tended to adopt a product-oriented approach when incorporating listening into their lessons and that the listening comprehension questions that are so familiar to many of us actually occupied 70% of the time devoted to "teaching" listening.

This imbalance may be partially due to the fact that many English language teaching (ELT) professionals have comparably little exposure to a variety of approaches for teaching listening strategies in their MATESOL and teacher training programs. Despite specific training in how to teach listening emerging as the number one "need" in Henrichsen's (1983) survey of educators and employers, it appears to receive relatively little attention in MATESOL curricula. Uber Grosse (1991) found that in the majority of TESOL programs she surveyed, while the teaching of writing, reading, and speaking received a fair amount of class time, listening pedagogy received almost the least coverage of all the topics on the syllabus, coming in ninth out of 10 topics. Perhaps this explains the findings of a study conducted by Emerick (2019), which found "language instructors, by and large, believed that direct, explicit listening instruction is essential in developing L2 listening skills, yet they report to only rarely provide process-oriented or metacognitive instruction for their students" (p. 115).

Another likely reason for this overreliance on the product-oriented approach to listening instruction is that most ELT materials provide product-oriented practice activities that require students to answer listening comprehension questions. Even though research into developing aspects of L2 listening acquisition has emerged in recent years (notably Field, 2008a; Brown, 2011; and Vandergrift & Goh, 2012), in a 2016 survey of several popular ELT course books, Nguyen and Abbott found that 92% of the listening activities in the texts were still product oriented. Though it is often the case that course materials do not reflect the findings of research in language acquisition, it is particularly problematic when it comes to listening instruction because many teachers haven't learned how to teach students to listen in their preservice training and, therefore, rely heavily on the approaches they see in their course books for "methodological support" (McGrath, 2013, p. 5).

What Teachers Need to Know

The mismatch between what learners need when it comes to developing strong listening skills and the limitations of many teacher training programs and published course materials has left TESOL practitioners with the tasks of figuring out what skills are necessary for students to learn to develop their listening proficiency and to create classroom lessons and activities that push learners toward this goal. We believe this book can assist instructors with these tasks. However, to fully access the suggestions in the following chapters, readers must understand several key terms.

Top-Down Listening Skills

Seasoned travelers may be familiar with the notoriously staticky announcements that pilots often make from the cockpit. Generally, pilots communicate messages about things like the travelling time and cruising altitude. We rarely panic when we can't hear every word clearly in these announcements because we are using our prior knowledge about air travel and pilot announcements to fill in the gaps. In other words, we are using our top-down processing skills to make sense of what we are hearing.

> Top-down processes involve the listener going from the whole—their prior knowledge and their content and rhetorical schemata—to the parts. In other words, the listener uses what they know of the context of communication to predict what the message will contain and uses parts of the message to confirm, correct or add to this. (Nation & Newton, 2009, p. 40)

Bottom-Up Listening Skills

When I first moved to Korea, I'd had absolutely no experience with the language. When I sat with my Korean colleagues, I felt like the sounds they were making simply washed over me; I had no way to even break the acoustic stream into identifiable sounds, much less understand how the sounds combined to form words and phrases. All the background knowledge in the world couldn't help me follow their conversation. In short, my bottom-up processing skills in Korean were nonexistent.

Bottom-up processing describes how a listener makes sense of an acoustic cluster. Just as readers use their bottom-up skills to decode print—identifying letters, understanding how they fit together to make words, and understanding how the words combine into sentences and paragraphs to tell a story or argue a point—"listeners draw primarily on linguistic knowledge, which includes phonological knowledge (phonemes, stress, intonation and other sound adjustments made by speakers to facilitate speech production), lexical knowledge and syntactic knowledge (grammar) of the target language" (Vandergrift & Goh, 2012, p. 18). Though strong listeners make use of both top-down and bottom-up processes, less competent listeners tend to rely more heavily on their bottom-up skills (Tsui & Fullilove, 1998).

Syllables

When I was in China on a tour of Beijing, the tour guide began telling an anecdote about a *sin-tist.* As I was listening, I was thinking, "What in the world is a sin-tist?" Within a few minutes I could understand that the speaker was telling a story about a *scientist,* but because he had pronounced the word with two syllables instead of three, I had a hard time following him. Language teachers often refer to syllables as the beats in a word. Another way to identify a syllable is to listen for the vowel sounds in a word. Teaching students about syllables is key for listening skill development because "learners accustomed to different phonological rules may not hear the syllable divisions in the same way" (Gilbert, 2008, p. 4).

IPA

"I have a cut. She is black and cute. I love her." I have sometimes found that when students make pronunciation errors, like not opening their mouths and dropping their jaw sufficiently so they are saying *cut* instead of *cat,* it can be difficult to correct them. They may not even be able to hear the difference between *cat* and *cut* if one or both of the vowel sounds don't exist in their native language. The subsequent conversation might sound like this:

> Teacher: "Not *cut, cat.*"
> Student: "Yes, *cut.*"

This exchange is probably familiar to many teachers. If students have trouble differentiating between sounds in English, having a way to show them which sound you are referring to can be helpful. The International Phonetic Alphabet (IPA) is one way of visually depicting sounds because it provides "a consistent one-to-one relationship between a written symbol and the sound it represent[s]" (Celce-Murcia et al., 2010, p. 3). There are several versions of the IPA, as well as other phonetic transcription systems. To ease confusion, teachers and their students will generally want to refer to the phonetic transcription system that appears in their textbooks; for this book, we've used the transcription system found in Celce-Murcia et al. (2010), for which a transcription key can be found on the last page of this book.

Lexical Segmentation

I grew up listening to an American song that was written in the 1940s but has since become a children's song, "Mairzy Doats." The song's lyrics are seemingly nonsensical: "Mairzy doats and dozy doats and liddle lamzy divey. A kiddle edivey do. Wooden chew?" I remember thinking they were so funny as I sang the song as a child. It wasn't until I was much older that I realized how the songwriters were playing with connected speech. In fact, if we want the sentences to make sense, we would read them as: "Mares eat oats and does eat oats and little lambs eat ivy. A kid will eat ivy, too. Wouldn't you?" The song lyrics demonstrate how English speakers link words in natural speech through *elision* and *assimilation*. Elision occurs when a sound is omitted as two words are connected; for instance in the song, the word *will* is contracted to [əl] and the sound /w/ is elided. Assimilation describes the transformation of two sounds into one. For example, in the song, the words *wouldn't you* are linked. The /t/ and the end of *wouldn't* and the /y/ at the beginning *you* are assimilated into the sound /ʧ/. The song also exemplifies how that can cause issues with listening comprehension, because "students are often stymied by what is arguably the commonest perceptual cause of breakdown of understanding: namely, lexical segmentation, the identification of words in connected speech" (Field, 2003, p. 327).

Weak Forms

A student in my English as a second language class was struggling with tech issues and had run into trouble when attempting to do some recording homework I had assigned the class. I gave him some troubleshooting instructions and the following week in the class I asked him if they had solved the problem. He responded "I can do the recording now." However, he said each word clearly, and as a result I couldn't tell if he was saying "I can do the recording" or "I can't do the recording."

When proficient speakers talk naturally, we often reduce some words, often function words, such as pronouns, articles, prepositions, and affirmative modal verbs (e.g., *can*). We tend to say content words, for instance nouns, adjectives, adverbs, and negatives (e.g., *can't*) more clearly. Proficient listeners' ears are trained to listen for stressed words, and they use what they know about the context, syntax, and grammar to fill in the gaps caused by the reduced function words. For instance, if the student had applied English speech rhythm when he said "I can DO the RECORDING NOW," I would have understood that the problem had been solved, but because he said *can* clearly, it sounded more like *can't*, and I was confused. Cauldwell (2018) refers to the syllables that occur in speech between stressed syllables as *squeeze zones* because the reduced syllables are squeezed between the clearly pronounced words. Not using squeeze zones can cause problems in speaking, and it's also true for listening, because "when listeners do not attend to (or are unaware of) subtle phonetic differences in English, communication can break down in interesting ways" (Celce-Murcia et al., 2010, p. 375).

Parsing

There is a funny meme that exists on the internet that contains the contrast between the sentences *Let's eat grandma.* and *Let's eat, grandma.* Of course, the humor stems from the fact that without the comma, the speaker is suggesting an unthinkable act; however, with the comma, the speaker is merely inviting a family member to a meal. These sentences not only look different, they sound different, too. The first sentence is said as one chunk or *thought group*. The second is broken into two chunks or *thought groups* by a little pause and change in intonation. A thought group is a "discrete stretch of speech that forms a semantically and grammatically coherent segment of discourse" (Celce-Murcia et al., 2010, p. 221).

Proficient listeners parse speech into thought groups using their knowledge of English. Sentence parsing requires knowledge of segmental phonology, including phonotactics (the permissible sound sequences in a language) and connected speech processes. A lack of this skill may result in learner failure to grasp the locution, the utterance itself. For instance, if we were to hear the sentence, "Let's eat, grandma," we would use what we know about pausing and intonation changes in English to understand that the speaker was inviting their grandmother to eat. If were unable to parse successfully, of course, we would be horrified by what we understood the speaker to be suggesting. The ability to parse a stream of speech into appropriate thought groups is extremely beneficial for English learners because it helps them comprehend and remember more of what they have heard (Harley, 2000).

Metacognition

When I moved to Belgium, I dusted off my high school French for daily encounters. My husband, however, studied German when he was younger and barely knew any French beyond what he learned in his workplace-sponsored orientation course. Interestingly, I noted that whenever we were out and about together, shopkeepers tended to direct their utterance toward him instead of me because he appeared to be the more proficient listener. This was infuriating, but it really caused me to think about what was going on. I reflected on the exchanges and came to understand that my husband is a calmer listener; because he was expecting to understand nothing, he was pleasantly surprised when he was able to follow what someone was saying. On the other hand, I was putting more effort into listening, making me an anxious conversationalist. Once I realized that, I tried to remember to relax more when I was listening. As a result, my comprehension actually improved. By thinking about my listening challenges, I was able to improve my skills. "Metacognition is, as it were, the ability to step back from the intense activities of learning, problem solving and communicating to becoming an observer, a critique [*sic*] and a commentator of one's own endeavors" (Goh, 2019, p. 2). If L2 listeners can be encouraged to reflect on what they know about how they listen, what they know about the listening task, and what they know about strategy use, their listening proficiency will increase (Vandergrift et al., 2006).

Listening is a complex process, and, because it happens inside our ears and brains, it can be incredibly challenging for language instructors to teach students how to listen and it can be difficult for students to identify what is going wrong when they don't understand. The overreliance that many published ELT listening resources place on top-down skill development and the overrepresentation of product-oriented listening practice in our classrooms have resulted in frustration among both teachers and students.

Fortunately, "research has also shown that systematic listening instruction can help improve students' ability to comprehend spoken language, which in turn can help enhance the acquisition process" (Renandya & Hu, 2019, p. 1). In other words, when we start to incorporate bottom-up skill development and metacognitive awareness-raising activities into our lessons, students can improve the skills that lead to increased comprehension for conversations, lectures, and extensive listening. "Efficient processing at the phoneme and syllable levels leads to accurate lexical segmentation at the word level. After words have been distinguished between one another, they are grouped into chunks by parsing processes at the syntactic and intonation levels" (Goh & Wallace, 2019, p. 1).

How This Book Can Help

The goal of this book is to provide teachers with research-based activities and teaching tips so that you can incorporate more listening instruction and focused practice into your lessons. As Wallace points out in Chapter 1 and Sheppard describes in Chapter 12, developing metacognitive awareness is a key aspect of L2 listening proficiency. After all, "without establishing why the errors occurred, we have no means of assisting learners to get it right next time" (Field, 2008a, p. 81).

Further chapters deal with the business of making meaning from a steady stream of unedited and therefore messy spontaneous speech. The activities presented by Jones and Siegel in Chapters 2 and 3, respectively, help students listen at the word level. In Chapter 4, Bogorevich and Kia suggest activities for helping students identify words in connected speech, a process referred to as lexical segmentation, which is "a major challenge for L2 listeners" (Vandergrift & Goh, 2012, p. 21).

Chapters 5, 6, 7, and 8 further propose additional strategies for helping students make sense of this "jungle of spontaneous speech, where the vegetation is crushed together in a messy and unruly manner which is quite unlike any orderly garden arrangement" (Cauldwell, 2014, p. 41), including using their knowledge of grammar (Rimmer, Chapter 5), understanding the message implied in a speaker's intonation (Reed, Chapter 6), listening for weak forms (Gay, Chapter 7) and making use of thought groups to boost comprehension and retention (McAndrews, Chapter 8).

Expanding from the metaphorical trees to the forest, in Chapter 9, Ryan recommends activities designed to help students participate more comfortably in conversations by strengthening their ability to predict turns and anticipate responses; in Chapter 10, Cole-French shares classroom activities targeting note-taking; and in Chapter 11, Ivone and Renandya advocate for extensive listening practice. We hope that the listening strategies and techniques that are addressed in the book bring a new understanding of listening challenges along with pedagogical tools to address them. We recommend that readers take the advice and suggestions from this volume and practice in class with your students.

References

Broersma, M., & Cutler, A. (2008). Phantom word activations in L2. *System, 36*, 22–34. https://doi.org/10.1016/j.system.2007.11.003

Brown, S. (2011). *Listening myths: Applying second language research to classroom teaching*. The University of Michigan Press.

Cauldwell, R. (2014). Listening and pronunciation need separate models of speech. In J. Levis & S. McCrocklin (Eds.), *Proceedings of the 5th pronunciation in second language learning and teaching conference* (pp. 40–44). Iowa State University.

Cauldwell, R. (2018). *A syllabus for listening: Decoding*. Speech in Action.

Celce-Murcia, M., Brinton, D. M., & Goodwin, J. M. (2010). *Teaching pronunciation: A course book and reference guide*. Cambridge University Press.

Elkhafaifi, H. (2005). Listening comprehension and anxiety in the Arabic language classroom. *The Modern Language Journal, 89*, 206–220. https://doi.org/10.1111/j.1540-4781.2005.00275.x

Emerick, M. R. (2019). Explicit teaching and authenticity in L2 listening instruction: University language teachers' beliefs. *System, 80*, 107–119. https://doi.org/10.1016/j.system.2018.11.004

Field, J. (2003). Promoting perception: Lexical segmentation in L2 listening. *ELT Journal, 57*, 325-334. https://doi.org/10.1093/elt/57.4.325

Field, J. (2008a). *Listening in the language classroom*. Cambridge University Press.

Field, J. (2008b). Revising segmentation hypothesis in first and second language listening. *System, 36*, 35–51. https://doi.org/10.1016/j.system.2007.10.003

Gilbert, J. B. (2008). *Teaching pronunciation Using the prosody pyramid*. Cambridge University Press.

Goh, C. C. M. (2019). Metacognition in listening. In J. I. Liontas (Ed.), *The TESOL encyclopedia of English language teaching*. Wiley Blackwell.

Goh, C. C. M., & Wallace, M. (2019). Lexical segmentation in listening. In J. I. Liontas (Ed.), *The TESOL encyclopedia of English language teaching*. Wiley Blackwell.

Graham, S., Santos, D., & Francis-Brophy, E. (2014). Teacher beliefs about listening in a foreign language. *Teaching and Teacher Education, 50*, 107–119. https://doi.org/10.1016/j.tate.2014.01.007

Harley, B. (2000). Listening strategies in ESL: Do age and L1 make a difference? *TESOL Quarterly, 34*(4), 769–776. https://doi.org/10.2307/3587790

Henrichsen, L. E. (1983). Teacher preparation needs in TESOL: The results of an international survey. *RELC Journal, 14*(1), 18–44. https://doi.org/10.1177/003368828301400102

McGrath, I. (2013). *Teaching materials and the roles of EFL/ESL teachers: Practice and theory*. Bloomsbury.

Mendelsohn, D. (2002). The lecture buddy project: An experiment in EAP listening comprehension. *TESL Canada Journal / Revue TESL du Canada, 20*(1), 64–73. https://doi.org/10.18806/tesl.v20i1.939

Mills, N., Pajares, C., & Herron, C. (2006). A re-evaluation of the role of anxiety: Self-efficacy, anxiety and their relation to reading and listening proficiency. *Foreign Language Annals, 39*, 276–295. https://doi.org/10.1111/j.1944-9720.2006.tb02266.x

Nation, I. S. P., & Newton, J. (2009). *Teaching ESL / EFL listening and speaking*. Routledge.

Nguyen, H., & Abbott, M. L. (2016). Promoting process-oriented listening instruction in the ESL classroom. *TESL Canada Journal / Revue TESL du Canada, 34*(11), 72–86. https://doi.org/1018806/tesl.v34i1.1254

Nunan, D. (1998). Approaches to teaching listening in the language classroom. In *Proceedings of the 1997 Korea TESOL Conference* (pp. 1–10). Korea Teachers of English to Speakers of Other Languages. https://koreatesol.org/sites/default/files/pdf_publications/KOTESOL-Proceeds1997web.pdf

Renandya, W. A., & Hu, G. (2019). Introduction to teaching listening. In J. I. Liontas (Ed.), *The TESOL encyclopedia of English language teaching*. Wiley Blackwell.

Richards, J. (2005). Second thoughts on teaching listening. *RELC Journal, 36*(1), 85–92. https://doi.org/10.1177/0033688205053484

Siegel, J. (2014). Exploring L2 listening instruction: Examination of practice. *ELT Journal, 68*(1), 22–30. https://doi.org/ 10.1093/elt/cct058

Tsui, A. B., & Fullilove, J. (1998). Bottom-up or top-down processing as a discriminator of L2 listening performance. *Applied Linguistics, 19*(4), 432–451. https://doi.org/10.1093/applin/19.4.432

Uber Grosse, C. (1991). The TESOL methods course. *TESOL Quarterly, 25*(1), 29–49. https://doi.org/10.2307/3587027

Vandergrift, L. (2004). Listening to learn or learning to listen. *Annual Review of Applied Linguistics, 24,* 3–25. https://doi.org/10.1017.S0267190504000017

Vandergrift, L., & Goh, C. M. (2012). *Teaching and learning second language listening*. Routledge.

Vandergrift, L., Goh, C. C. M., Mareschal, C. J., & Tafaghodtari, M. H. (2006). The Metacognitive Awareness Listening Questionnaire (MALQ): Development and validation. *Language Learning, 56,* 431–461.https://doi.org/10.1111/j.1467-9922.2006.00373.x

TAMARA JONES has taught in Russia, Korea, England, and Belgium. She is currently the associate director of the English Language Center at Howard Community College in Columbia, Maryland, USA. Tamara holds a PhD in education from the University of Sheffield in the United Kingdom.

CHAPTER 1

MATTHEW P. WALLACE

Metacognitive Awareness for Listening

Listening in Real Life

As a researcher of second language (L2) listening, I have devoted my career to understanding the nature of listening and identifying how individual differences in listeners affect comprehension and how listening teachers and their practices can improve listening ability. My motivation to research this area emerged during my time as an English as a foreign language teacher in Japan, where an experience with one class in particular spurred my interest in this topic. I was tasked with improving the listening proficiency for a class of lowly motivated 2nd-year senior high school students. The goal of most students in Japan is to become proficient enough in English to perform well on high-stakes assessments, like university entrance exams or the Test of English as a Foreign Language, on which listening is a key component. Confident that I would be able to help my students do well on their tests, I armed myself with my trusty audio player, comprehension questions, and transcripts every week.

The lessons themselves followed what is commonly described as the text-based approach (Vandergrift & Goh, 2012; also called comprehension approach; Field, 2008a) to teaching listening and involved first introducing the topic of the upcoming text and ensuring the students were familiar with the key terms. I played the audio twice while students answered comprehension questions. After the second listen, I gave students the answers to the questions and showed them how to find the answers in the transcript. The students initially appreciated being able to listen multiple times to the same text, and the explanations for answering the questions prepared them well for similar tasks they would face in upcoming tests. However, as the semester drew on, I started to notice some dissatisfaction from the class. They seemed bored, were still not very motivated to listen, and perhaps most importantly, the accuracy of their comprehension did not seem to be getting better. This all culminated in the class performing no better on the midterm exam than they had on the previous semester's final exam! How could this be after weeks of listening practice?

Talking with the students about how the class was going revealed some things for which I was not prepared. The students enjoyed the topics of the listening tracks but felt that the tracks were not improving their ability to listen. They felt that they understood how to answer comprehension questions better, but when they came across a word or chunk of language that they could not understand, they did not know how to handle it. They wanted to learn strategies to help them overcome this difficulty because their current strategy, focusing narrowly on that piece of language and ignoring everything else, was not working, and their anxiety to listen grew each time they encountered this situation. When I asked if the words they misunderstood were new to them, they said that most of the time they knew the words but did not recognize them, and the reason was because the speech was too fast and the words were imperceptibly clumped together. Another issue they raised was that the topics that the class discussed before the listening did not always match the content of the listening text. They thought that the text would be consistent with what they expected it to be about, and when it wasn't, they completely misunderstood what was said and ultimately gave up and stopped listening.

Listening in the Research

The issues raised by the students in my class may be attributed to problems associated with metacognition (also called metacognitive awareness). Metacognition is the ability to step back from what we are currently thinking about to observe and evaluate our thoughts (Vandergrift & Goh, 2012). It is a three-dimensional construct consisting of metacognitive knowledge, metacognitive experience, and use of metacognitive knowledge (also called metacognitive strategy use; Vandergrift & Goh, 2012).

Metacognitive knowledge involves three knowledge bases that interact with one another during a cognitive activity (Flavell, 1979):

1. *Person knowledge*: knowledge a person has about themself and their capabilities
2. *Task knowledge*: knowledge of the nature and demands of tasks
3. *Strategy knowledge*: knowledge of what strategies are available to complete tasks and how to use them

Metacognitive experience refers to the previous experiences in which metacognitive knowledge was used to complete tasks. Finally, **use of metacognitive knowledge** refers to the efficiency with which metacognitive knowledge and experience are used to complete tasks.

Learners use these metacognitive resources whenever they complete listening tasks. Learners are aware, though perhaps implicitly, of how well they listen in the target language, how to complete similar listening tasks to the one they are currently undertaking, and how effective listening strategies they know may be used to accomplish the current listening task. For example, my Japanese students' previous experience with listening in

English informed them of their listening capabilities. They were aware of how successful or unsuccessful they had previously been in comprehending English speech, giving them at least some tacit understanding of their listening competence. My students' prior experience in completing multiple-choice tasks informed how they approached completing the multiple-choice tasks in my class. Likewise, their experience in using strategies to comprehend target language speech and complete comprehension tasks informed what strategies they used to comprehend the texts that I gave them and answer the questions that I posed.

Individual differences in metacognitive awareness purportedly explains variance in L2 listening comprehension performance (Goh & Hu, 2014; Vandergrift et al., 2006; Zeng, 2012). In other words, listeners who have more person, task, and strategy knowledge and the ability to use that knowledge efficiently tend to perform better on L2 listening tasks than those with less knowledge. This is because having greater metacognitive resources affects how listeners approach listening tasks. Listeners efficient in metacognition tend to plan, monitor, and evaluate what they do as they listen, as opposed to listening in a random or incidental way (Goh, 2008). These three actions—planning, monitoring, and evaluating—which are also referred to as metacognitive processes (Vandergrift & Goh, 2012), form the center of metacognitive approaches to teaching listening, the aim of which is to increase efficiency in using metacognitive resources to accomplish listening tasks.

Individual differences in metacognition can explain why listening behaviors vary for more and less skilled listeners. When less skilled listeners experience decoding problems, they tend to narrowly focus their attention on working out those issues immediately and miss subsequent information provided in the speech. Because their attentional focus is not on the ongoing text, they miss out on understanding the overall meaning intended by the speaker(s) (Field, 2004). In contrast, bottom-up processing by more skilled listeners is automatized and allows them to focus on monitoring their comprehension of the text. More skilled listeners also experience decoding issues, but will continue listening to the text and revisit ambiguous parts after they have processed larger chunks of speech because the subsequent information may help disambiguate what was misperceived earlier. In other words, skilled listeners tend to reflect on and evaluate their performance after completing a listening task.

Another challenge for less skilled listeners is that they struggle with revising their interpretations of an ongoing text when incoming information contradicts initial expectations and/or information that has been provided in the co-text (Field, 2008b). This may result from inaccurate decoding of a word or phrase early in the text and then misattributing all subsequently decoded information as being related to that topic. The mental representation of that text would likely be quite different than what the speaker intended. Skilled listeners actively monitor their comprehension and will abandon and adjust their initial hypotheses about a listening text should additional information contradict those hypotheses. This process of monitoring and reflecting helps ensure that interpretations are accurate and coherent.

So the question becomes, what can we do about these issues facing our students? The approach I advocate for here echoes that made by Vandergrift and his colleagues (2006):

A metacognitive approach to teaching listening that is supplemented by activities targeting problematic bottom-up processes is ideal. It may be argued that because most of the issues facing the learners are bottom up that the pedagogical approach should focus on overcoming those issues. However, focusing primarily on bottom-up approaches may not address the issues in metacognition that affect listening comprehension. Bottom-up approaches have been criticized for not giving learners adequate exposure to extended discourse, which prevents them from being able to construct their own meaning of speech on a regular basis. These approaches generally give students extensive drill work but insufficient opportunities to practice what they have drilled in authentic contexts.

In contrast, the metacognitive approach aims to enhance metacognitive processes holistically (Cross, 2015) and has enjoyed much success in improving L2 listening comprehension in the empirical literature (e.g., Bozorgian, 2014; Fahim & Fakhri Alamdari, 2014; Goh & Taib, 2006; Vandergrift & Tafaghodtari, 2010). The main criticism levied against the metacognitive approach is that it may not directly address problems in listening but helps learners become autonomous in increasing their knowledge. This claim is supported by recent empirical studies that have shown that metacognitive awareness has an indirect effect on listening performance. The results of these studies indicated that metacognitive awareness may have helped listeners gain domain-specific knowledge (e.g., target language vocabulary; Vandergrift & Baker, 2015; 2018; and topical knowledge; Wallace, 2020) that is then used to comprehend speech.

Listening in the Classroom

Metacognitive Pedagogical Sequence

To address issues in listening related to inefficient metacognition, teachers can use the metacognitive pedagogical sequence (Cross, 2011; Vandergrift, 2004; Vandergrift & Goh, 2012; Vandergrift & Tafaghodtari, 2010). The aim of the sequence is to improve learners' metacognitive processes and help them overcome problems that they may encounter as they listen. Specifically, the sequence targets the ability to plan before an activity, monitor comprehension and overcome listening difficulties as they arise while listening, and evaluate performance on listening tasks after completing them. To date, the metacognitive pedagogical sequence is the most comprehensive and flexible approach to improving metacognitive awareness. It has enjoyed much success in the empirical literature in improving L2 listening comprehension for advanced-level adult English as a foreign language learners in Japan (Cross, 2011), beginner- and intermediate-level university learners of French in Canada (Vandergrift & Tafaghodtari, 2010), intermediate- to advanced-level university English learners in Iran (Fahim & Fakhri Alamdari, 2014), and elementary school children in Singapore (Goh & Taib, 2006).

The role of the teacher during the sequence is to initially serve as a model and guide for the learners, but this role is lessened as the learners increase their metacognitive processes and become more self-directed listeners. The sequence draws upon the process approach to teaching listening, which helps students view listening events as a process rather than a single product to decipher (Vandergrift & Tafaghodtari, 2010). There have been several versions of the sequence used in the literature, but the sequence described in this chapter is similar to Vandergrift and Goh's (2012) version. It consists of five stages of activities that coincide with five phases of the listening process. This sequence is flexible in that it may be applied to a generic listening activity or one for a specific context and can be applied when there are preset comprehension tasks and when there are none. I first describe the sequence in general and then explain how it can be applied to materials that you may be currently using.

Stage 1 (Prelistening): Planning Before a Listening Activity

The aim of this stage is to develop the habit of planning what students will do before they engage in listening tasks. First, introduce the topic and text type of the upcoming text. Elicit from students what they know of the topic, how text types like the one they are about to listen to can be organized, and what words or phrases in the target language they may hear in the text (also see Chapter 4 for more on segmenting streams of speech). The information can be elicited by posing questions to the entire class and having students respond individually. However, many language learning classrooms have students who may be reluctant to volunteer in front of their peers without additional support. As an alternative, pose these questions to pairs or groups so that shyer students have the opportunity to actively participate in the task. When the students report to the class overall, they will feel more confident because their ideas have already been validated by their peers. This can also be turned into a fun competition by setting a time limit and awarding points for each guess.

After eliciting what the students know of the topic, text structure, and language that could be used in the text, guide them to use this knowledge to make predictions about the upcoming text. Students will likely need support in how to do this initially, so consider modeling a think-aloud protocol to help students verbalize their thoughts. Think-aloud protocol involves speaking out thoughts as they enter our mind while completing tasks (Dornyei, 2007). It gives insight into the thinking processes as they are unfolding; doing this helps students see how to condense information to write predictions. The predictions generated in this stage should be written down so that students can use them as a guide while they listen and then reflect on their accuracy afterwards. The degree of teacher engagement in writing predictions and planning before the text should be reduced over time so that students become autonomous, self-directed learners.

One point of caution should be made here about the prelistening phase of the lesson sequence. Field (2008a) recommends that this stage should be short in comparison with the other listening stages. He warns that giving too much attention to the topic, structure, and language to be encountered before listening may do students a disservice and limit their opportunities to interpret spontaneous speech. This would deprive them of much needed practice at listening in authentic listening encounters.

Stage 2 (Listening 1): First Verification

During the first listen, students (1) evaluate how accurately their predictions match what they heard in the text and (2) add additional information about the content of the text.

If the predictions are inaccurate, students write down what is different in their notes. After listening, students share their notes and/or compare their answers to comprehension questions with a partner or group. Students discuss their understanding of the text and identify areas of misunderstanding that can be given more attentional focus when they hear the text again. Identifying areas of miscomprehension for subsequent attention helps students plan for their next listening effort. This stage helps students monitor their comprehension by using their own predictions as a set of expectations for what the content is about and then guides them into evaluating those predictions against the incoming information from the speech and revising them as necessary.

Stage 3 (Listening 2): Second Verification

During the second listen, students make adjustments to their notes again and add new information as needed to confirm their understanding of the text. The point of the notes is not to try to re-create the entire text, but to identify the main points and details of the text and be able to generate a basic outline of the talk or to complete comprehension tasks. Students discuss their understanding of the text and/or compare answers to comprehension tasks with their partner or group again. Then, lead a whole-class discussion to reconstruct the main points and important details of the text. The discussion allows students to identify what they were unable to understand in the first two listens. Like Stage 2, this stage gives students opportunities to monitor and evaluate comprehension of a text and then plan how to approach a subsequent listening task.

Stage 4 (Listening 3): Final Verification

Students listen to the text again, but this time for information from the class discussion that they were unable to understand on their own. Consider introducing the transcript of the text at this stage so that students may make the phoneme-grapheme connection, identify sounds that were especially challenging to understand (e.g., from connected speech), and recognize word boundaries. Reading along with the audio can be helpful in improving segmentation, a noted challenge for L2 listeners. If the level of the listening text is not too difficult, this stage may be optional.

Stage 5 (Postlistening): Reflection and Goal Setting

The final stage involves reflecting on the performance in the lesson overall and offering a critical evaluation of it (also see Chapter 12 for more on the benefits of analyzing listening successes and challenges). Students are encouraged to evaluate

- how effective their approach was to listening,
- what aspects of listening they found challenging,
- how effective their strategies were in helping them overcome those challenges, and
- what they will do in the future should they experience those challenges again.

To make this part of the metacognitive process more meaningful and salient, students should write down and read these reflections before subsequent listening lessons. You may want to collect and offer comments on these reflections to give students feedback on their ongoing development. As well, students may enjoy having the opportunity to discuss their observations about their own metacognition with a partner or in small groups. Hearing about other students' challenges and "aha moments" can create a sense of support and solidarity for struggling listeners, thereby making a difficult task more pleasurable.

The metacognitive pedagogical sequence can be adapted to use with most commercially available listening textbooks, in which the exercises usually follow the process approach to teaching listening, involving pre-, while-, and postlistening activities. Like the metacognitive pedagogical sequence, the first activities elicit what students know about the topic through discussion and use vocabulary drills to preteach key terms. What is sometimes missing in these materials is the key part of Stage 1 of the metacognitive pedagogical sequence, which is to guide students into making predictions about what they are about to hear based on the topics and vocabulary words introduced. It is essential for teachers to ensure that students make this connection between what they have been discussing and learning and what they may hear in an upcoming text.

Commercial textbooks typically then offer students opportunities to listen to a text and complete comprehension activities. These activities are often split into two stages. First, students listen and complete tasks eliciting comprehension of the main ideas or gist of the text. Then they listen again and complete activities for details of the text. You have a few options at this point to adapt Stage 2 (first verification) and Stage 3 (second verification) of the metacognitive sequence. (1) You can have students use the predictions they generated from Stage 1 as a note-taking guide as they listen, then complete the comprehension activities immediately after the listening text is completed, and finally evaluate the accuracy of their predictions. (2) You can ask students to complete the comprehension activities as they listen and then verify the accuracy of their predictions. Allow students to discuss their comprehension of the texts with a partner or group after each listen, and to lead a whole-class discussion about the main points and relevant details after the second listen.

Commercial textbooks usually end the sequence of activities with opportunities to expand on the ideas that were discussed in the text (e.g., through group discussion). Before or instead of leading students through this activity, consider incorporating Stage 4 (final verification) of the metacognitive pedagogical sequence by giving students the transcript of the audio so they can follow along as they listen one final time. The expansion activity usually marks the end of the listening sequence for commercial textbooks, but I encourage you to add Stage 5 (reflection and goal setting) to your sequence. Because class time can be limited, consider spending one or two classes teaching students how to do this and then eventually move this final stage outside of class.

Metacognitive Strategy Instruction

Improving metacognition may also be achieved by focusing narrowly on increasing metacognitive strategy knowledge and use. The empirical research has shown that metacognitive strategy instruction can improve L2 listening comprehension for beginner-level

(Coskun, 2010) and intermediate-level (Rahimirad & Shams, 2014) university students and intermediate-level high school students (Graham & Macaro, 2008). These studies have utilized a variety of techniques for teaching strategies, but they generally embed strategy-building activities within the three-stage listening sequence (i.e., pre-, while-, and postlistening). Strategies can be either directly introduced and practiced (explicit instruction) or presented as activities to complete within the lesson without mention of their purpose (implicit instruction). Regardless of the manner of presentation, metacognitive strategy instruction has been shown to be effective at improving comprehension and metacognitive awareness (Rahimirad & Shams, 2014). Unfortunately, though, there remains little consensus regarding what principles govern how a strategy-based program should be developed (Graham & Macaro, 2008). Therefore, as a starting point, the metacognitive pedagogical sequence can be used as a model for how metacognitive strategies can be embedded within the lesson sequence.

The benefits of a strategy-based approach are that students will be given opportunities to improve their metacognitive strategy knowledge and use; however, the effects may be limited to only strategies and ignore the other dimensions of metacognitive knowledge (person and task knowledge). Further, it has been argued that teaching the strategies of skilled listeners may be inappropriate because the linguistic knowledge differences between skilled and unskilled listeners cause the use of the strategies to be different. Skilled listeners use their strategies more efficiently than less skilled listeners because they have more knowledge and experience with the language from which to draw. Despite this criticism, strategy instruction has been shown to help listening comprehension in less skilled listeners.

In addition to teaching strategies to students directly, you may consider supplementing your instruction with the following activities designed to improve metacognitive awareness.

Strategy Checklists

An indirect approach to improving metacognitive awareness is to give students a checklist of strategies that they can use as a reference throughout a listening lesson and reflect on afterwards (Graham & Macaro, 2008; Vandergrift, 1999). The metacognitive strategies provided on the checklist (see Flowerdew & Miller, 2005, pp. 73–74) should be divided among the three metacognitive processes—planning, monitoring, and reflection and evaluation—with a description of the strategy and an example of each. Leave extra space on the checklist within each section for students to add their own strategies or those that are discussed in class. If students are of limited linguistic proficiency, consider asking them to translate each strategy into their first language so that they are clear about each strategy's meaning. The list should also contain a grid on another page that allows students to tick off which strategies they used during a listening lesson and a score indicating their performance on a listening task.

Before class, have the students take out the checklist and review the strategies that can be applied during each stage of the lesson. Also have them review their previous performance so that they understand what strategies they used and how successful their listening performance was. After the lesson is over, have the students tick which strategies they used and indicate their score on comprehension tasks. If specific comprehension tasks are not used in the lesson, have them indicate what percentage of the speech they understood during the lesson. Also, when ticking which strategies they used, have students mark the strategies that were helpful for them in understanding what they heard with a circle ("O") and those that they used but were not helpful with a cross ("X"). If the strategy was not used, then the space should be left blank. Doing this can help students understand how their strategy use has helped them understand the listening texts and that not every strategy is appropriate to use in every listening situation.

Tables 1 and 2 show examples of what these checklists may look like.

Table 1. Strategy Side of Metacognitive Checklist

Strategies	**Description**
Planning	*Before listening . . .*
1. Advanced organization	I thought of the structure of the text I was about to hear.
2. Selective attention	I thought about what specific information I wanted to listen for.
Monitoring	*While listening . . .*
3. Comprehension monitoring	I continually checked my understanding of the text to make sure it made sense to me.
4. Mental translation	I tried not to translate every word as I listened.
Reflection/Evaluation	*After listening . . .*
5. Task performance evaluation	I thought back about how well I performed on the listening task.
6. Comprehension evaluation	I thought back about how much of the listening text I understood.

Table 2. Performance Evaluation Side of Strategy Checklist

Date	**30 June**	**3 July**	**7 July**
Performance	75%		
Planning			
1. Advanced organization	0		
2 Selective attention	0		
Monitoring			
3 Comprehension monitoring	0		
4 Mental translation	X		
Reflection/Evaluation			
5 Task performance evaluation			
6 Comprehension evaluation	0		

Certainly, a strength of the checklists is that they help students see how their strategy use may change over time. By tracking their performance and strategy use throughout a language course, students and the teacher may get a sense of the strategies that students use during a listening lesson. However, it is important for you to make students aware that even though there is a list of possible strategies to be used while listening, not all of them may be relevant to accomplishing every listening task. Students should be using the most appropriate strategies to accomplish that task, and if they are found not to be, then you can address this with subsequent instruction.

Another advantage of the checklists is that they can be easy and flexible to use. The students can pull out the checklists for most listening tasks and tick off which strategies they used and then put them away afterwards. As well, the strategy checklist can help students track their own progress and, as a result, they may gain confidence in their listening abilities and find listening activities to be more manageable.

Use of checklists also comes with a few limitations. As with all self-reported techniques, using checklists assumes that students will accurately recall what they did during a lesson. Even though they may have the list of strategies in front of them during the lesson, the accuracy of their reflections is subject to human error. It may also be challenging for you to directly observe how effectively the students are using the strategies in class. Finally, because checklists provide only a description of a strategy, students are not given a model of how it can be used. This drawback can be overcome by modeling how to use strategies through additional instruction. In this sense, checklists may serve a supporting role as supplemental materials during the metacognitive pedagogical sequence or in strategy instruction.

Metacognitive Awareness Listening Questionnaire

A similar approach to using the metacognition checklist is to use the Metacognitive Awareness Listening Questionnaire (see Vandergrift et al., 2006; (www.academia.edu/3186922/The_metacognitive_awareness_listening_questionnaire_Development_and_validation). The questionnaire consists of 21 statements that aim to measure five dimensions of metacognition:

1. Directed attention: how well students regain their focus if they lose it during a listening task
2. Problem solving: how well listeners overcome comprehension or processing problems as they listen
3. Planning and evaluation: how well listeners plan before they listen and evaluate their performance after they listen
4. Mental translation: how well listeners avoid mentally translating what they hear
5. Person knowledge: how well students maintain a positive attitude toward listening

Completing the questionnaire is expected to raise student awareness to these dimensions and improve their metacognitive knowledge. The questionnaire can be delivered to students throughout a language course. At first, explain what the questionnaire is, what it is used for, and what it aims to measure. Then, explain that good listeners are those who are able to address the dimensions from the questionnaire and that students will complete it repeatedly over the course of the semester to see how their metacognitive knowledge may change.

Directly explaining the value of the questionnaire to students will help them see its importance in helping them improve their listening ability. Periodically collect the questionnaires throughout the course and calculate average scores for each dimension on the questionnaire and on the questionnaire overall. This will give you some insight into how students are developing their metacognitive awareness and diagnostic information about which dimensions are not being adequately developed.

Listening Diaries

Listening diaries can be a useful tool to help students reflect on and evaluate their listening experience (Goh, 2000), identify their weaknesses, and plan for future listening tasks (Goh, 1997; Vandergrift & Goh, 2012). Diaries require students to write about their listening experience on a consistent basis. You have three options when asking students to write in their diaries. Entries can be made at regular intervals (interval-contingent; e.g., once a week), when prompted by the teacher (signal-contingent), or whenever a specific listening event occurs (event-contingent; e.g., when students listen in the target language outside of class; Dornyei, 2007). Diary entries are written in response to prompts aimed at eliciting reflections of the listening event and metacognitive awareness demonstrated during it. Vandergrift and Goh (2012, p. 133) offer several example prompts for listeners:

- Reflections on a selected listening event
  - What was the listening event?
  - Did you understand what you heard?
  - What did you do to help your understanding?
  - Are you pleased with the results?
  - Would you do things differently next time?
- Self-evaluation of skills learned from listening lessons
  - List the listening skills you have been developing during the last week (e.g., listening for details in a description; inferring speaker attitude from tone).
  - How well do you think you have learned each of these skills?
- Immediately after a lesson
  - What strategies did you use during the listening tasks?
  - What made listening easy or difficult for you?
  - How do you feel about the class today? Why do you feel this way?

The strength of using diaries for improving metacognitive awareness is that it gives students a means to reflect deeply about their listening experiences. Unlike the think-aloud protocols that require students to verbalize what they think as a listening experience unfolds or immediately afterwards, diaries allow students to more clearly articulate their ideas because they can take their time and revise their thoughts as they write them out. When using diaries for class, collect them and offer feedback on entries so that students are aware of how effectively they are using and developing metacognitive processes.

Use of diaries also has drawbacks. Certainly, the biggest one is that they can be time consuming for students to write and for teachers to read. It is also easy for students to forget to write in their diary, which could cause the inconsistent benefit among learners. Despite these limitations, diaries can have a profound impact on developing metacognitive awareness for learners.

Supplemental Bottom-Up Activities

To address the limitation that metacognitive approaches to teaching listening inadequately address specific listening problems, bottom-up activities should be used to supplement the metacognitive pedagogical approach (Vandergrift & Goh, 2012; Vandergrift & Tafaghodtari, 2010). This can be done in two ways.

A first option is to embed bottom-up activities within the third-listening phase of the approach, when students can receive the transcript to identify sounds that they were unable to understand. These activities may include dictation, partial dictation, minimal pair activities, or activities that Field (2008a) lists as being helpful for improving decoding problems (see Chapters 3, 4, 5, 7, and 10 for more on helping students overcome listening challenges associated with decoding).

A second option is to alternate lessons between those focusing on improving metacognition and those improving bottom-up processing. The specific bottom-up processes that are targeted may be identified in the final verification stage of the metacognitive pedagogical sequence when students use the transcript to find sounds that they were unable to understand in previous listens. After students identify sounds that are especially challenging, you can plan a sequence of classes to address them. The activities in such classes may follow a present, practice, and produce structure. For example, present students with speech that is challenging to segment:

> *whadaya* = what do you
>
> *wanna* = want to

Then, have them transcribe sentences with the target sounds within them.

> A: Whadaya wanna do tomorrow after school.
>
> B: I wanna go to the movies.

Finally, have students complete comprehension tasks based on speech that has the targeted sounds and sounds that have been previously targeted. This last stage is important so that students are given opportunities to encounter problematic sounds in extended discourse. These activities should be incorporated within an overarching metacognitive instructional framework to dually address specific listening problems and train learners to become self-directed listeners.

In this chapter, I advocate for teachers to focus on improving metacognition in their learners. Doing so can improve students' listening ability and help them to become autonomous learners. I have recommended several pedagogical options you may consider incorporating within your classroom, either explicitly or implicitly, to improve metacognition. Bottom-up listening activities are also recommended to address the limitation that metacognitive teaching approaches inadequately address specific listening problems.

References

Bozorgian, H. (2014). The role of metacognition in the development of EFL learners' listening skill. *International Journal of Listening, 28*(3), 149–161. https://doi.org/10.1080/10904018.2013.861303

Coskun, A. (2010). The effect of metacognitive strategy training on the listening performance of beginner students. *Research on Youth and Language, 4*, 35–50.

Cross, J. (2011). Metacognitive instruction for helping less-skilled listeners. *ELT Journal, 65*, 408–416. https://doi.org/10.1093/elt/ccq073

Cross, J. (2015). Metacognition in L2 listening: Clarifying instructional theory and practice. *TESOL Quarterly, 49*, 883–892. https://doi.org/10.1002/tesq.258

Dornyei, Z. (2007). *Research methods in applied linguistics*. Oxford University Press.

Fahim, M., & Fakhri Alamdari, E. (2014). Maximizing learners' metacognitive awareness in listening through metacognitive instruction: An empirical study. *International Journal of Research Studies in Education, 3*(3), 79–91. https://doi.org/10.5861/ijrse.2014.762

Field, J. (2004). An insight into listeners' problems: Too much bottom-up or too much top-down? *System, 32*, 363–377. https://doi.org/10.1016/j.system.2004.05.002

Field, J. (2008a). *Listening in the language classroom*. Cambridge University Press.

Field, J. (2008b). Revising segmentation hypotheses in first and second language listening. *System, 36*, 35–51. https://doi.org/10.1016/j.system.2007.10.003

Flavell, J. H. (1979). Metacognition and cognitive monitoring: A new area of cognitive-developmental inquiry. *American Psychologist, 34*, 906–911. https://doi.org/10.1037/0003-066X.34.10.906

Flowerdew, J., & Miller, L. (2005). *Second language listening: Theory and practice*. Cambridge University Press.

Goh, C. (1997). Metacognitive awareness and second language listeners. *ELT Journal, 51*, 361–369. https://doi.org/10.1093/elt/51.4.361

Goh, C. C. M. (2000). A cognitive perspective on language learners' listening comprehension problems. *System, 28*, 55–75. https://doi.org/10.1016/S0346-251X(99)00060-3

Goh, C. C. M. (2008). Metacognitive instruction for second language listening development: Theory, practice and research implications. *RELC Journal, 39*, 188–213. https://doi.org/10.1177/0033688208092184

Goh, C. C. M., & Hu, G. (2014). Exploring the relationship between metacognitive awareness and listening performance with questionnaire data. *Language Awareness, 23*, 255–274. https://doi.org/10.1080/09658416.2013.769558

Goh, C., & Taib, Y. (2006). Metacognitive instruction in listening for young learners. *ELT Journal, 60*, 222–232. https://doi.org/10.1093/elt/ccl002

Graham, S., & Macaro, E. (2008). Strategy instruction in listening for lower-intermediate learners of French. *Language Learning, 58*, 747–783. https://doi.org/10.1111/j.1467-9922.2008.00478.x

Rahimirad, M., & Shams, M. R. (2014). The effect of activating metacognitive strategies on the listening performance and metacognitive awareness of EFL students. *International Journal of Listening, 28*(3), 162–176. https://doi.org/10.1080/10904018.2014.902315

Vandergrift, L. (1999). Facilitating second language listening comprehension: Acquiring successful strategies. *ELT Journal, 53*, 168–176. https://doi.org/10.1093/elt/53.3.168

Vandergrift, L. (2004). Listening to learn or learning to listen. *Annual Review of Applied Linguistics, 24*, 3–25. https://doi.org/10.1017/S0267190504000017

Vandergrift, L., & Baker, S. C. (2015). Learner variables in second language listening comprehension: An exploratory path. *Language Learning, 65*, 390–416. https://doi.org/10.1111/lang.12105

Vandergrift, L., & Baker, S. C. (2018). Learner variables important for success in L2 listening comprehension in French immersion classrooms. *Canadian Modern Language Review, 74*, 79–100. https://doi.org/10.3138/cmlr.3906

Vandergrift, L., & Goh, C. C. M. (2012). *Teaching and learning second language listening: Metacognition in action*. Routledge.

Vandergrift, L., Goh, C. C. M., Mareschal, C. J., & Tafaghodtari, M. H. (2006). The metacognitive awareness listening questionnaire: Development and validation. *Language Learning, 56*, 431–462. https://doi.org/10.1111/j.1467-9922.2006.00373.x

Vandergrift, L., & Tafaghodtari, M. H. (2010). Teaching L2 learners how to listen does make a difference: An empirical study. *Language Learning, 60*, 470–497. https://doi.org/10.1111/j.1467-9922.2009.00559.x

Wallace, M. P. (2020). Individual differences in second language listening: Examining the role of knowledge, metacognitive awareness, memory, and attention. *Language Learning*. Advance online publication. https://doi.org/10.1111/lang.12424

Zeng, Y. (2012). *Metacognition and self-regulated learning (SRL) for Chinese EFL listening development.* (Unpublished doctoral dissertation). National Institute of Education, Nanyang Technological University, Singapore.

MATTHEW P. WALLACE is an assistant professor in the Department of English at the University of Macau. His current research interests include second language listening comprehension, language assessment fairness, and language learner motivation.

CHAPTER 2

TAMARA JONES

Fostering Word Recognition

Listening in Real Life

As a Canadian, I took French classes throughout elementary and secondary school and even in university, but language learning never came easily to me. Because I grew up in a bilingual country, I was often exposed to French print even outside the classroom, on product packaging, in government documents, and on street signs. However, I come from a small city in British Columbia, where there weren't many native French speakers, so in my formative years I had few opportunities to hear a lot of French that was not spoken by my teachers and classmates or the speakers on the class cassette tapes.

It wasn't until many years later, when I moved to a French-speaking region in Belgium, that I had any cause to regret the imbalance of my French skills. To participate in Belgian society, I had to do a lot more speaking and listening than I had done when I was growing up in Canada. For instance, while I was living there, I participated in several local clubs that held regular meetings conducted entirely in French. I could usually follow the gist of the conversation, but often the details were lost on me.

One evening, as I was walking toward the building where meetings were often held, I saw another club member walking away from the building. After greeting me, she said something to me that I could not understand. I asked her to repeat it once, which she did. I still had no idea what she was saying. I figured it had something to do with the club meeting, but I was too embarrassed to ask her to repeat herself a third time, so I smiled and nodded and then continued to walk toward the door. Once I turned the corner to enter the building, I saw a sign that said *la réunion est annulée*. As soon as I saw the words in print, I understood that the woman had been trying to tell me the meeting was cancelled. After all, I knew the words, *réunion* and *annulée*. However, I was astonished to realize that, even though I had learned and remembered the words, I couldn't recognize them when they were said out loud. As it turns out, my experience was not at all unusual.

Listening in the Research

Unsurprisingly, several studies (Bonk, 2000; Staehr, 2009; Cheng & Matthews, 2018) have linked a robust vocabulary with better listening comprehension. Confronting an unfamiliar word within a stream of speech can derail a listener because "when listeners encounter a word they don't know, they frequently respond by focusing on that word and they stop listening to the rest of the text" (Brown, 2011, p. 7). This is hugely problematic for our learners, as that means students need to know 6,000 to 7,000 word families to reach the text coverage of 98% (Nation, 2006) required to adequately comprehend a spoken text. Clearly, one important step in boosting listening proficiency is developing an extensive vocabulary.

However, simply remembering a large number of words is not enough; students also need to know what the words sound like so they can identify them in speech. In her catalogue of the top 10 real-time listening challenges faced by English learners, Goh (2000) describes students' inability to recognize the spoken forms of words they know as the second most common obstacle to listening comprehension. Some of the participants in Goh's study reported that at times they heard words that seemed familiar to them, but the stream of speech progressed so quickly they didn't have time to think about the meaning of the words. Other students described experiences similar to mine, in that the words they could easily understand in print were incomprehensible to them in speech.

Goh (2000) attributes this inability to recognize known words to difficulties matching the sounds to script. In other words, when we listen, our ears are hit with clusters of acoustic features and we must decode the clusters, or match them with our knowledge of what sounds they represent. As proficient English listeners, we hear some acoustic cues, match them to sounds that we have stored in our long-term memory, match the sounds to a word, and finally match the word to a meaning. For instance, we might hear an acoustic cluster, match it with the sounds /skuwl/, connect those sounds with the word *school*, and understand that a school is a place where people go to learn. For proficient listeners, this process happens at lightning speed and usually completely subconsciously; however, for language learners, there are many occasions for difficulty. Students may hear the acoustic cluster and not be able to attribute any sounds to it, or they may accurately recognize the sounds, but be unable to connect them to words. Alternatively, they might be able to hear the words, but not know their meanings. In my case, I don't believe I even connected the acoustic clusters to any sounds. The woman was simply speaking too fast and I was too embarrassed to ask her to slow down and repeat herself a third time. According to Goh (2000), my French sound-to-script relationship was not fully automatized, which resulted in my underdeveloped listening vocabulary.

For English learners, memorizing vocabulary based primarily on how it looks is problematic because the sound spelling correspondence in English is extremely loose (see Chapter 7 for more on the spelling of weak forms). Though a few consonants are more or less reliable (/v/ is always spelled with a *v*, and *v* is always pronounced /v/), the majority of both consonants and vowels are unpredictable. For instance, the consonant /p/ can be spelled with *p* or *pp*. In addition, when a *p* is paired with an *h*, the resulting combination sounds like /f/. English language students also often find it confusing that the letter *p* sounds different depending on where it appears in a word (see Chapter 3 for more on how the location of sounds can affect their pronunciation). If it appears at the beginning of a word or stressed syllable, as in *party* or *compare*, it is aspirated, meaning that the speaker releases a puff of air when they say /p/ ([pʰ]). However, when *p* or *pp* comes at the beginning of an unstressed syllable, as in *complicate*, and when *p* appears at the end of a word or syllable, like *top*, the speaker presses their lips together and simply stops the air flow. There isn't an easily discernable difference between /p/ at the beginning and /p/ at the end of word, but they are not exactly the same. The sound spelling correspondence for vowels is even more unstable. For example, the possibilities for writing the sound /ay/ include *ie* (*tie*), *i* (*hi*), *igh* (*bright*), *y* (*my*), *i*+consonant+*e* (*write*), and *y*+consonant+*e* (*type*). As well, the same vowel combinations can have different sounds. Think about the *ea* combination; it can be pronounced as /iy/ like in *bead*, but also as /ɛ/ like in *bread*.

To identify what specific challenges students face when decoding acoustic clusters, Harada (1998) categorized English learner listening errors in greater depth. When he analyzed the errors his advanced English learners made as they transcribed a 10-minute segment from a U.S. university lecture, he also found ". . . that nonnative speakers' listening can be very inaccurate, and the inability to hear content words can lead to wrong schemata and finally to communication breakdown" (Harada, 1998, p. 57). His examination of the mishearings of content words revealed that the vast majority of mistakes (about 34%) were segment substitutions, such as hearing the word *defending* as *depending*. In other words, students heard the acoustic cues and ascribed the wrong sounds to them, causing a breakdown at the first step of the decoding process. Segment deletion, such as hearing the word *playing* but understanding *paying*, made up nearly 11% of the listening mistakes. These errors are worrying for English language teaching professionals because content words, such as *defending* and *playing*, tend to contain the most important information in the phrase or sentence, and "even the best top-down listener would have difficulty making sense of a passage when such key words are misunderstood" (Celce-Murcia, Brinton & Goodwin, 2010, p. 368).

Another challenging obstacle for learners decoding naturally occurring speech is the presence of reduced sounds in unstressed syllables and function words (also see Chapter 7 for more information about how sounds change in weak forms). Vowel sounds in stressed syllables are crucial signals for listeners. According to Grosjean and Gee (1987), native English speakers store vocabulary in phonological chunks, and the stressed syllable of a word provides an access code for the listener. For instance, in the word *photographer*, the stressed syllable [tʰɑg] provides key information about the word. As Brown (1990) explains,

> the stress pattern of a polysyllabic word is a very important identifying feature of the word. . . . We store words under stress patterns . . . and we find it difficult to interpret an utterance in which a word is pronounced with the wrong stress pattern—we begin to "look up" possible words under this wrong stress pattern. (p. 51)

However, while the stressed vowels are usually pronounced clearly, and so provide acoustic cues that are at least possible for listeners to match to sounds stored in their long-term repertoire, the vowels in unstressed syllables are usually reduced to an /ə/ sound. For instance, in the word *photographer*, the stressed syllable is pronounced clearly, but the other syllables are "muffled" (Gilbert, 2008, p. 21), so the word sounds like [fəˈtʰɑg rə fəʳ]. All of the other vowels, the *o*, *a*, and *e*, are reduced to the same short sound. Therefore, not only do English listeners need to match the clear acoustic cues to sounds, they also have to match the diminished cues to the sound /ə/ and then figure out which letter that sound represents. Clearly, the common process of learning vocabulary by studying a printed list of words is insufficient for English listeners.

Listening in the Classroom

The good news is that, just are there are many ways to unpack the listening challenges faced by English learners, there are also many things English language teaching professionals can do to help their students become more skilled listeners.

Teaching Sound Recognition

According to Harada (1998), the number one cause of misunderstanding content words is segment substitution, or hearing one sound instead of another. It's easy to see why this is likely to happen, even if all the acoustic cues in a word are pronounced clearly, when one considers the English consonant and vowel inventory in comparison to that of our students' first languages (L1s). For instance, Arabic speakers often have a hard time distinguishing between the /p/ and /b/ sounds because the /p/ sound does not exist in Arabic (Avery & Ehrlich, 2008); as a result, when Arabic students hear a /p/ acoustic cue, they may assign it a /b/ sound, so the word *pop* might be mistaken for *bob*. Similarly, Mandarin speakers often cannot easily perceive the difference between the /æ/ and /ɛ/ sounds (Avery & Ehrlich, 2008), so these learners might think of the word *pen* when they hear the word *pan*. "As English speakers, we make use of something like 45 sounds while having only 26 letters in our alphabet" (Nilsen & Pace Nilsen, 2010, p. 5), and this understandably presents challenges for speakers whose L1 contains fewer or different sounds.

Because listeners' perception of acoustic cues is filtered through their knowledge of their L1 sounds, English language students need practice hearing and identifying English consonant and vowel sounds. The first step in this process is introducing students to those sounds that are interfering with their listening comprehension. When introducing an English phoneme, it can be helpful to use a sagittal diagram to support explicit instruction about the voicing, place of articulation, and manner of articulation. As well, it may be beneficial to use International Phonetic Alphabet (IPA) symbols or, if using the sagittal diagram, The Color Vowel Chart™ (Taylor & Thompson, 2009), which is composed of colors and words, to help learners conceptualize the difference between sounds. Students often initially need to visualize the contrasting sounds in order to understand that minimal pairs actually contain different sounds, as the contrasts may sound identical to them.

For instance, for the Arabic-speaking students struggling to differentiate between /p/ and /b/, you can show on two sagittal diagrams the similar lip and tongue placement for /p/ and /b/, while drawing students' attention to the primary difference, the unvoiced quality of /p/ and the vocalization of /b/. To help students feel the difference, you can encourage students to place their hand on their throat as they alternate between /p/ and /b/, noticing how their vocal chords vibrate only when saying /b/. Because the /p/ and /b/ IPA symbols correspond nicely to the letters associated with the sounds for *p* and *b*, you and your students should feel quite comfortable using phonetic symbols to identify the different sounds and for feedback, as in, "I heard you say this sound (point to /b/) and not this sound (point to /p/)."

Teaching students to hear all of the 15 English vowel phonemes can be more challenging. Not only is the North American vowel inventory more complex than that of many of our learners' L1s, but the way we describe vowels in terms of tongue height, lip rounding, frontness, and tenseness is harder for students to see, feel, and replicate. For the Mandarin-speaking students who can't hear a difference between /æ/ and /ɛ/, while explaining that the /æ/ is low, front, and lax and the /ɛ/ is mid, front, and lax, you might choose to use a sagittal diagram, and because jaw positioning differs for /æ/ and /ɛ/, you can hand out small mirrors or have students use a mirror app on their smart phones. You can act as a model, encouraging students to watch their mouth and then look in their mirrors as they try to replicate the movements.

Target Sound Cards

Even once students are aware of the difference between the sounds, they need a great deal of practice to reinforce the contrasts so that when they hear acoustic cues, they are able to automatically match them with sounds. One activity that helps students to practice identifying sounds involves making one set of index cards or slips of paper for each student with the target sounds written clearly across the top. For instance, for the Arabic speakers, each student would get two cards or pieces of paper that look like this:

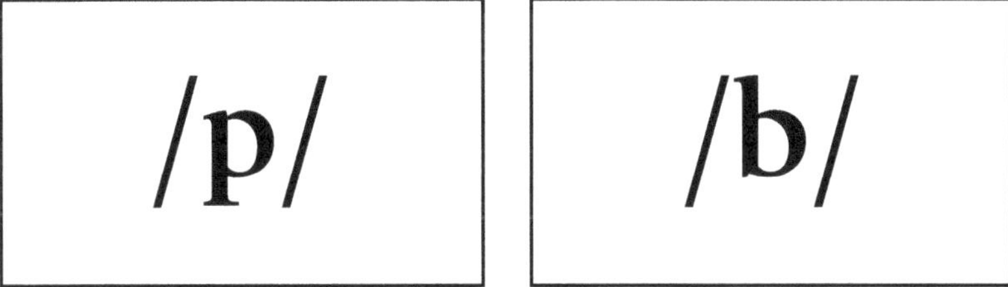

For the Mandarin speakers, the cards would look like this:

/æ/ black cat	/ɛ/ red dress

(For the vowel cards, it can be helpful for students to see the IPA symbols and the words, as the symbols are often difficult for them to remember. Because the purpose isn't for them to memorize the IPA, but rather to identify a target sound, you may want to consider this scaffold.)

In addition to one set of cards for each student, prepare a list of words, randomly assembled, that contain the target sounds. For instance, to practice /p/ and /b/, you might write a list containing words such as *path, box, bike, crumple, mapping, boast, cob, stable, pin,* and *pup.* To practice /æ/ and /ɛ/, the list could contain words such as *bread, mast, land, ran, flex, vet, fatter, rant, leather,* and *neck.* In class, distribute the cards to each student and then call out the words on the list, pausing after each one to give time for students to hold up the corresponding sound card. This activity not only gives the students valuable practice identifying sounds, but it also provides you with a quick snapshot of which sounds the students are struggling to identify and which ones they have mastered.

Target Sound Flyswatter Game

Another activity that provides practice with sound identification is the flyswatter game. Just as with "Target Sounds," prepare a list of words containing the target sounds. In addition, bring several flyswatters of different colors to class. Once class begins, write the phonetic symbols (or color phrases) using large characters on the board and divide the students into several groups, giving each group a different color flyswatter. The students line up in their groups in front of the board with the first student holding the flyswatter. As you call out the first word on your list, the students with the flyswatters race to swat the corresponding symbol. For instance, if you say *bread,* the students holding the flyswatters would race to hit the /ɛ/ symbol or, alternatively, the phrase *red dress.* The first group to correctly identify the sound gets a point. The students holding the flyswatters pass them to the next student in the line and then move to the back of the line.

This is a fast-paced, engaging activity that students love. They often get so excited that implementing a few "rules" is a good idea:

1. Limit students to one swat per turn.
2. Remind students not to hit others with the flyswatter, even jokingly.
3. Instruct students to keep their flyswatter in place once they have swatted. Sometimes students will hit the symbol and move their flyswatter away before you can clearly see which team should be awarded the point.
4. Explain to students that, in addition to being a fun activity, the flyswatter game helps them practice identifying the sound quickly, as they will have to when listening to naturally occurring speech.

Ear-training practice like in the preceding exercises serves to help students "practice the distinctions that experience has taught an L1 listener to make between words that are closely similar. It is even possible that a record of confusability of certain words forms part of the L1 listener's lexical knowledge" (Field, 2008, p. 168). Perhaps, had I been given the opportunity to practice distinguishing between similar sounds in French, I may have built up a more accessible and more complete inventory of French sounds in my long-term memory and would have made faster and more successful matches between the acoustic cues the woman's speech contained and the sounds of French.

Teaching Sound-Spelling Correspondence

As students become more comfortable identifying English sounds, instructors can also focus on introducing English sound-spelling correspondences. This is an extremely important step, as most of our students learn vocabulary from printed lists; however, it is often overlooked completely in listening instruction. For instance, because so much of my exposure to French was through print, I don't know how words are supposed to sound, so I apply a quasi-English pronunciation to French words. Thus, to help our students automatize the process of connecting the words they are hearing to how they look and sound in their brains, we need to bring spelling out of writing lessons and into listening lessons.

Stirling (2011) presents a list of the different ways the sounds of English can be spelled. However, use such a list with caution, because students may be overwhelmed by the "109 ways to spell the 24 consonant sounds and 149 ways to spell the 20 vowel phonemes" (Stirling, 2011, p. 43). Thus, rather than offering students a daunting list, particularly when it comes to vowel sounds, you may want to look to Carney's (1994) data on how frequently vowel spellings are pronounced in certain ways. For instance, the sound /æ/ is spelled with an *a* (as in *cat*) 91% of the time. The other 9% of the time, /æ/ can be spelled with *au* (*laugh*), *ai* (*plaid*) and *i* (*meringue*). Instead of teaching all the possible spellings of phonemes, you may wish to focus on the most common and then address additional spellings as they arise. Students are often frustrated by the complexity and unreliability of English spelling patterns, and so it can be helpful to remind them that children in English-speaking countries all around the world have to study spelling "rules" in school.

Practice With Sound-Spelling Texts

A practice activity you can use to reinforce spelling patterns involves presenting students with a level-appropriate text that contains several examples of the target sound. Phonics materials are excellent sources for reading passages that focus on specific sounds. However, you can also either pull readings from existing course materials or even create your own texts that are appropriate and specific to your learners.

If a sound has a large number of potential spellings, the text should contain a variety of possible spellings and focus only on one sound. For instance, *Stories with a Twist* (Hess, 2017) includes a story about a policeman that contains six examples of the 11 possible spellings for the sound /iy/. In class, you can distribute a copy of the text and a highlighter to each student and then read the passage aloud, encouraging the listeners to highlight the words that they hear contain the target sound.

Dictations

Dictations are also an incredibly effective tool for helping students associate sounds with spelling patterns. To help students focus on target sounds, it can be useful to present a form of gapped dictation in which students are given a list of words that have the target sounds removed. For example, to practice /æ/ and /ɛ/ contrast, the list of the words *when, act, breath, next, flash, pack, wealth, help, pants* and *band* might look like this:

1. wh_____n	6. p_____ck
2. _____ct	7. w_____lth
3. br_____th	8. h_____lp
4. n_____xt	9. p_____nts
5. ch_____t	10. b_____nd

As you read out the list of words, the class fills in the gaps with the appropriate spelling.

These kinds of activities are not particularly innovative, and teachers of young learners, as well as instructors who work with students with limited or interrupted formal education, will already be familiar with activities that help students decode the English sound-spelling correspondence. However, it has not always been an obvious necessity in the listening classroom. "Spelling extrapolation is an area that currently receives little attention in listening instruction. . . . Exercises should aim to create awareness of the underlying spelling system, not to teach individual word forms" (Field, 2008, p. 171). Because students often learn vocabulary from printed lists, it is imperative that they also learn the sounds associated with spelling patterns so that they can more quickly and accurately identify the words when they are used in speech.

Teaching Syllables

When focusing on matching the acoustic clusters with English sounds and the sounds with spelling patterns, it is common for teachers to primarily use one-syllable words. Dealing with multisyllabic words creates a whole new set of listening challenges; however, these words also make up the vast majority of the words listeners encounter. Interestingly, Harada's (1998) research cataloguing the patterns of misheard content words reveals that syllable insertion makes up 4% of word-level listening errors and syllable deletion accounts for nearly 9% of these errors. In other words, not hearing the correct number of syllables in a content word causes almost 13% of all content word mishearings. These errors may be attributable to the resyllabification that English words often undergo when they are said by nonproficient speakers (Gilbert, 2008). For instance, Korean does not allow word-final sibilants, so Korean speakers may be tempted to add a vowel sound to the ends of these kinds of words, especially when they occur at the end of the sentence, pronouncing the word *church* as [ˈʧɝ ʧiy], thereby incorrectly adding a syllable. For many other learners, if a letter appears in a word, it's pronounced. In English, conversely, speakers delete unstressed vowels in the middle of certain words when they follow stressed syllables. This is often why students mispronounce the word *chocolate* (normally two syllables) as [ʧɑ kow lɑ tɛ]. Therefore,

> while the number of syllables in a word is usually obvious to a native speaker of English, learners accustomed to different phonological rules may not hear the syllable divisions in the same way. Since this seriously affects both intelligibility and listening comprehension, time must be spent training students' ears to notice the number of syllables in the words they learn. (Gilbert, 2008, p. 4)

For students to learn to hear the syllables in English words, teachers can explicitly explain that a syllable is a unit of speech that contains a single vowel sound. (Though somewhat limited, this definition is arguably sufficient for the majority of our students for ELT instructional purposes.) Then, as students learn new words, time should be set aside for them to also identify the number of syllables in those words.

Quality Choral Repetition: Syllables

Perhaps the easiest and most efficient way to incorporate this kind of learning into vocabulary development is through choral repetition combined with body movements. When introducing new vocabulary, it is essential to have students repeat the words aloud with you acting as the model and then saying the words again with the class. "The teacher prompts students to listen first and then, 'Say it with me.' This is different from 'listen and repeat' because the sound of the teacher's voice is needed to carry the chorus of student voices along" (Miller & Jones, 2016, p. 91). Gilbert (2008) often refers to this as *quality choral repetition*.

For students learning to identify the number of syllables in words, *quality choral repetition* features movement, such as tapping a pencil or clapping as the repetition occurs. For instance, if students are learning vocabulary associated with school supplies, you might have them repeat words such as *pencil* and *eraser*. As students look at the words (to reinforce the sound-spelling correspondence) and chorally repeat with you, they can tap a pencil with each syllable.

> *Teacher*: pencil
>
> *Teacher and Students*: pen (tap) cil (tap)
>
> *Teacher*: eraser
>
> *Teacher and Students*: e (tap) ra (tap) ser (tap)

In this way, students get immediate feedback about the number of syllables because you are tapping along with them, making the repetition even more valuable for weak listeners.

Syllable Categorization Practice

In addition to choral repetition, students benefit from other practice with identifying the number of syllables in a word. For homework, after introducing the vocabulary words in the class, you might assign a categorization activity to encourage the class to review the number of syllables in the words. For the classroom objects, the handout might look like this:

backpack	chair	computer	desk	dictionary
eraser	paper	pen	pencil	table

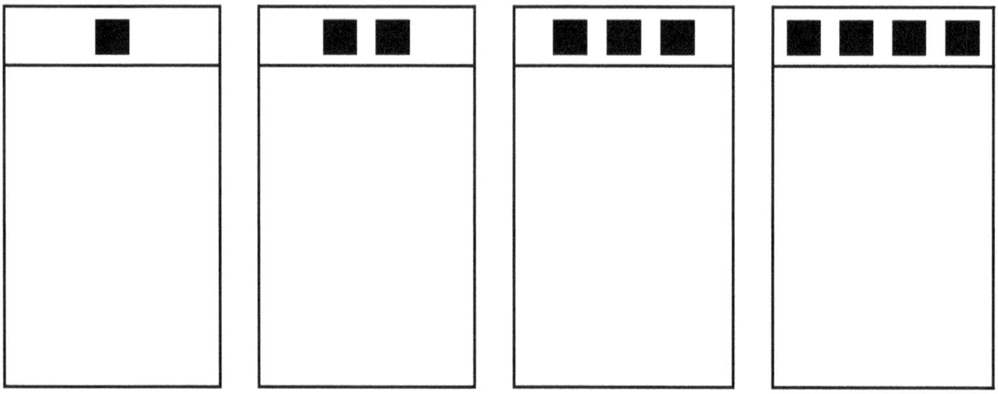

■	■ ■	■ ■ ■	■ ■ ■ ■

At home, students then hav be to retrieve the pronunciation of the word from their memory along with the appropriate number of syllables, presumably requiring them to repeat the word aloud several times, and then write the word in the appropriate column.

Alternatively, you might encourage group work and incorporate kinesthetic learning by creating sets of index cards for the students with one target vocabulary word written on each card and having students work in partners to separate the words into groups according to their syllable counts. Research (Joe, 2010) suggests that the frequency with which learners encounter words, even if some of those encounters are context-free, is more crucial to retention than simply encountering new words once or twice in a context-rich text. Therefore, these kinds of activities are enormously beneficial not only in terms of listening comprehension, but also for the development of student word banks.

Pronunciation experts have long understood that correctly identifying the number of syllables a word contains is not necessarily a straightforward task for many English learners; however, it is a vital step toward comprehensibly pronouncing words. Listening instruction has not been as quick to embrace the addition of syllable practice. Nonetheless, because students' listening errors can be caused by the incorrect insertion or deletion of a syllable in a content word, it is clear that when students are learning new words, they also need to learn the syllable count so they can be prepared to accurately hear the word in speech.

Teaching Word Stress

In addition to accurately counting the number of syllables in a word, English learners must also be able to identify the stressed syllable of the word. As previously stated in this chapter, proficient English listeners store words in their long-term memories by their stressed syllables. For example, when considering the vocabulary list of classroom items, the word *computer* would be stored by the syllable /pyuw/. The information contained in the stressed syllable is an essential key to understanding the word when it is said aloud.

"After all, if learners have failed to learn the stress pattern for a new word, they may also fail to recognize that word when it occurs in spoken form" (Gilbert, 2008, p. 6). Just as with syllables, it is useful for instructors to introduce the concept of word stress to learners explicitly. Speakers of other languages need to understand that the vowel sound of a stressed syllable is said more clearly and at a higher pitch and that it is held for a longer time. Students also often benefit from attention drawn to the contrast between stressed and reduced syllables in a word. They need to understand that in the word *computer*, the vowel sound of the stressed syllable, /pyuw/, is said more loudly, longer with a higher pitch and more clearly than the vowel sounds in the other syllables, /kəm/ and /tə^r/, which have been reduced to the schwa /ə/ sound.

Quality Choral Repetition: Stress

Once this concept is clear, whenever students learn new words, they should also learn their stress patterns. Again, *quality choral repetition* provides a wonderful opportunity for the reinforcement of word stress. Gilbert (2008) recommends giving each student a thick rubber band that they hold in both hands and stretch on the stressed syllable as they are chorally repeating the words with you.

> *Teacher*: pencil
>
> *Teacher and Students*: pen (pull) cil (relax)
>
> *Teacher*: eraser
>
> *Teacher and Students*: e (relax) ra (pull) ser (relax)

Through the effort of stretching a thick rubber band, students are able to feel the stressed syllable, thereby internalizing the pronunciation of the word. After the choral repetition, permit students time to mark the stress patterns on the vocabulary words in their lists. Students can highlight or underline the stressed syllables. Alternatively, they can draw small circles over the unstressed syllables and a bigger circle over the stressed syllable in each word. English learners will benefit from the repeated encounters with the vocabulary, as they reinforce the essential aural characteristics of the words that enable listeners to understand the words in speech.

Quick Stressed Syllable Check

In order to quickly determine whether students are able to identify the stressed syllables in the words they hear, you may want to incorporate an activity that focuses solely on listening for the stress. Before the class, prepare a list of target words. During the lesson, read the list aloud, pausing between each word to give students a chance to identify first the number of syllables and then the stressed syllable by holding up the corresponding number of fingers. For example, if the word is *computer*, the students should hold up three fingers to indicate there are three syllables and then two fingers to indicate they hear the stress on the second syllable. This exercise allows you to assess on the spot whether students can identify the stressed syllables. It also gives the students immediate feedback if you then show the word along with the syllable count and stressed syllable.

Learning to identify the stressed vowel sound in English words can be very beneficial for English language students. Although only 2% of the misheard content words in Harada's (1998) study were associated with wrong word stress, it still represents a significant barrier to listening comprehension. Mishearing the stress of the content words that the woman outside the meeting in Belgium said to me certainly contributed to my inability to understand her. Because I had little opportunity to hear French as I was learning it, I applied English stress patterns to the words I saw in print and tucked them away into my long-term memory. So, in my mind, *réunion* had the stress on the second syllable, the way *reunion* does in English, but in French *réunion* is stressed on the last syllable. Clearly, my idea of how the words should sound was a barrier to my understanding of how they actually sounded.

For a long time, the listening practice activities in many ELT textbooks have provided primarily top-down skill building, such as schema activation. However, all the context in the world didn't help me understand what the woman was saying to me all those years ago in Belgium. I was just outside the meeting hall, I recognized the speaker as a club member, and she was walking away even before the meeting started. If this had been a textbook activity and I had been sitting in a language classroom, surely I would have been able to brainstorm her message as a possibility. However, in real life, language learners don't always have time to brainstorm about the message in an unexpected conversation. They aren't provided with a tidy list of key vocabulary to listen for, and, unlike in my case, the consequences of mishearing may, at times, be devastating. Therefore, English language teaching professionals need to incorporate more bottom-up skill building into listening lessons.

References

Avery, P., & Ehrlich, S. (2008). *Teaching American English pronunciation*. Oxford University Press.

Bonk, W. (2000). Second language lexical knowledge and listening comprehension. *International Journal of Listening, 14*, 14–31. https://doi.org/ 10.1080/10904018.2000.10499033

Brown, G. (1990). *Listening to spoken English*. Longman.

Brown, S. (2011). *Listening myths: Applying second language research to classroom teaching*. The University of Michigan Press.

Carney, E. (1994). *A survey of English spelling*. Routledge.

Celce-Murcia, M., Brinton, D., & Goodwin, J. (2010). *Teaching pronunciation: A course book and reference guide*. Cambridge University Press.

Cheng, J., & Matthews, J. (2018). The relationship between three measures of L2 vocabulary knowledge and L2 listening and reading. *Language Testing, 35*(1), 3–25. https://doi.org/10.1177/0265532216676851

Field, J. (2008). *Listening in the language classroom*. Cambridge University Press.

Gilbert, J. B. (2008). *Teaching pronunciation using the prosody pyramid*. Cambridge University Press.

Goh, C. (2000). A cognitive perspective on language learners' listening comprehension problems. *System, 28(1)*, 55–75. https://doi.org/10.1016/S0346-251X(99)00060-3

Grosjean, F., & Gee, J. (1987). Prosodic structure and spoken word recognition. *Cognition, 25*, 135–155. https://doi.org/10.1016/0010-0277(87)90007-2

Harada, T. (1998). Mishearings of content words by ESL learners. *The CATESOL Journal, 10,* 151–171.

Hess, N. (2017). *Stories with a twist* (2nd ed). ALTA English.

Joe, A. (2010). The quality and frequency of encounters with vocabulary in an English for academic purposes programme. *Reading in a Foreign Language, 22*(1), 117–138.

Miller, S., & Jones, T. (2016) Taking the fear factor out of integrating pronunciation and beginning grammar. In T. Jones (Ed.), *Pronunciation in the classroom: The overlooked essential* (pp. 89–102). TESOL Press.

Nation, I. S. P. (2006). How large a vocabulary is needed for reading and listening? *The Canadian Modern Language Review, 63*(1), 59–82. https://doi.org/10.26686/wgtn.12552221

Nielsen, D. L. F., & Pace Nilsen, A. (2010). *Pronunciation contrasts in English* (2nd ed.). Waveland Press.

Staehr, L. S. (2009). Vocabulary knowledge and advanced listening comprehension in English as a foreign language. *Studies in Second Language Acquisition, 31,* 577–607. https://doi.org/10.1017/s0272263109990039

Stirling, J. (2011). *Teaching spelling to English language learners.* Lulu.

Taylor, K., & Thompson, S. (2009). The Color VowelTM chart. http://www.colorvowelchart.org/index.php?option=com_content&view=article&id=47&Itemid=56

TAMARA JONES has taught in Russia, Korea, England, and Belgium. She is currently the associate director of the English Language Center at Howard Community College in Columbia, Maryland, USA. Tamara holds a PhD in education from the University of Sheffield in the United Kingdom.

CHAPTER 3

JOSEPH SIEGEL

Recognizing Morphological Markers for Improved Listening Ability

Listening in Real Life

One day when walking on a university campus where I worked, I saw a friend from a distance. We waved to each other, and then she called out to me. Even though we could see each other, we were still too far apart for me to hear her clearly. The gusts of wind didn't help the communication, either. Was it "I call you" she said? Something like that. She repeated, a bit louder but still I couldn't make it out clearly. It was probably either "I called you" or "I'll call you." I remember being confused about what I should do. I couldn't hear the verb conjugation correctly and was stuck between these two viable alternatives. Either my friend had called me and I missed the call, meaning she might be upset that I hadn't yet returned the call and I should call her back as soon as I could. Or she said she *will* call me. In that case, all I needed to do was wait.

My struggle to decipher this seemingly simple message hinged on my ability to hear and process morphological markers in speech. In this case, it was either the past tense *-ed* [d] or the contracted form of "I will." I knew I was missing something in this listening experience, because "I call you" is a rather odd thing to say to someone. Grammatically correct, yes, but not pragmatically appropriate. Yet, I was confused because I couldn't quite catch either the [d] or [l] I was listening for.

This type of listening experience emphasizes that each individual phoneme and morphological marker carries with it significance for the listener. Without recognizing all of the intended information a speaker is sending or encoding, a listener may be left wondering about actual intent and may misinterpret, or at least struggle to immediately interpret, a message. This particular situation involved two native English users, and the clarity of morphological markers in listening is even more important for second language (L2) English users (e.g., Karimi, 2012). This importance, particularly the endings on regular nouns and verbs, is addressed elsewhere in this volume (see Chapter 6) and in the following review of the literature.

Listening in the Research

As highlighted by Goh and Wallace (2018), one of the main challenges L2 listeners face is lexical segmentation, which refers to the cognitive activity of chunking and decoding aural input into meaningful and manageable units in order to facilitate comprehension (also see Chapters 4, 5, and 6). Parsing the speech stream requires that listeners recognize where one word ends and the next begins, a task that can be extremely demanding for L2 listeners who may ascribe their difficulty to the rapid rates of speech they encounter (e.g., Goh, 2000; Hasan, 2000). Cauldwell (2013) describes the "sound substance" as "the blur of the speech stream" (p. 16) that the listener needs to attend to in real time. Deconstructing and reconstructing that blur into meaningful input nearly instantaneously is a requisite listening skill. Lexical segmentation occurs in reading as well; however, in that skill, the blank white space between words signals the segmentation. Listeners are left to do the same work without the visual support of the written words and empty spaces on the page. However, when trying to decipher aural input, memory and the "perpetual appearing, disappearing and replenishing act" (Cauldwell, 2013, p. 20) occurs as speech is processed and more input becomes available.

Though abilities for L2 aural comprehension gradually develop through exposure and explicit practice, one overt linguistic aspect that listeners can utilize to improve their lexical segmentation skills is morphological markers (MMs). The ability to recognize MMs is part of the more general concept of morphological awareness, defined by Karimi (2012) as "the ability to understand the morphemic structure of words" (p. 451). Morphemes are "minimal units of meaning or grammatical function" (Yule, 2017, p. 73). They contain "semantic, phonological and syntactic properties that clearly express the role of a particular word in its linguistic context (e.g., the –s, in the verb 'rides')" (Karimi, 2012, p. 452). That is, morphemes carry consequential information related to a word's meaning, and the ability to recognize morphemes in the speech stream greatly increases a listener's comprehension ability.

Though morphemes are very important for grammatical understanding, most L2 learners and teachers do not immediately connect the term *morpheme* with listening. Instead, it is more commonly associated with linguistic studies, grammar, spelling, and writing. As well, the notion of morphological awareness has often been applied to research in the receptive skill of reading but has been less understood and is only recently receiving attention from researchers in relation to listening (Gottardo et al., 2018).

Field (2003) points out that there has been an overemphasis on top-down, contextual, higher level understanding at the expense of "the primacy of the speech signal" (p. 325) and advocates for more attention to lexical segmentation and word boundary identification when listening. Students who misinterpret the difference between *won't* and *want* or who miss the grammatical meaning of the phoneme /v/ in the contracted *I've* would benefit from such explicit instruction and practice (also see Chapter 2 for more information about how the misperception of phonemes can cause misunderstandings). Siegel and Siegel (2015) conducted a study that involved a range of bottom-up activities, including dictation, sentence level prediction, and word counting exercises in an effort to improve students' bottom-up skills, and found those activities to improve student listening comprehension. In addition, Kissling (2018) demonstrated how pronunciation instruction can also help enhance bottom-up processing for listening. Though neither of these studies focused exclusively on MMs, morphological awareness and lexical segmentation were at least indirectly included and recognized as being basic building blocks for listening.

Two types of morphemes generally come in to play with regards to listening ability. One is derivational morphemes. These include prefixes such as *re–*, *non–*, and *dis–*, and suffixes such as *–ism*, *–ment*, *–ful*, and *–ize*, which allow users to make new words and which may but do not necessarily change the part of speech (e.g., friend + *–ly*; friend + *–ship*). The other type of morpheme is inflectional; this type indicates the grammatical function of a word. For English nouns and verbs, information such as number or tense and aspect is conveyed either in the stem of irregular nouns (*child; children*) or verbs (*go; went/gone*) or as an attached, bound suffix for regular nouns (boy + *–s*) or verbs (walk + *–ed*). Bound inflectional noun and verb endings in English can be particularly difficult morphemes for L2 learners because of the variety of ways in which they can be pronounced (e.g., [t], [d], [ɪd] for verbs and [s], [z], and [ɪz] for nouns and for third-person, singular, present tense verbs; also see Chapter 6 for information about the effect bound inflectional noun and verb endings can have on connected speech). Failure to supply these morphemes in spontaneous speech or read aloud tasks despite success on discrete declarative knowledge tasks has been the focus of previous research in L2 learning (e.g., Lardiere, 2003; Jiang, 2007).

So, in the opening anecdote, when I was standing in the wind, straining to hear my friend, I was struggling to identify the inflectional morpheme related to verb tense, the past tense [d] on the word *call* or the contracted [l] sound of the auxiliary verb *will* after *I*. Recognizing MMs is one valuable way to segment words and accurately comprehend certain aspects of a spoken message, such as singular-plural and tense.

Another concept related to MMs is *morphological congruency*, which refers to the morphological distance between one's first language (L1) and the target L2 (Jiang et al., 2011). Though all languages have mechanisms to mark number, tense, and aspect, when this is done lexically rather than by means of a bound morpheme on a regular stem, as it is in English, students may have trouble producing and recognizing the English MM. For example, when Jiang et al. (2011) compared L1 Russian and L1 Japanese learners of English, the results of a reading task showed that the L1 Russian group was more attuned to plural errors. Because Russian includes plural forms of nouns and Japanese does not, the findings support the hypothesis that the proximity of L1 morphology to a target L2 may affect morphological awareness in the L2. As Jiang et al. (2011) note, morphological congruence refers to specific morphemes contained within languages rather than to generalizations about the entire languages. Thus, identifying and understanding morphological differences between an L1 and an L2 can help facilitate listening skills in the L2.

Such knowledge may be particularly helpful to teachers and students who share an L1; however, teachers with multilingual classes may need to expand their knowledge of students' L1 morphology to take advantage of these possible connections. A valuable resource is the second edition of *Learner English* (Swan & Smith, 2010), which compares morphology and other features of 22 languages to English. Additionally, teachers could work to raise their students' metalinguistic awareness of the differences between English and their L1s by engaging in targeted questioning about how things like plurals and the past tense are indicated in students' languages.

To help L2 listeners recognize the importance of bottom-up aspects of listening, teachers have been implementing a range of activities targeting the linguistic "nuts and bolts" that are necessary for accurate aural understanding. As Field (2008) points out, word boundaries, particularly those of content words, are often marked by prefixes, suffixes, or verb conjugation markers. These linguistic elements carry important meaning for spoken messages, even if they are often of lower prominence when used by L1 speakers (Field, 2008). Proficient users are adept at attending to such MMs because they occur so frequently in spoken communication.

Several L2 listening researchers emphasize that teachers should be incorporating aspects of lexical segmentation (of which MMs is one) in language classrooms to explicitly interact with and decode incoming speech (e.g., Goh & Wallace, 2018; Graham, 2017; Vanderplank, 2013). In one study focusing specifically on MMs in listening through transcription, Karimi (2012) found that explicit instruction on English morphology helped the listening performance of preuniversity students as measured by transcription tests. The study involved 40 preuniversity students who were divided into control and experimental groups. Analysis of preintervention dictation tests showed no significant differences in student listening ability between the two groups. The experimental group then received a total of 5 hours of instruction focused on both inflectional markers (e.g., *–ing*, *–ed*) and derivational markers (e.g., *–tion*, *–ly*, and *–er*). Posttests results showed that the intervention group made gains of 2.9 words on average, in comparison to a –0.8 word decline for the control group. When comparing these results using an independent samples t-test, significant differences between the experimental and control groups were found, indicating that the gains by the experimental group were likely attributable to the MM-focused instruction. Karimi (2012) observed that morphological awareness "can be thought of as a bottom-up cognitive process that attempts at deriving the meaning of the message based on the analysis of the morphemic structure of the incoming data" (p. 457). In other words, based on the evidence, explicit instruction on morphology for English words can positively affect listening ability.

L2 morphological awareness also develops through natural exposure and immersion experiences (e.g., without explicit classroom instruction). In one study, the word segmentation ability of Japanese learners of L2 English improved in correlation with the length of time spent in an English-speaking environment (Ito & Strange, 2009). The researchers described how students in their study struggled to use allophonic signals for lexical segmentation. Allophones, or the variations in the way phonemes are pronounced, can be very challenging for learners to hear and say (also see Chapter 2). For instance, in English there is a difference in how /t/ is articulated in the words *top* (where it is aspirated) and *stop* (where aspiration is blocked by the fricative /s/ in the consonant cluster). In other languages, such as Thai or Hindi, these are recognized as two different sounds, or only one sound may exist, as in Spanish where word initial /t/ sounds are not aspirated. Ito and Strange's (2009) research demonstrated that even though the students struggled to use allophonic signals for segmentation purposes, they were able to recognize and use aspiration and glottal stops (the manner of consonant articulation in which the speaker cuts off air at the glottis, as in "uh oh") with increasing effectiveness. For example, the phrases *keeps talking* and *keep stalking* may sound very similar except for the aspirated [t^h] in the former. If a listener fails to recognize the /s/ in *keeps* as the word boundary, a domino effect will be that they fail to identify the initial [t^h] in *talking* as the beginning of that word; thus, they misinterpret the entire phrase. In relation to glottal stops, such as the difference between *an itch* and *a niche*, the Japanese learners performed better, registering 91% correct recognition. Results showed different perceptual patterns by the Japanese L2 English users compared to their native speaker counterparts and that length of stay in an English-speaking country can help increase perceptional abilities. Taken together with the classroom- and instruction-based findings in the previous paragraph (i.e., Karimi, 2012), the results of Ito and Strange (2009) suggest that both explicit systematic in-class instruction and real-world exposure support L2 learners in developing morphological awareness.

As the discussion thus far makes clear, the role of grammar in the listening act is important, as morphological awareness can aid lexical segmentation and therefore increase listening accuracy. Whereas bottom-up processing for listening and classroom activities targeting it have become more prevalent in research and pedagogic literature, much of the work remains at a rather general level and does not focus specifically on MMs as key tools L2 listeners can use to attend to and unlock meaning. Research (e.g., Karimi, 2012) has demonstrated how explicit in-class instruction can help learners take advantage of MMs in listening. Such instruction may be more accessible and time efficient than developing similar skills over longer periods of time in immersion programs (e.g., Ito & Strange, 2009). The pedagogic activities described in the next section are meant to provide teachers and students with exercises that highlight MMs with respect to other aspects of bottom-up processing.

Listening in the Classroom

The following activities are organized into two categories. The first focuses exclusively on MMs as they present themselves in single words. The second centers on MMs and their integration into the speech stream, which the listener must act on in order to accurately parse the "blur."

Focusing on Morphological Markers in Individual Words

Explicit Teaching

Introduce the concept of MMs and show students how they may already be familiar with both derivational and inflectional morphemes. Examples related to other content and skills in the English language classroom will likely be available, such as from reading assignments and grammar worksheets. Using word pairs (woman/women; finger/fingers; play/played) can be a simple way to reinforce the grammatical differences between these similar sounding words. Emphasize the important role MMs play in listening and illustrate with a personal example like that described in the opening anecdote. Though the notion of explicit, teacher-fronted instruction for listening may seem old-fashioned to some, the direct, efficient nature of such an approach can be valuable and effective.

Word Lists

Prepare short lists of similar words. Students hear a set of four unconnected words and need to pick out which one is different. Following are several examples.

Example 1. Focusing on the allomorphs, or variations of the past tense morpheme *-ed* ([t], [d], [ɪd])

Say: "Walked, talked, looked, tried" and ask which word sounds different from the others.

Answer: *Tried* is the only one with [d] marking the past tense. The others have [t], which may be aspirated [tʰ], for example when occurring in sentence final position, as in the following sentences: *They walked. They talked. They looked.*

Example 2. Focusing on the MM for regular plural countable nouns

Say: "Cats, mats, bat, pats" and ask which word sounds different from the others.

Answer: *Bat* is the only singular noun; the others are plural

Example 3. Focusing on the final *-s* allomorphs

Say: "Dishes, kisses, doors, wishes"

Answer: Three of the words share the extra syllable [ɪz], but the plural marker for *doors* does not add an extra syllable

Example 4. Focusing on voicing distinction

Say: "Dogs, cats, cows, birds"

Answer: Three share voiced [z] and *cats* ends with voiceless [s]

Example 5. Focusing on the MM for irregular singular-plural

Present a set of options to students indicating singular (1) and plural (1+). Students listen and then identify the pattern and label the items.

Say: "Men, woman, man, women"

Answer: 2 morphemes: man + plural; one; one; 2 morphemes: woman + plural

Before giving students the correct answers, encourage them to compare their guesses with a partner. Prompt students to ask each other questions like "Do you think the first one was one or more than one?" and "Could you tell the difference between the similar-sounding words?" Following is an illustrative conversation sample following cumulative stem and affix practice:

Student A: Do you think the first word, *cats*, was one or more than one?

Student B: More than one. I heard [ts] for the first one, not [t].

Student A: Yeah, I thought so too. How about the second word? I thought just one. The teacher said *woman* not *women*.

Working with a partner makes listening more of a social activity in which students can (a) confirm their answers; (b) ask for help; and (c) get unstructured practice in repeating the list of words, thereby applying their listening ability to their own pronunciation. Depending on the proficiency level of the student group, you can make adjustments to the difficulty level; for example, shorter words that students are already familiar with (e.g., of immediate relevance to everyday life) and/or words that students have recently encountered in other activities could be options for lower level learners. These easier adaptations could be used to target the A2 level on the Common Framework of References for Languages (CEFR), where grammatical focus for students includes "[using] simple structures, but [the learner] still systematically make[s] basic mistakes" (Council of Europe, 2001, p. 114). To make the activity more challenging, multisyllabic words can be used.

Affix Awareness

Prepare a list of words that include several different affixes. The list should also include affixes that are shared between at least some of the words (e.g., *government, disappear, tardiness, carelessness, revisit, thoughtfulness, hopeless, rearrange*). Students listen to the list and write down any affixes that occur more than once. Students then compare their answers with a classmate, after which you can check answers in plenary.

As part of the peer-to-peer discussions, you can include grammar extension (i.e., converting words to different parts of speech, e.g., the noun *government* converting to *govern* [verb] or *governing* [verb, gerund, or participial adjective]) and/or vocabulary extension activities (i.e., using the identified affix to say or write three additional words that include the same affix, e.g., using the *dis–* in *disappear* to list *disadvantageous, disbelieve,* and *disobey*).

This activity can be used in conjunction with vocabulary learning. For instance, when students learn new words from a reading passage or vocabulary list, these words can be incorporated into this MM-focused listening exercise to give extra exposure and take advantage of recycling opportunities. As emphasized by Nation (2014), learners benefit from multiple repetitions of and encounters with words, and an activity like this one presents opportunities to facilitate such encounters at regular intervals. Thus, the MM listening aspect can be integrated with other types of language practice.

Parsing and Morphological Markers in the Speech Stream

Counting Words

Select specific utterances from any type of listening text (from a textbook or authentic material). As students listen, they count the number of words they hear. One option is for students to count with their fingers (assuming the utterance is 10 words or fewer). Another is to have students make short marks on a note paper to indicate each word they hear. Remind them that contractions are generally counted as two words. Students then compare with classmates to see if they agree on how many words they heard.

Sentences for beginning students might include vocabulary items most relevant to learners' immediate needs:

a. I usually wake up at 8 o'clock. (7 words)
b. My sister and I go to school every day. (9 words)
c. What's your favorite food? (5 words)

Intermediate level learners might need to recognize sequencing and causation:

a. After we finish, let's take a walk. (8 words)
b. We have to hurry because I don't want to be late. (12 words)
c. I don't really understand where he went. (8 words)

At more advanced levels, you might target more complex structures, such as conditionals or reported speech or include lower frequency vocabulary:

a. If you don't have time to help me, then I'll ask somebody else. (15 words)
b. My mom asked me whether or not I'd had any trouble in school today. (15 words)
c. That sector was established as a consequence of the catastrophe. (10 words)

Because it is important for learners to be able to visualize the number of words they just heard, you can share the correct answers either by counting on your fingers and/or by writing the sentence on the board and counting along with students. When the sentences are written, you can also illustrate where aspects of connected speech may confuse students in their counting efforts (e.g., *wanted* + *to* = *wannedta*; *don't* + *really* = *donreally*).

Counting Words With . . .

Similar to the "Counting Words" activity, in this version of the activity, you indicate one or more MMs for students to focus their listening attention on. For instance, you might tell students to count the number of words with the regular past tense sounds [d], [t], and [ɪd] in the following story:

> Yesterday, I was so busy. First, I cleaned my bathroom quickly. Then I met my friend for breakfast and we chatted the morning away. I realized how late it was. I raced to the supermarket and picked up a cake for my daughter's

birthday. After that, I hurried to my dentist appointment. I arrived at home after 5:00.

Beginning learners might focus only on one type of sound (e.g., the [d] in *cleaned, realized, hurried,* and *arrived*), while more advanced learners could attend to more than one sound during a single listening (e.g., the [d] in *cleaned,* the [t] in *raced* and *picked,* and the [ɪd] in *chatted*). You can also vary the rate of speech and emphasis you place on certain sounds to accommodate learners of different proficiencies. When you draw students' attention to and contrast the similar sounds within longer stretches of speech, students will become more adept at noticing and producing the distinct sounds. This type of practice focuses student attention on specific morphemes and their contributions to the lexical segmentation process. This practice can be applied to various grammatical tenses and thus provides another opportunity for listening practice integrated with other language skills. Other options could be counting words with different types of plural formations ([s], [z], [ɪz]) or words with certain part of speech markers (e.g., *–ment, –ize*).

Same or Different?

In this activity, Prepare two sentences or utterances that are either identical or nearly identical. You can create these utterances or source them from available materials. Tell students they will hear two sentences, A and B. They may be exactly the same or have a slight difference. Students listen first to determine if the sentences are the same or different. If students detect a difference, they need to either write it down or quietly tell a classmate what the difference is. The following contrived utterances serve as examples:

1. A: I want to go to the supermarket to buy apples.
   B: I wanted to go to the supermarket to buy apples.
2. A: I wanted to go to the supermarket to buy apples.
   B: I've wanted to go to the supermarket to buy apples.
3. A: I won't go to the supermarket to buy apples.
   B: I've wanted to go to the supermarket to buy apples.

Orthographically, the past tense and past participle endings (*–ed*) are visible, as are the contracted auxiliary verbs (have: *–ve*; will not: *won't*). Likewise, the infinitive form of the verb (*to go*) follows the verb *want* but not the auxiliary *won't*. In continuous oral speech, noticing these distinctions is facilitated by knowledge of the co-occurring grammar (also see Chapter 5 for information on the role grammar knowledge plays in listening comprehension). Samples like those shown in 2 and 3 should not be used at beginning proficiency levels where perfect tenses, for example, have not yet been introduced into the curriculum.

To increase the difficulty, more than one morphological change can be added, where students need to listen for *any differences,* as opposed to only one:

A: I want to go to the supermarket to buy an apple.
B: I wanted to go to the supermarket to buy apples.

This activity can be used to target particular parsing problems that a certain student or group of students may be experiencing.

Affix Transcription

Prepare a short transcript that corresponds with a listening text (from a textbook or sourced from the internet). In preparing the transcript, remove affixes, such as derivational prefixes or suffixes and inflectional suffixes. Also insert numbered blanks before or after each and every word that has an affix removed. As students listen to the text (either read aloud or played digitally), they write in any affixes they hear. In this way, the exercise is similar to a traditional gap-fill activity but is meant to draw students' attention to lexical segmentation and the beginnings and endings of words. To make the task easier or more difficult, vary the speed of the text. Adding pauses is another option that can help lower level students.

The following example is modified from a TED Talk by Gary Kovacs (2012) on internet safety:

> "We are [1]leav___ our [2]birthday___, our [3]place___ of [4]resid___, our [5]interest___ and _____[6]preference_____, our [7]relation___, our [8]financ___ [9]histor___ [online]."

A second example comes from lyrics to the song "American Pie" by musician Don McLean:

> "I can't remember if I [1]cr___ when I [2]hear___ about his widowed bride but something [3]touch___ me deep [4]___side the day the music [5]di___."

This type of activity can also serve the purpose of reinforcing certain grammatical points that have been studied previously in class (e.g., the past tense or singular/plural). Though some students could make educated guesses and apply their grammatical knowledge to complete the exercise, you could also pose questions in which you say something that goes against student expectations in order to keep the emphasis on listening using MMs. At the same time, it could be enlightening for you and students to explore how using grammatical knowledge can facilitate completing the gap-fill without even listening, thereby presenting an opportunity to draw on students' grammatical knowledge and show how it can be used when listening.

Dictation and Circle

Dictation has often been cited as a useful way to help students develop bottom-up listening skills (e.g., Siegel & Siegel, 2015). The typical dictation activity involves students listening and writing verbatim what they hear. It can sometimes lack clear pedagogic purpose, especially when related to listening comprehension. After all, students could copy down what they have heard without actually understanding the message. In this variation of the traditional dictation activity, you draw explicit attention to a specific MM. Thus, the teaching purpose aligns with listening to MMs and the relationship between sounds and grammar. Students circle the MM they have written down following the listening and dictation, as in the following example, from a lesson focused on the sounds of plural noun endings ([s], [z], [ɪz]):

Example

Say: "I just bought some apples, two cartons of milk, a bag of doughnuts, and three packages of cookies at the store."

Students: Transcribe the sentence and then circle: the final *–s* on *apples, cartons, doughnuts, packages,* and *cookies*.

As a reminder, when doing dictations, you should pause after each phrase, rather than reading sentences word by word. Once you have read the text a couple of times, students can compare with a classmate and then you should show the completed text. Then, students can circle the final *–s* and identify which sound each one makes (apples [z], cartons [z], doughnuts [s], packages [ɪz], cookies [z]) and then repeat the words with the correct sounds. Like the previous activity, this exercise could easily be used as review of the three ways to pronounce the plural ending and/or to reinforce previously covered grammar points (e.g., count noun plural: add *–s*).

Because so much other work in language learning involves morphemes, and because those morphemes carry crucial information for accurately expressing and understanding messages, activities focused on MMs in listening can add new dimensions to listening activities while at the same time reinforcing grammar, vocabulary, and parts of speech. This chapter has illustrated the value of incorporating both derivational and inflectional morphemes into listening practice to further develop students' bottom-up listening abilities. None of the activities presented in this chapter can stand alone as the sole focus of a listening lesson. Instead, teachers might consider using one or more of the exercises in conjunction with the listening texts they use in class. Such an approach can provide more balance in listening rather than focusing only on comprehension questions (Field, 2008), listen-answer-check sequences (Siegel, 2014), or top-down aspects of listening. Morphological markers, along with several other bottom-up elements of language in general and listening in particular discussed in this volume (connected speech, intonation, lexical bundles, etc.), play important roles in the comprehension process and deserve to be highlighted in the L2 classroom.

References

Cauldwell, R. (2013). *Phonology for listening: Teaching the stream of speech*. Speech in Action.

Council of Europe. (2001). *Common European framework for reference of languages: Learning, teaching and assessment*. Cambridge University Press.

Field, J. (2003). Promoting perception: Lexical segmentation in L2 listening. *ELT Journal, 57*(4), 325–334.

Field, J. (2008). *Listening in the language classroom*. Cambridge University Press.

Goh, C. (2000). A cognitive perspective on language learners' listening comprehension problems. *System, 28*(1), 55–75.

Goh, C., & Wallace, M. (2018). Lexical segmentation in listening. In J. Liontas (Ed.), *TESOL encyclopedia of English language teaching*. Wiley Blackwell. https://doi.org/10.1002/9781118784235.eelt06003

Gottardo, A., Mirza, A., Koh, P. W., Ferreira, A., & Javier, C. (2018). Unpacking listening comprehension: The role of vocabulary, morphological awareness, and syntactic knowledge in reading comprehension. *Reading and Writing, 31*, 1741–1764.

Graham, S. (2017). Research into practice: Listening strategies in an instructed classroom setting. *Language Teaching, 50*(1), 107–119.

Hasan, A. (2000). Learners' perceptions of listening comprehension problems. *Language, Culture and Curriculum, 13*(2), 137–153.

Ito, K., & Strange, W. (2009). Perception of allophonic cues to English word boundaries by Japanese second language learners of English. *Journal of the Acoustical Society of America, 125*, 2348–2360.

Jiang, N. (2007). Selective integration of linguistic knowledge in adult second language learning. *Language Learning, 57*(1), 1–33.

Jiang, N., Novokshanova, E., Masuda, K., & Wang, X. (2011). Morphological congruency and the acquisition of L2 morphemes. *Language Learning, 61*(3), 940–967.

Karimi, M. (2012). Enhancing L2 students' listening transcription ability through a focus on morphological awareness. *Journal of Psycholinguistic Research, 42*(5), 451–459.

Kissling, E. (2018). Pronunciation instruction can improve L2 learners' bottom-up processing for listening. *The Modern Language Journal, 102*(4), 653–675.

Kovacs, G. (2012, February). *Tracking our online trackers* [Video]. TED Conferences. https://www.ted.comtalks/gary_kovacs_tracking_our_online_trackers/transcript?language=en

Lardiere, D. (2003). Second language knowledge of [±past] and [±finite]. In J. Liceras, H. Zobl, & H. Goodluck (Eds.), *Proceedings of the 6h generative approaches to second language acquisition conference* (pp. 176–189). Cascadilla Press.

McLean, D. (1971). American pie. On *American pie* [album]. United Artists.

Nation, P. (2014). How much input do you need to learn the most frequent 9,000 words? *Reading in a Foreign Language, 26*(2), 1–16.

Siegel, J. (2014). Advice in listening instruction: Degrees of transferability. *International Journal of Innovation in ELT and Research, 3*(2), 121–138.

Siegel, J., & Siegel, A. (2015). Getting to the bottom of L2 listening instruction: Making a case for bottom-up activities. *Studies in Second Language Learning and Teaching, 5*(4), 637–662.

Swan, M., & Smith, B. (Eds.). (2010). *Learner English: A teacher's guide to interference and other problems* (2nd ed.). Cambridge University Press.

Vanderplank, R. (2013). Listening and understanding. In P. Driscoll, E. Macaro, & A. Swarbrick (Eds.), *Debates in modern languages education* (pp. 53–65). Routledge.

Yule, G. (2017). *The study of language* (6th ed.). Cambridge University Press.

JOSEPH SIEGEL is associate professor (docent) in English at Stockholm and Örebro Universities in Sweden, where he teaches TESOL methodology, linguistics, and applied linguistic research methods courses. He holds a PhD in applied linguistics from Aston University and an MA (TESL/TEFL) from the University of Birmingham. His recent publications are on the topics of second language notetaking, English as a medium of instruction lecture comprehension, listening pedagogy, and pragmatic instruction.

CHAPTER 4

VALERIA BOGOREVICH AND ELNAZ KIA

Segmenting Streams of Speech in University Discourse: The Role of Lexical Bundles

Listening in Real Life

For the past 6 years, we have been teaching English for academic purposes courses at an intensive English program in the United States. Our students' levels are mostly intermediate to advanced and their goal is to pass all the English classes to graduate from our program and start studying at a university. Because neither of us started speaking English as our first language but rather studied English outside of the United States in a formal setting, it was not shocking to us that our students struggled with their listening comprehension. As teachers, we broke the lectures down into parts, created listening organizers, and developed numerous comprehension questions. In turn, our students spent hours of class time reading the questions carefully, listening to lectures, relistening multiple times, and still could not answer most of the questions correctly or accurately summarize a lecture. Therefore, after one of the curriculum meetings, we decided to go back to gap-fill and transcription tasks. Why? Because we both agreed that those were the only exercises that significantly boosted our listening skills many years ago when we used to be language learners. Gap-fill and transcription benefited our speech recognition skills by teaching our brain to automatically process speech and translate what sounds like one word into multiple words (e.g., "mgonatak" into "I am going to talk").

We knew that asking our students to transcribe a whole 4-minute lecture would be too ambitious, so we decided to focus on specific phrases that would aid students' listening comprehension. We created a gap-fill activity by cutting out important transitions, such as "My main argument is that" and "I strongly believe that" and leaving one long line for the students to fill in the gaps (see Example 1). Unfortunately, not a single student was able to reconstruct the gapped elements from listening close enough to call their performance "good" or "excellent."

Example 1: Gap-filling example with a solid line

What students hear: Another point is that animals suffer in circuses.

What students see: ______________________________ animals suffer in circuses.

After our students have completed such activities several times, we could see common patterns. Students would write "you point you" instead of "your point of view," "it well know the" instead of "it's well known that," "furstval" instead of "first of all," and "it similar" instead of "it's similar to." Of course, we expected the gap-fill activity to be a hard task, but we did not know that the parsing ability of our conditionally admitted university students was at such a low level. We wanted our students to keep practicing such tasks but knew that their motivation would most probably plummet if they kept struggling that much and seeing grades showing low performance. Therefore, we decided to make the task a bit easier by providing one gap for each omitted word, making the gaps longer or shorter depending on how many letters each word has (see Example 2).

Example 2: Gap-fill example with a broken line

What students hear: At the same time, there are many other ways of improving the conditions.

What students see: _____ ________ _______________ _____________, there are many other ways of improving the conditions.

Additionally, we asked our students to complete error-correction activities; for each phrase in which they had an error, students practiced writing and pronouncing the correction five times. We also provided an option to redo the activity for a higher grade. As a result, our students told us that activities like these opened their eyes (or rather tuned their ears?).

Listening in the Research

Listening plays an important role in learning languages and in higher education. However, many second language (L2) learners struggle to understand information from listening. L2 listening can be considered more challenging than other language learning skills because of its spontaneity and transient mode (Cutler, 2012). In other words, in the real world, students cannot go back and listen again to a sentence. Therefore, they have to decode speech quickly, which is a complicated procedure: Students need to process the meaning of running words and phrases to be able to recognize the overall meaning and detailed information. According to students' self-reports, two of the main challenges in listening comprehension are the inability to identify familiar words in fast-speed speech and understanding the overall message (Vandergrift & Goh, 2012). Students associate these difficulties with issues regarding segmentation of streams of speech (Goh, 2000).

Unlike in writing, where there are spaces in-between words, spoken discourse does not have clear word boundaries. Thus, identification of word boundaries and parsing the continuous speech stream into individual words is a fundamental skill for L2 language learners (also see Chapters 5 and 6 for more information about parsing speech). O'Mally et al. (1989) mentioned parsing as one of the three areas that distinguished effective listeners from ineffective listeners because effective listeners focus on larger units rather than words. The positive impact of parsing activities on learners' listening comprehension is also supported by research studies on bottom-up listening activities (e.g., Leonard, 2019; Siegel & Siegel, 2015; Goh, 2000).

Research on segmenting streams of speech includes studies on idioms, collocations, formulaic sequences, multiword units, prefabricated units (Wray, 2002), and lexical bundles (Biber et al., 1999). Though all of these streams of speech are composed of multiple words and are independently meaningful, they differ in terms of frequency and idiomaticity. In this chapter, we focus on lexical bundles, which are extended collocations defined as sequences of three or more words that frequently co-occur in spoken and written discourse (e.g., "do you know what," "going to talk about," "it is important to"; Biber et al., 1999).

One of the reasons why this chapter focuses on lexical bundles as opposed to other streams of speech is that lexical bundles are frequency based (Biber & Barbieri, 2007). That is, they are not identified based on human intuition or hunches. Instead, they are picked using a corpus computational technique considering the number of times they appear in a range of texts. Therefore, we can conclude that they are the most common phrases or clauses used in a given discourse. Another reason for the importance of lexical bundles is that they are crucial in understanding classroom teaching because they are extremely frequent in spoken academic discourse (Biber et al., 2004; Nesi & Basturkmen, 2006). According to Biber (2006), the frequency of use of lexical bundles in classroom teaching is twice the frequency in conversations and four times the frequency in textbooks.

Understanding lexical bundles in listening can also be challenging for students because bundles include function words and prepositions (Reppen, 2018) that are frequently reduced in speech (also see Chapter 7 for more on weak forms). In addition, despite being frequent, lexical bundles are not obvious to listeners because of their incompleteness and because they are basically fragments that frame other information (Biber et al. 2004; Byrd & Coxhead, 2010; Simpson-Vlach & Ellis, 2010). Another factor that challenges listeners is the storage and retrieval process of lexical bundles. The high frequency and multifunctionality of lexical bundles suggest that they are prefabricated (Biber & Barbieri, 2007), and prefabricated word sequences are, for native speakers of English, "stored and retrieved whole from memory" (Wray, 2002, p. 9). However, according to Conklin and Schmitt (2012), nonnative speakers are more inclined to process prefabricated units one word at a time. This suggests that we should include explicit instruction of lexical bundles in L2 learning classrooms.

In addition, learning lexical bundles can help L2 listeners better understand academic lectures. Listening to lectures is known to be cognitively demanding because it involves multitasking: decoding long streams of speech and understanding complex ideas while simultaneously processing the information projected on slides and taking notes (Nesi &

Basturkmen, 2006). Because lexical bundles usually function as signposts or discourse signals (Reppen, 2018), learning them can help the listeners predict upcoming topics and ideas and subsequently make relevant inferences. Teaching students to recognize lexical bundles in university lectures will also help them comprehend speech more easily by lowering the cognitive load of listening. Importantly, lexical bundles help listeners follow the higher level information in the lecture and consequently better understand the overall meaning (Csomay & Cortes, 2010). In a study on the effect of using micro-markers (e.g., *well, so*) and macromarkers (e.g., lexical bundles such as "what I'm going to talk about today") in academic lectures on students' comprehension, it was found that students do better on listening comprehension tasks after listening to lectures that used macromarkers alone (Chaudron & Richards, 1986, as cited in Neely & Cortes, 2009).

Building on the aforementioned findings, many studies have examined the effect of direct and indirect instruction of lexical bundles on students' listening comprehension. Liu (2012) noted that multiword units were not salient to students, and, therefore, students did not easily notice them, and this was because of the incompleteness of the multiword constructions. As a result, Liu suggested a partial filling activity in which some of the lexical elements of the bundle were filled while others were replaced by schematic linguistic representations. An example would be changing "it is important to" to "it is important to + verb phrase." Based on the results of this study, explicit noticing of lexical bundles with linguistic cues is more effective than incidental learning of bundles (i.e., noticing bundles in a complete context). The author claims that explicit noticing of bundles will raise learners' awareness. These results were further confirmed by Thomson (2016), who mentions that matching lexical cues with the associated words in the texts further engages learners in this process and promotes better initial uptake.

Another approach to raise the salience of lexical bundles for students could be textual enhancement (e.g., underlining, highlighting). In a study on collocations, underlining the multiword units in spoken and written texts led to more uptake. For example, students in the experimental group used more of the collocations in their speech (Boers et al., 2006). Based on the review of the literature, we can conclude that explicit instruction of lexical bundles improves listeners' comprehension and leads to early uptake.

Listening in the Classroom

Lexical Bundles in Academic Lectures

Teaching academic listening might seem to be an extremely hard task because lectures are usually long and information dense. Sometimes, teachers do not know what they need to focus on in their classrooms, as their B1 or B2 level students (according to the Common European Framework of Reference for Languages; Council of Europe, 2001) may often guess instead of answering main idea and detail questions and cannot summarize the information from lectures. Creating activities for students that focus on listening for lexical bundles can be compared to teaching the meaning of road signs to a novice driver. Automatic processing of lexical bundles will help future university students become more alert when professors identify the topic of the lecture, signal a change of topic, emphasize important information, and give examples.

The following paragraphs provide descriptions of various activities that teachers can easily implement in their classrooms. For most of the activities, teachers need to listen to the lectures or conversations that students are going to listen to in class beforehand and create a list of lexical bundles that appear in those lectures or conversations. Teachers can also refer to Nesi and Basturkmen (2006), which provides 20 of the most frequent lexical bundles in lectures. Additionally, some activities require teachers to provide students with transcripts. For most of the activities, options are given for how teachers can make the activity more or less difficult for their students.

Ordering

In class, hand out or project the list of phrases (see Example 3) and play the lecture to students. Students listen to the lecture and number lexical bundles in order of appearance in the lecture. If you would like to make this activity more challenging, then add two or more extra phrases to the list that do not appear in the lecture.

Example 3: Ordering activity

Number the expressions in the order you hear them in the lecture.

Expression	#
another point is that	
that's a good example of	
to argue against the issue	
my main argument is that	
that's what I'm going to talk about today	

To add a communicative element to this straightforward activity, ask students to have a conversation to compare their answers. This example can be projected to facilitate such conversations:

A: Which expression was first?
B: I think it is . . .

A: Oh, great! I have the same!
B: Yay! What about the second?

A: I am not sure, but I think it is . . .
B: Oh, really? I have . . .

A: Hmm, I have that one for number . . .
B: I see, okay, I think you are right. Let's move on to number . . .

Classification

Choose two or more lectures to play for students. As in the previous activity, students receive a list of lexical bundles. The students need to not only number the bundles in the order of appearance but also categorize which bundles were used in which lecture (see Example 4).

Example 4: Classification activity

Listen to the lectures. Choose which expressions from the box appear in which lecture. Make sure to write down the expressions in the order they appear in each lecture.

Order	Lecture 1	Lecture 2	Lecture 3
# 1			
# 2			
# 3			

Scramble

Students receive a transcript of the lecture that they are going to listen to. In the transcript, the components of each lexical bundle are scrambled. For example, instead of "despite some differences between," students see "between despite differences" and instead of "first of all" they see "of first all." The students' task is to unscramble lexical bundles while listening to the lecture. This activity can provide needed scaffolding for lower proficiency learners.

Gap-Fill

Give the transcript of the lecture with gaps instead of lexical bundles to students coupled with a box containing lexical bundles. Students listen to the lecture and fill in the gaps by choosing which phrases from the box they hear in the lecture (see Example 5). You can make this activity more challenging by adding distractors in the form of additional lexical bundles that do not appear in the lecture. To add even more rigor, the distractors might be similar sounding phrases, such as "the other example" and "another example."

Example 5: Gap-fill activity

Listen to the lecture and use the expressions from the box to fill in the gaps in the transcript.

another point is that	that's a good example of	to argue against the issue
my main argument is that	what I'm going to talk about today	

Many of you probably know that climate change is a huge issue on the news today. So, as a biology professor and an environmental activist, I focus on how climate change is affecting species around the world. [1]__________________________is the adverse effects of climate change on polar bears. Hmm, well [2]______________ ____________ humans are the biggest threat to polar bears. It is human activity and nothing else that has led the poor bears to the brink of extinction.

Transcription

This activity is a more difficult version of the previous one ("Gap Fill"). The only difference between the two is that this option does not provide students with a list of words in a box to choose from. Therefore, this exercise can be more time consuming and, perhaps, is better suited for higher level learners or reserved for at-home work.

To prepare this activity, create a transcript of a lecture with gaps instead of lexical bundles beforehand. Students use the transcripts while listening and write down the missing words. To make this activity easier, you can substitute the solid gap line (__________) with a broken line (____ ______) to help students identify how many words each gap includes and even provide the first or last letter (or both) for each word (___r ________e; f____ e________; or f_r e______e). Such an activity might be time consuming if the students struggle with spelling in addition to listening.

To scaffold further, show or write on the board the list of bundles for a minute so that students have time to familiarize themselves with the bundles (however, it should be made clear that students cannot write them down for use during the activity). After that, students listen to the lecture and write down the bundles for each gap. The next step can be asking students to compare their answers with a partner before you review the activity with the whole class. For homework practice, you might want to assign longer lectures or TED Talks (10–20 mins), encouraging students to listen and pause as many times as they need to identify every single word in each bundle.

Production

As discussed in Chapters 1 and 6, there is some evidence that production can lead to better perception (see Flege, 1995; Flege et al., 1999; Best, 1995; Best & Tyler, 2007; Huensch & Tremblay, 2015). For this activity, ask students to create their own mini-lectures on a given topic using a specific number of lexical bundles from a list.

The first step in creating such an activity would be providing the students with an example mini-lecture that fits the content of the unit and a list of lexical bundles that are typical of presentations, such as the following:

- Today, I am going to talk about
- Now, let's move on to
- As you can see in the picture
- the graph shows

After that, the students can work in small groups of three or four people at home to write their mini-lectures. In class, students use a checklist (see Example 6) while listening to their classmates' presentations to identify which bundles were utilized in each mini-lecture. To verify if the students check-marked the right lexical bundles, you can create an answer key while listening and project it after all the students are finished with their presentations. As an alternative, you can organize a discussion after each mini-lecture where the audience members compare answers in groups and then the presenter shares a slide or handout with the expressions they used.

Example 6: Checklist

	Group 1	Group 2	Group 3	Group 4
Now, let's move on to				
According to the pie chart				
we strongly oppose				
supports the argument				

This activity can be completed by listening to the recorded lectures played in class or presented live. This can be a whole-class activity if all the students listen to each group mini-lecture or a small-group activity if only two or three groups of students listen to each other's mini-lectures. Alternatively, in order to save class time, you can assign this task as homework by using the Flipgrid website (info.flipgrid.com; see more in Stoszkowski, 2018) to organize a space for the students to share their video mini-lectures. Students can also use Zoom (www.zoom.com) to record and then share their video mini-lectures via email or a shared drive, like Google Drive. This way, the classroom can be flipped—the students listen to the mini-lectures at home and come to class to discuss what bundles they heard.

Mingling Activity

This activity should be introduced to students as a midterm or final review activity once the target lexical bundles have been studied. Compile all the bundles and create a list. Each student gets several cards with beginnings and ends of lexical bundles. For instance, random students receive "I strongly," "example of," "believe that," and "that's a good." Ask all the students to mingle and find a match for their bundle half. Once all the students find their matches, play a sentence that contains these lexical bundles. Those students who had parts of that bundle need to stand up and write their parts next to each other on the board.

Background Knowledge

Lexical bundles can be used in prelistening activities to activate students' background knowledge. Create a stack of cards with one or more lexical bundles written on each card. Before listening to a lecture, students randomly pick one card and read the bundles on it. Then, announce the topic of the lecture to the students, and they write down one or more sentences using lexical bundles on the card that they might hear in the lecture.

For example, a student gets a card with "today we'll focus on" and the topic of the lecture is "alternative energy." That student can write, "Today we'll focus on alternative energy and other renewable energy sources." Optionally, ask several students to share their example sentences with the class or exchange their examples with a partner in order to highlight the lexical bundles in their partner's example sentences.

The next step focuses on developing students' metacognitive ability, which is important for L2 learners (Goh, 2008; Vandergrift & Tafaghodtari, 2010). Students need to compare their predictions with what they actually heard in the lecture. To this end, ask students to mark if their sentence was (a) similar, (b) close, or (c) not close at all to what they heard in the recording. This step will help learners to exercise their ability to assess their predictions and discard incorrect guesses more easily and quickly.

Field Trip

Because students will need access to mainstream academic classes for this activity, it might not be feasible for all teachers, but only for those who teach at pathway or sheltered programs. However, as an alternative, you can substitute real-life lectures with recorded full-length academic lectures. Such lectures can be found online on MOOCs (e.g., Coursera, EdX, Khan Academy, FutureLearn, Open2Study, Open Yale Courses) or via YouTube lecture compilations (e.g., by Vanderbilt, Carnegie Mellon University, Massachusetts Institute of Technology, University of New Brunswick, and other well-known universities).

Ask students to observe a regular academic lecture and take notes on what kind of formulaic expressions they heard in this lecture. Students can work in groups (if they are taking the same mainstream class) or individually. This assignment can be turned into a writing or a speaking mini-project if you ask students to tally the number of times they heard each lexical bundle and to create a pie chart or a bar graph describing how frequent each expression was. If speaking is the target, students can prepare short presentations about the class they observed and the frequency of the bundles in that class. Alternatively, students can turn in written reports with the same information.

Function Words

As illustrated in Lacroix et al. (2016), and as we've seen constantly in our own classrooms, students struggle to hear function words when listening to lectures (also see Chapter 7 for a discussion about listening for weak forms). This activity provides an additional focus on the function words that lexical bundles comprise (see Example 7). Because function words are naturally reduced and not emphasized or stressed in speech (Celce-Murcia et al., 2010), they are harder to hear; therefore, some scaffolding is needed to prepare the students for this listening activity. Ask the students to break into pairs or groups of three to discuss the sentences beforehand. The focus of this discussion should be on utilizing students' knowledge of English grammar and syntax in order to predict the missing function words.

Example 7: Function words activity

Listen to the sentences to complete lexical bundles.

1. ___ argue ____ ____ issue, we have Jon Longa who is a well-known author and anthropology professor.

2. People who avoid regular exercise have lower immune systems. ______ results _____ more colds and flues that such people get throughout the year.
3. When I gave you ____ example ____ water flowing through the tubes, I forgot to mention that the pressure of water ____ similar ____ voltage in electricity.

Because listening to function words takes a long time (students need to listen to the same sentence repeatedly to discern the missing words), using longer lectures might be too time consuming in the classroom. Thus, consider using lecture excerpts that can be either one sentence long or contain several sentences connected by the same idea.

Error Correction

You can focus on grammar while teaching listening for lexical bundles. For example, give students lecture transcripts or lecture excerpts that include several sentences in which lexical bundles include typical grammar and spelling errors. As shown in Example 8, this activity can be made easier if the bundles are underlined so that the students know where to focus their attention. Additionally, you can focus on problematic grammar aspects, such as *–ed* and *–s* endings that students tend to not hear (also see Chapter 3 for more on listening to morphological markers). First, students try to correct the errors, either individually or in pairs, without listening. Second, the students listen to the lecture to check if they corrected the mistakes accurately.

Example 8: Error correction activity

Read the lecture excerpts, which contain grammatical errors. First, try correcting the mistakes based on your grammar knowledge. Second, listen to the excerpts to check your work.

1. In his book, Cook argue against this issues.
2. In the past, many people strong believe that the Sun goes around the Earth.
3. I can see some difference with his early writing, before 1996, and his later books.
4. Other things are the they have distinct likes and dislikes.

YouGlish

YouGlish is a website that searches for specific words or phrases in 50 million YouTube videos (see more in Karatay, 2017 and Miller, 2019). Depending on frequency and length of an expression, it can return thousands of videos (e.g., "for example" has 95,043 occurrences) or hundreds ("it's a good example of" has 221 occurrences). Figure 1 shows search results for "another point is that." In this case, choose which video out of 343 videos you would like to play in class. YouGlish returns a compilation of videos, and you can use "back" and "forward" buttons to play the videos.

For this YouGlish activity, choose several specific lexical bundles that you would like your students to focus on in class. Type the lexical bundle in the search box of the YouGlish website and play five or more videos with that expression. While listening,

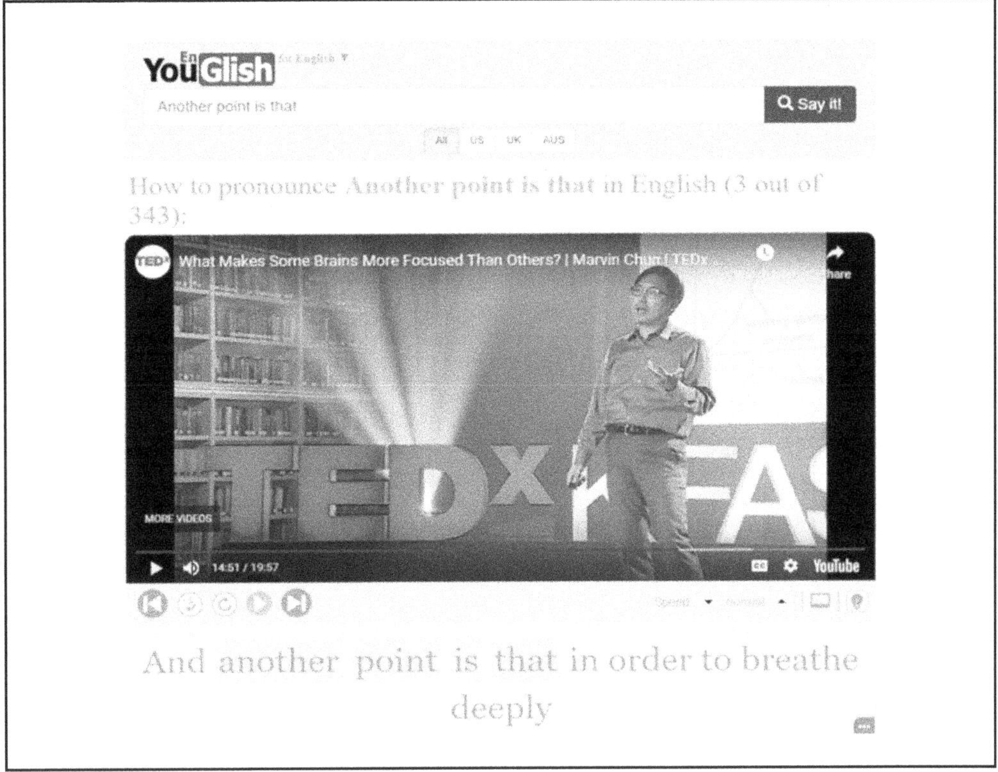

Figure 1. YouGlish results for "another point is that."

students are trying to identify which lexical bundle is repeated in the played videos. It is important not to project the videos for this activity because YouGlish shows the transcripts for each video with the search words highlighted (see Figure 1).

YouGlish can also be used to practice pronunciation of selected lexical bundles. You can focus on students' convergent production of target expressions because improved production can possibly lead to improved perception of such expressions from listening (e.g., Casserly & Pisoni, 2010; Reed & Michaud, 2011).

Lexical Bundles in Academic Interactions

Lexical bundles are important not only when students are practicing listening to lectures, but also when teachers prepare students for classroom discussions, which are a common means of instruction in the United States. All the previously described activities in this chapter to practice lexical bundles in lectures can be also used to practice lexical bundles common in academic interactions. The following two examples show how lexical bundles that are common for interaction can be practiced in a classroom.

Lists

This simple activity can be used to create lists of bundles for future use in speaking or other activities. Provide a list of isolated bundles to students with one word missing from each bundle (see Example 9). The students look the list over first and then listen to a recorded conversation in which the bundles are used. This activity has an example of a simple conversation that would be suitable even for elementary level students. To make the task accessible for lower level students, only content words should be omitted, and all the function words left unchanged. However, if the target audience is at a higher proficiency level, the opposite can be done.

Example 9: Lists of lexical bundles

Look at the list of expressions. Each expression is missing one word. Listen to the conversation and complete the bundles.

1. ____ are you doing here
2. I _____ to see
3. I have a _______ about
4. Oh, I ____
5. I don't _____

Shi: Hey, Alexis!

Alexis: Oh, hi, Shi! How are you doing?

Shi: I'm doing great! And you?

Alexis: I am good too. What are you doing here?

Shi: Hmm, I want to see Dr. Jarrasko because I have a question about the midterm.

Alexis: Oh, I see!

Shi: Yeah, but I am not sure where the office is. Do you know?

Alexis: Uh-uh, sorry! I don't know!

Shi: It's okay!

Alexis: Oh look, there's Adah! Maybe she knows. Let's ask her!

Shi: Yeah!

Alexis: Adah!

Conversations

Revisiting the benefits of production for perception (e.g., Casserly & Pisoni, 2010), this activity focuses on students' ability to use lexical bundles in their own speech. For this exercise, you can use the lists generated in the previous activity as well as provide your own lists of lexical bundles. Provide students with a topic that they are likely to be given for a discussion in a university session. If students' majors are known, the topic can be major specific. The directions can specify how many expressions you want each student to use in one conversation (e.g., use at least three lexical bundles) or simply direct students to use as many as they can. The conversations can be done in pairs or in small groups. (See Example 10.)

Example 10: Conversations

For this group conversation, you and your partners will discuss the following statement: "Fossil fuels are finite resources; thus, our nation must focus on harnessing wind and sun power for our needs." Use as many expressions from the box as you can.

what I mean	good point	in other words	are you saying	okay, but	yeah, but
I see what you are saying	I see your point	another thing is	another point is that		

English learners face numerous challenges related to parsing streams of speech and breaking connected speech into individual words, particularly in long lectures. Expressions that seem clear to proficient listeners ("I'm going to talk") may sound incomprehensible to learners (*mgonotak*) as they struggle to understand reduced words and word boundaries. If students can learn to identify lexical bundles in those streams of speech, their listening will become more efficient.

This chapter has provided a number of bottom-up listening and speaking activities that can be incorporated as-is or with modifications. As well, we have suggested several activities that help students memorize the lexical bundles. As the literature reviewed in the chapter corroborates, English language teachers need to explicitly teach lexical bundles to students to help them better comprehend long speeches. After the lexical bundles have been explicitly introduced, we would encourage teachers to incorporate some of these activities with the goal of lessening listeners' cognitive load by training students' brains to automatize the parsing process. The chapter has suggested modifications for each activity to make them suitable for a variety of students, ranging from beginning to advanced English proficiency levels. Learning to listen for lexical bundles is an important step in developing listening fluency and one that merits the use of precious class time.

References

Best, C. T. (1995). A direct realist perspective on cross-language speech perception. In W. Strange (Ed.), *Speech perception and linguistic experience: Issues in cross-language research* (pp. 171–204). York Press.

Best, C. T., & Tyler, M. D. (2007). Nonnative and second-language speech perception: Commonalities and complementarities. In O. S. Bohn & M. J. Munro (Eds.), *Language experience in second language speech learning: In honor of James Emil Flege* (pp. 13–34). John Benjamins. https://doi.org/10.1075/lllt.17.07bes

Biber, D. (2006). *University language: A corpus-based study of spoken and written registers* (Vol. 23). John Benjamins. https://doi.org/10.1075/scl.23

Biber, D., & Barbieri, F. (2007). Lexical bundles in university spoken and written registers. *English for Specific Purposes*, *26*(3), 263–286. https://doi.org/10.1016/j.esp.2006.08.003

Biber, D., Conrad, S., & Cortes, V. (2004). *If you look at . . .*: Lexical bundles in university teaching and textbooks. *Applied Linguistics, 25*(3), 371–405. https://doi.org/10.1093/applin/25.3.371

Biber, D., Johansson, S., Leech, G., Conrad, S., & Finegan, E. (1999). *Longman grammar of spoken and written English*. Longman.

Boers, F., Eyckmans, J., Kappel, J., Stengers, H., & Demecheleer, M. (2006). Formulaic sequences and perceived oral proficiency: Putting a lexical approach to the test. *Language Teaching Research, 10*(3), 245–261. https://doi.org/10.1191/1362168806lr195oa

Byrd, P., & Coxhead, A. (2010). On the other hand: Lexical bundles in academic writing and in the teaching of EAP. *University of Sydney Papers in TESOL, 5*, 31–64.

Casserly, E. D., & Pisoni, D. B. (2010). Speech perception and production. *Wiley Interdisciplinary Reviews: Cognitive Science, 1*(5), 629–647. https://doi.org/10.1002/wcs.63

Celce-Murcia, M., Brinton, D. M., & Goodwin, J. M. (2010). *Teaching pronunciation hardback with audio CDs (2): A course book and reference guide*. Cambridge University Press.

Conklin, K., & Schmitt, N. (2012). The processing of formulaic language. *Annual Review of Applied Linguistics, 32*, 45–61. https://doi.org/10.1017/s0267190512000074

Council of Europe. (2001). *Common European framework of reference for languages: Learning, teaching, assessment*. Cambridge University Press.

Csomay, E., & Cortes, V. (2010). Lexical bundle distribution in university classroom talk. In *Corpus-linguistic applications* (pp. 153–168). Brill | Rodopi. https://doi.org/10.1163/9789042028012_011

Cutler, A. (2012). *Native listening: Language experience and the recognition of spoken words*. MIT Press. https://doi.org/10.7551/mitpress/9012.001.0001

Flege, J. E. (1995). Second language speech learning: Theory, findings, and problems. *Speech Perception and Linguistic Experience: Issues in Cross-Language Research, 92*, 233–277.

Flege, J. E., MacKay, I. R., & Meador, D. (1999). Native Italian speakers' perception and production of English vowels. *The Journal of the Acoustical Society of America, 106*(5), 2973–2987. https://doi.org/10.1121/1.428116

Goh, C. C. (2000). A cognitive perspective on language learners' listening comprehension problems. *System, 28*(1), 55–75. http://dx.doi.org/10.1016/S0346-251X(99)00060-3

Goh, C. (2008). Metacognitive instruction for second language listening development: Theory, practice and research implications. *RELC Journal, 39*, 188–213. http://dx.doi.org/10.1177/0033688208092184

Huensch, A., & Tremblay, A. (2015). Effects of perceptual phonetic training on the perception and production of second language syllable structure. *Journal of Phonetics, 52*, 105–120. https://doi.org/10.1016/j.wocn.2015.06.007

Karatay, Y. (2017). YouGlish.com (Review). In M. O'Brien & J. Levis (Eds.), *Proceedings of the 8th annual pronunciation in second language learning and teaching conference* (pp. 254–259). Iowa State University.

Lacroix, J., Reed, M., & Harbaugh, A. (2016). The effect of metacognitive strategy instruction on L2 learner beliefs and listening skills. In J. Levis, H. Le, I. Lucic, E. Simpson, & S. Vo (Eds.), *Proceedings of the 7th annual pronunciation in second language learning and teaching conference* (pp. 76–87). Iowa State University.

Leonard, K. R. (2019). Examining the relationship between decoding and comprehension in L2 listening. *System, 87*, 102–150. https://doi.org/10.1016/j.system.2019.102150

Liu, D. (2012). The most frequently-used multi-word constructions in academic written English: A multi-corpus study. *English for Specific Purposes, 31*(1), 25–35. http://dx.doi.org/10.1016/j.esp.2011.07.002

Miller, M. (2019). YouGlish [Review]. *TESL-EJ, 23*(2). https://www.tesl-ej.org/wordpress/issues/volume23/ej90/ej90m1/

Neely, E., & Cortes, V. (2009). A little bit about: Analyzing and teaching lexical bundles in academic lectures. *Language Value, 1*(1), 17–38.

Nesi, H., & Basturkmen, H. (2006). Lexical bundles and discourse signaling in academic lectures. *International Journal of Corpus Linguistics, 11*(3), 283–304. https://doi.org/10.1075/ijcl.11.3.04nes

O'Mally, J. M., Chamot, A. U., & Küpper, L. (1989). Listening comprehension strategies in second language acquisition. *Applied Linguistics, 10*(4), 418–437. https://doi.org/10.1093/applin/10.4.418

Reed, M., & Michaud, C. (2011). An integrated approach to pronunciation: Listening comprehension and intelligibility in theory and practice. In. J. Levis & K. LeVelle (Eds.), *Proceedings of the 2nd annual pronunciation in second language learning and teaching conference* (pp. 95–104). Iowa State University.

Reppen, R. (2018). Teaching lexical bundles: Which ones and how? In E. Hinkel (Ed.), *Teaching essential units of language: Beyond single-word vocabulary* (pp. 186–200). Routledge. https://doi.org/10.4324/9781351067737-8

Siegel, J., & Siegel, A. (2015). Getting to the bottom of L2 listening instruction: Making a case for bottom-up activities. *Studies in Second Language Learning and Teaching, 5*(4), 637–662. https://doi.org/10.14746/ssllt.2015.5.4.6

Simpson-Vlach, R., & Ellis, N. C. (2010). An academic formulas list: New methods in phraseology research. *Applied Linguistics, 31*(4), 487–512. http://dx.doi.org/10.1093/ applin/amp058

Stoszkowski, J. (2018). Using Flipgrid to develop social learning. *Compass: Journal of Learning and Teaching, 11*(2). https://doi.org/10.21100/compass.v11i2.786

Thomson, H. E. (2016). Presenting lexical bundles for explicit noticing with schematic linguistic representation. *TESL-EJ, 20*(2).

Vandergrift, L., & Goh, C. C. (2012). *Teaching and learning second language listening: Metacognition in action*. Routledge. https://doi.org/10.4324/9780203843376

Vandergrift, L., & Tafaghodtari, M. (2010). Teaching L2 learners how to listen does make a difference: An empirical study. *Language Learning, 60*(2), 470–497. http://dx.doi.org/10.1111/j.1467-9922.2009.00559.x

Wray, A. (2002). *Formulaic language and the lexicon*. Cambridge University Press. https://doi.org/10.1017/cbo9780511519772

VALERIA BOGOREVICH is an English as a second language community college professor at Arizona Western College. She holds a PhD in applied linguistics from Northern Arizona University. Her research interests include second language listening, speaking, and pronunciation.

ELNAZ KIA is a postdoctoral research associate at the Second Language Teaching and Research Center at the University of Utah, where she oversees developing and maintaining multilingual learner corpora. She holds a doctorate in applied linguistics from Northern Arizona University. Her research focuses on corpus linguistics, second language pragmatics, corpus-based pedagogy, and spoken academic discourse.

CHAPTER 5

WAYNE RIMMER

Parsing Streams of Spoken Speech

Listening in Real Life

Early on in my career, at the back end of the 1990s, I was teaching English as a second language to teenagers in an international school in Moscow. The Friday afternoon slot at the end of a long week was always challenging as I realized that no one was really in the mood for ploughing through the textbook. Scratching my head, in a then rare gesture at autonomy, I asked my class for their suggestions for finishing the week. After discounting some ideas on health and safety grounds, the class voted from a shortlist. "Songs" was the winner, which sounded fine to me, especially as songs were supposed to be good for listening practice and many of my learners struggled with listening.

In the preinternet era, getting hold of songs and lyrics was not so easy and although students contributed some material, I had to fall back on the limited CD collection I'd brought to Russia in my suitcase. Thursday evenings became transcription time as I'd listen to the track over and over until I had the lyrics down. Most of the songs the students had never heard of, and this was definitely true of "Flowers Never Bend With the Rainfall" by Simon and Garfunkel (Simon, 1966), a hippy-era song of alienation and soul-searching. Luckily, this was one of those nice CDs where the lyrics were on the jacket, so it wasn't hard to produce a gap-fill to play the "What was that word?" game (my sole recourse for teaching listening at the time). However, there was one sequence where it wasn't the vocabulary causing the confusion:

> So, I'll continue to continue to pretend
> My life will never end

One student, Oksana, asked me what this meant. In true Socratic style, I turned the question back to her. Oksana thought it could mean two things: the first that the singer wants to go on pretending he won't die; the second that he actually thinks he won't die.

I looked at it again and realized that the absence of punctuation at the end of the first line of the couplet, common in poetry, makes for a subtle ambiguity. However, when I replayed it, I heard a terminal boundary between *pretend* and *My*, showing that Oksana's second interpretation was the correct one.

It was a minor incident, but I afterwards I wondered exactly how a listener could resolve an ambiguity which existed on the page, and the answer here was grammatical, not lexical. If the two lines were in the same sentence, the second line a nominal clause functioning as object of *pretend*, this would favor a version where the singer knows he is self-deluded. In this case, the listener would hear enjambment, in which the second line smoothly follows on from the first. If, as actually sung, the second line begins a new sentence, showing the singer is certain of his immortality, the listener will separate the lines prosodically.

This showed me that grammar has a role to play in how listeners deconstruct a spoken sequence and give it meaning. Knowing the sound shapes of the words is not enough; they have to be given a syntactical representation based on the larger sound sequence they are contained in. Oksana found conflicting interpretations of the song because she could not relate what she was hearing to a single grammatical structure compatible with one meaning. In other words, it was a parsing issue.

Listening in the Research

Parsing is a process that follows perception and consists of "establishing a grammatical structure that puts those sounds and syllables together and trying to identify words that might fit those grammatical slots" (Graham & Santos, 2015, p. 12). A sentence from a listening text in Abrahams (2017), a speaking and listening skills textbook chosen because, as noted by Thoms et al. (2018), it is a rare example of an open educational resource in English language teaching, illustrates parsing:

> "The changes that she made helped her learn English more quickly"
> (Abrahams, 2017, p. 86)

This is a complex sentence with the following syntactical structure:

Sentence					
Subject		**Predicate**			
The changes that she made		helped her learn English more quickly			
Noun	**Postmodifier**	**Main verb**	**Object**	**Complement**	**Adverbial**
The changes	that she made	helped	her	learn English	more quickly.

In the recording, this is heard as two tone units:

> The changes that she made // helped her learn English more quickly

It is common for subjects, especially complex noun phrases (i.e., those with modifiers), to be separate tone units (Cruttenden, 2014, pp. 284–285). The listener must work out that *made* is not a main verb but part of a relative clause giving more detail about the subject. What comes next should then be processed as the predicate of the sentence, rather than an independent unit. This is a very neat example, typical of teaching materials, in that the utterance corresponds to a written sentence. However, as I will discuss, authentic language often does not equate to sentences spoken aloud, which considerably complicates the task of parsing.

What comes out of the empirical research into parsing and listening is summarised in the following sections.

1. Parsing Is Not Unequivocally a Bottom-Up Process

A purely serial account of listening assumes that lexis and grammar are processed before and independently of discoursal features. In this theoretical position, parsing is a bottom-up process which needs to be completed before higher order cognitive strategies, such as contextual clues and real-world knowledge kick in. As Rukthong and Brunfaut (2020) note in a review of current models of listening comprehension, this is the predominant representation of parsing.

However, an alternative position is that processing strategies happen in parallel rather than sequentially and listeners use a combination of linguistic and nonlinguistic clues in conjunction. To illustrate, Rukthong and Brunfaut's (2020) study of performance on listening summary tasks showed listeners to prioritise strategies according to the task and their own proficiency. Though this study showed parsing to be a core strategy in listening, the implication is that parsing could be bypassed completely if there were other clues available to process the utterance.

The tension between sequential and parallel accounts of parsing is contentious (see van Gompel & Pickering, 2007, for a full technical discussion). However, both camps recognise parsing as a critical aspect of listening comprehension.

2. Punctuation Provides a Clue to Parsing

As the diachronic corpus study of Sun and Wang (2019) shows, the two main functions of punctuation in English have been syntactical and rhetorical, both aimed at clarifying meaning. There is evidence that intonation operates in a similar way in speech in order to facilitate parsing (also see Chapter 8 for more on parsing speech). Drury et al. (2016) investigated whether commas and prosodic breaks have parallel functions through a silent reading task where native speakers signaled the acceptability of parallel sentences (* indicates error):

> John said Mary was the nicest <u>girl</u> at the party.
> John said Mary was the nicest <u>boy</u>* at the party.
> John, said Mary, was the nicest <u>girl</u>* at the party.
> John, said Mary, was the nicest <u>boy</u> at the party.

Without commas, the gender-marked noun is the complement of *Mary*. With commas, the same noun is the complement of *John* with *said Mary* in parenthesis. The commas also change the pronunciation, as parenthetical matter typically is spoken with a separate tone unit at a lower pitch (Hewings, 2017, p. 122). The study found that readers showed great accuracy in recognizing under time constraints the acceptability of sentences when commas changed the syntax. This was used to support a hypothesis that punctuation acts as subvocal signal of prosodic boundaries; in other words, reading involves listening to oneself composing a mental representation of how the sequence is pronounced. From a second language (L2) listening angle, it is a useful strategy for students to recognize similarities between punctuation and intonation in determining grammatical structure.

The most commonly treated example of this in teaching materials is the distinction between restrictive and nonrestrictive relative clauses, as in:

a. My sister who is 30 lives in Virginia.
b. My sister, who is 30, lives in Virginia.

In sentence (a), the relative clause is restrictive as it postmodifies the head noun and gives information to identify the sister (the speaker probably has several sisters). In (b), the relative clause is nonrestrictive as it is a supplement and provides background information (the speaker probably has only one sister). There would also typically be different pausing:

a. My sister who is thirty // lives in Virginia
b. My sister // who is thirty // lives in Virginia

Punctuation and intonation are at the fringes of most curricula, yet this is a clear example where the relationship impacts parsing and thus comprehension.

3. Authentic Language Challenges Parsing

Parsing is not the beginning of the listening process, and the "garbage in, garbage out" principle basic to computer science and neuro-linguistic programming (Srinivasa-Desikan, 2018) makes parsing reliant on the quality of the input. Perception may be impaired as natural features of connected speech, such as elision and assimilation, distort the message for listeners: Cauldwell (2014) gives numerous examples within and beyond word boundaries (also see Chapters 3, 4, and 6 for more information about lexical segmentation). Listeners do not have the written form to fall back on, so there may be errors at the decoding stage which, independent of whether parsing is a serial or parallel process, will impact the accuracy and completeness of the utterance available for parsing. Worryingly, this phenomenon is not restricted to low-proficiency students. In a study of Common Framework of References for Languages (Council of Europe, 2001) B2 level students on preuniversity courses in the United Kingdom, Field (2011) found among other issues that only 7% of listeners could decode *we've* from a lecture. An accumulation of decoding errors would not provide a reliable string to be parsed.

Furthermore, parsing is arguably a strategy better adapted to reading than listening because it is sentence, not utterance based. The complete, fully grammatical sentence is the model we use to teach language and skills. This convenience of a sentence-based discourse is maintained by the listening materials in English language teaching resources, as illustrated by the aforementioned sentence from Abrahams (2017). However, research using authentic language samples has challenged this depiction. Much of what we listen to outside of the classroom is not a series of well-formed sentences but utterances which, because of the constraints of real time production, may not conform to standard grammar. Examples taken from the comprehensive treatment in Biber et al. (1999) are features of dysfluency, for instance ellipsis and repetition. The nature of spoken speech thus complicates the process of parsing for second language (L2) learners, and this challenge increases the further speech departs from a formal variety, such as a prepared lecture, to casual usage, especially conversation.

To illustrate from a colloquial register, consider an excerpt from the spoken data of Corpus of Contemporary American English (Davies, 2020). It is taken from a CNN crime documentary:

> There was something going on back then that we need to find out what the piece of the puzzle is.

The syntax breaks down at *what* because *what* appears to function as object of *find out*. This is ungrammatical if *find out* is initially parsed as part of the nominal underlined with the relative pronoun *that* as object. The change of object midsentence represents anacoluthon, the disruption of one syntactical construction by another; Quirk et al. (1985) give an example of anacoluthon in the same context of postmodification (p. 1299). Readers do not need to deal with anacoluthon, unless the writer's intention is deliberately rhetorical, but listeners might, and rule-based parsing could not account for the structure.

To summarise, research primarily within a psycholinguistic paradigm has identified parsing as a crucial strategy to identify grammatical relations within a sentence. This remains valid regardless of theoretical positions on the degree to which parsing operates independently or in collusion with top-down strategies. There is also evidence that pronunciation facilitates parsing in a similar way to how punctuation defines phrase-clause structure in writing. However, theories of parsing generally assume a written and idealised model of language with the sentence as the core unit made up of a complete set of words that are individually distinct. This means that native speakers are better equipped to adapt parsing to the messier patterns of oral production than learners. L2 listeners need explicit guidance in parsing speaking, and this is the focus of the following section.

Listening in the Classroom

Most of these activities in the format presented do not claim authenticity in terms of replicating the type of extended listening learners will experience outside the classroom. Their function is to prepare learners for listening to grammar in a controlled setting where the teacher can isolate issues and provide focused feedback. The rationale is that the more sensitive students are to the grammar of the utterance, the more rapid and accurate their parsing will be.

Several exercises involve dictation. Cognitive accounts of dictation, most notably Oller (1979), credit dictation as a valuable tool in testing or teaching listening and writing because it taps the parsing process. In taking dictation, learners need to hold a chunk of spoken language in working memory and parse it under time constraints. Dictation initially fell out of favor in the communicative era because it seemed artificial and old school, but classic titles, such as Davis and Rinvolucri's (1988) *Dictation: New Methods, New Possibilities*, saw a reappreciation of the technique. Rimmer (1997) also showed that dictation is a valid pronunciation, and by extension listening, activity if the chunking of the text preserves the prosody of discourse. Dictation is also resource free, so of universal application.

Garden Path Sentences

Sentences are built incrementally, word by word, so parsing assigns an early syntactic structure to the input. That parsing is then confirmed as more information is received. However, this initial parsing may turn out faulty, and "the term garden-path effect refers to a reader's feeling of being led astray by syntactic preferences while reading a sentence" (van Gompel, 2013, p. 116). The classic example from Bever (1970) is, "The horse raced past the barn fell" (p. 316). Until *fell*, the sentence would have been parsed as subject-verb-complement:

Subject	**Verb**	**Complement**
The horse	raced	past the barn

However, *fell* must be the main verb, so the sentence has to be reparsed as subject-verb.

Subject	**Verb**
The horse raced past the barn	fell

Raced is reassigned to postnominal status.

In van Gompel's (2013) definition, the garden path sentence is predominantly discussed as a written artefact (hence the reference to a *reader* who is *reading*). This is rational, as garden path sentences are complex in the final analysis, and often rather contrived. An argument is not being made that garden path sentences are typical of authentic listening; as noted in the preface to this section, they are tools for teaching parsing.

Suggested Procedure

1. Dictate to students "The man sent the flowers was pleased." Ask students at what part of the sentence they got confused (probably at *was*). With the help of the class, write two parsings on the board to show the different grammatical analyses. (Note, though, that it's not helpful to use with students metalanguage (semitechnical terminology used to analyze or describe language) such as *parsing*, which is not commonplace in English language teaching materials.)

Subject	Verb	Object
The man	sent	the flowers

Subject	Verb
The man sent the flowers	was pleased

2. Preteach any vocabulary in the sentences that students may be unfamiliar with. Divide the students into pairs. Tell them to take turns dictating the garden path sentences once to each other.

Student A

1. While I was surfing the Internet went down.
2. The government plans to increase prices failed.
3. They painted the wall with cracks.
4. When Sally eats food gets thrown.

Student A Parsings

1. [While I was surfing the Internet = subordinate clause]
2. [While I was surfing // the Internet went down = subordinate clause + main clause]
3. [The government // plans // to increase prices = subject + verb + infinitive complement]
4. [The government plans to increase prices // failed = subject + verb]
5. [They // painted // the wall // with = subject + verb + object + adverbial]
6. [They // painted // the wall with cracks = subject + verb + object]
7. [When Sally eats food = subordinate clause]
8. [When Sally eats // food gets thrown = subordinate clause + main clause]

Student B

1. The woman sent to her house was happy.
2. As Liz was washing the dishes fell.
3. When Mike called his mother was happy.
4. The boat floated down the river sank.

Student B Parsings

1. [The woman // sent // to her house = subject + verb + indirect object]
   [The woman sent to her house // was happy = subject + complement]
2. [As Liz was washing the dishes = subordinate clause]
   [As Liz was washing // the dishes fell = subordinate clause + main clause]
3. [When Mike called his mother = subordinate clause]
   [When Mike called // his mother was happy = subordinate clause + main clause]
4. [The boat // floated // down the river = subject + verb + complement]
   [The boat floated down the river // sank = subject + verb]

3. Students check they have written down the sentences correctly. They then work together to parse each sentence twice as in the example (alternative parsings are included on the cards for your reference). They could draw boxes or arrange Cuisenaire rods (Legos may be easier to obtain) to show the difference.
4. Younger learners and those with less metalinguistic awareness could represent the alternative parsings with drawings. For instance, "The man sent the flowers was pleased" could show a sketch of a man handing over a bouquet next to a smiling man receiving a bouquet.
5. A fun extension could be for learners to make up their own garden path sentences to dictate to new partners and then parse in the same way.

Notes

You can find many examples of garden path sentences through search engines, but be careful not to introduce low-frequency usage. For example, "The old man the boat" only works if learners understand that *man*, though typically a noun, is also a verb.

Categories

The clauses that students hear in a variety of speech acts often correspond to tone units. For this reason, it is useful for students to be able to parse clauses because they then have a framework for processing what they hear. Though clauses can vary tremendously in length and lexis, the number of syntactical patterns is finite (Biber et al., 1999, p. 141), so teaching them within a listening focus is realistic.

Suggested Procedure

1. Number a sample of clause patterns (the number and complexity depending on learners' proficiency) on the board, for example:

Subject + Verb + Subject Complement *It looks a real mess.*	1
Subject + Verb + Object *I didn't expect that kind of treatment.*	2
Subject + Verb + Object + Object *My sister lent me fifty dollars.*	3
Subject + Verb + Object + Object Complement *Who called me stupid?*	4

2. Read out clauses that correspond to the categories on the board. Examples follow, but you could use clauses from your textbook (written texts or the audioscripts) to recycle the content:

   a. Not many people understand his paintings. (2)

   b. Susan's mother is a high school teacher. (1)

c. The police want him found. (4)
d. The text message we got explained everything. (2)
e. Mary heard the children shout to her. (4)
f. The manager offered us a pay increase. (3)
g. It doesn't feel like summer. (1)
h. Did you give her the right password? (3)

Students number the clause according to the category type. Check students' answers.

3. Read out the clauses again. Students should write down and parse the full clause.

Notes

- To make the clauses longer, increasing the listening load, but keeping the clause pattern, add optional sentence constituents, such as adverbials and adjectives. For example, "Not many people <u>really</u> understand his <u>early</u> paintings."
- This is an effective exercise for introducing spoken utterances that do not fit into the canonical patterns so that students realize the limitations of parsing based on written language. An example is dislocation of clause elements, for instance what Carter and McCarthy (2006) call a header:

> <u>The teacher with glasses</u>, he seems very nice. (Carter & McCarthy, 2006, p. 193)

The noun phrase underlined is moved in front of the Subject-Verb-Subject Complement clause (Category 1 in the sample clause chart) to give extra detail. It would also be heard as a separate tone unit. Authentic language will supply many such examples of spoken grammar and give students experience of a range of accents. Recommended is TubeQuizard (tubequizard.com), a free ready-made English language teaching resource for capturing YouTube speech.

Mutual Dictation

Students will be familiar with mutual dictation, a standard classroom activity where they work in pairs to complete the same text, taking turns to read their incomplete version to each other, so it will need little introduction.

Suggested Procedure

1. Put students into pairs and give each student a different copy, A or B, of the text. Pre-teach any vocabulary you think students might be unfamiliar with and drill the pronunciation. Allow students some time to read their text and, if necessary, practise reading it aloud.

A

A man was driving down the road, ______________________. It was a pretty quiet day ______________________. ______________________, he saw a strange sight. ______________________ surrounded by what looked like a group of penguins. ______________ the driver said to himself ______________. Being a friendly kind of guy, ______________________. The driver of the van, ______________________, ______________________. "Could you help me out?" ______________. "This van has broken down again ______________. Could you take these penguins to the zoo? ______________________." The man thought it would be okay ______________________. A few hours later that afternoon ______________________ to find her penguins. ______________________. She then spent ages frantically driving around town ______________________. Just as she was giving up hope, ______________________. Relieved and angry at the same time, ______________________. The answer she got from the man was "______________________ so we took in a movie."

B

______________________, thinking about his plans for the evening. ______________ and there wasn't much traffic about. All of a sudden, ______________. There was a van parked at the side of the road ______________. 'Very strange!' ______________ as he stopped his car right next to the van. ______________________, he thought he might be of some help. ______________________, a woman in her late thirties, looked at him very gratefully. '______________?' she asked the driver. ______________________ and I'll have to wait ages for the rescue service. ______________________. They won't be much trouble to you." ______________________ and squeezed all the penguins into his car. ______________________ the van driver drove to the zoo ______________________. The zoo keeper hadn't seen them. ______________________ looking for any sign of the penguins. ______________________, she saw the penguins coming out of a movie theater with the man. ______________________, she asked what had been going on. ______________________ "We had been to the zoo ______________________."

2. Tell students to take turns reading out their text for the other student to fill in. Monitor and make sure that students are reading out the missing sections as complete chunks, not word by word.
3. Tell students to compare their texts and check answers.

Notes

- As a follow-up, ask students to identify the narrative tenses in the text and their link with pronunciation. For example, the past continuous is often used in a subordinate clause to give background to the main action and thus is a separate tone unit.

  Just as she was giving up hope // she saw . . .

  This will help listeners to distinguish between the main point and details.

- You can find plenty of ready-made mutual dictations on the internet, sometimes for groups rather than pairs, but check that the missing sections are of utterance length (a complete thought group). For example, using the following sentence, it would work much better to gap the underlined section in (b) than (a).

  It must have been a shock when he saw the penguins in the cinema.

  a. It must have been a shock when he saw the penguins at the movie theater.
  b. It must have been a shock when he saw the penguins at the movie theater.

Dictogloss

Dictogloss involves students working in groups and reconstructing a short text, which is read aloud. The text is read aloud several times in its entirety, but it is not split into sections with pauses for writing as in a classic dictation. Because the text is too long for students to hold in working memory, the aim is not for students to write it down faithfully. Students' task is to pool their notes of the language and main ideas heard to produce a version of the text that makes sense and is grammatical.

The procedure, described in detail in Wajnryb (1990), is claimed to involve all four skills:

1. listening to the text
2. writing it down
3. speaking to other students about the text and composition process
4. reading their own version as it takes shape

Parsing enables students to break down the volume of text into recognizable structures, which may form a framework for their written text. Often, as in Wajnryb (1990), texts are chosen based on their language features, for example several examples of a particular verb tense, so dictogloss can practice parsing within the confines of one language area.

Suggested Procedure

1. Introduce the topic of the text, in this example, sleep, with some questions for students to discuss in groups. For example, "How long did you sleep last night? Did you have any dreams?"
2. Put students into groups and explain the dictogloss task. Tell students that they will not be able to remember the text, so they must listen carefully and make notes. Read the text once.

We spend one third of our lives asleep, but science can't really explain why we sleep. We do know that we need sleep and we can live for longer without food than without sleep. A good night's sleep is important, and most people fall asleep after 10 or 15 minutes. If you can't do this, switch off all your electronic devices in the evening and have a milky drink before bed. If this doesn't work, try counting sheep!

3. Give students time to work in groups and compare their notes. Read the text a second time.
4. Students complete their texts. Tell students to make a copy of their joint text (if it is handwritten, by taking a photograph on their mobile device). Arrange new groups of students so they can share and compare their versions. You may want the groups to write a final version based on the features of the texts they share.

Notes

- An extra step, not encouraged in the standard procedure, would be to present the original text to the students to exploit parsing (also see Chapter 1 for a detailed explanation of how seeing the transcript benefits L2 listeners). Ask students to identify which sections of the text they found difficult to understand. This is a time to highlight the link between grammar and listening. For example, the subordinate clause *if this doesn't work* would be heard as a full tone unit.
- To scaffold the task, the pretask stage can be extended; for example, preteach vocabulary or read the text out more times. As with all dictation, do not compensate by reading out the text unnaturally slowly or disrupting the tone units.

Praat

There is no proven correlation between incorporation of technology and pedagogic effectiveness. Indeed, a common warning is that technology is often used for show rather than after consideration of the learning context (e.g., Kirkwood & Price, 2014). However, learners fed on technology in their everyday lives may respond positively to digital solutions. Praat (www.praat.org; Boersma & Weenink, 2020) is a well-known freeware for phonetic analysis which allows you to view and print sequences of spoken language so learners can see what they hear. Designed and regularly updated by Paul Boersma and David Weenink at the University of Amsterdam, Praat can be downloaded for free, and its popularity with linguists has led to (external) user manuals and YouTube videos which are useful for navigating the product. Praat is designed for phoneticians rather than teachers, so many of the functions may not be relevant for English language teaching; however, Mills (2020) recommends Praat for visual feedback for learners. Mills (2020) also makes the point that some learners would be impressed by the scientific appeal of Praat.

Suggested Procedure

1. Tell students to download Praat from the website (www.praat.org).
2. Following the onscreen instructions, record an utterance and generate the sound graph. Play the recording and show students the graph. You may want to print it out if you can't project the image or share it. To illustrate, see Figure 1.

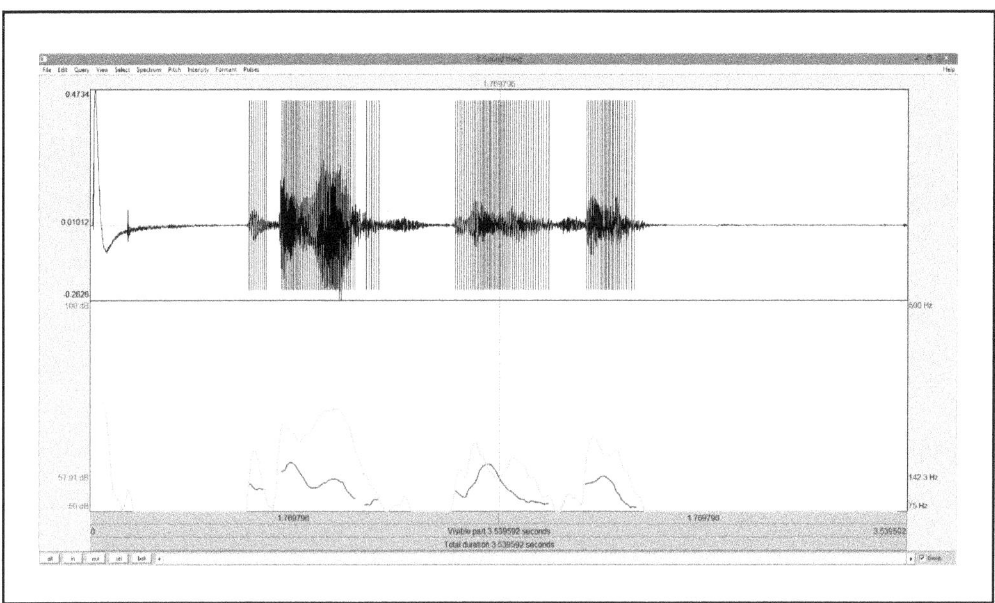

Figure 1. Praat example sound graph. Utterance: *The thing is, I'm not really sure.*

The top half of the graph shows the waveform and the lower half the intensity.

3. It is clear that the utterance is heard as two units. Tell students to parse it.

Subject	Verb	Complement
The thing	is	I'm not really sure

Point out that *The thing is* represents a common chunk and it is set off prosodically from its complement by a fall-rise intonation (Marks & Bowen, 2012, p. 148; use *the thing is* and variations with the same phonology, such as *the problem is*, to practise intonation). As a grammar note you could add that the option of adding the complementizer *that* (*The thing is* <u>*that*</u> . . .) excludes an interpretation of *The thing is* as an adverbial.

4. Tell learners to repeat the utterance and record it on Praat. They should then listen to themselves and produce the sound graph. Explain that their sound graphs will differ because every voice has a fingerprint.
5. Have learners repeat recording, listening back, and parsing with different utterances. You could concentrate on a specific grammatical structure, for example conditional sentences; work on sequences that learners have found problematic in listening exercises; or just let them have fun. Praat also allows you to upload sound files and long stretches of speech, for example songs, and analyse selected portions.

Notes

- If you don't have technology, a simple method of giving visual feedback is for learners to draw, using their own annotation, what they hear.
- There are similar online tools which work on the basic principle of recording speech to listen back to and then parse. These often have the advantage of working happily on mobile devices such as phones, providing students with listening practice whenever the occasion arises. A really simple but flexible example is Vocaroo (vocaroo.com), whose minimalist homepage just has a recording button. One metalistening activity using Vocaroo might be for instructors to record feedback on parsing for students to listen to.

Listen Back

Field (2009) advocates working on smaller segments of speech within the longer texts, often lasting several minutes, that populate textbooks. The standard procedure is for students to answer comprehension questions after listening to a whole text played once or twice. As an alternative, Field (2009) suggests instructors stopping the recording at selected points and having the students reconstruct as much as they can of what they have just heard. This microlistening strategy can be exploited in parsing.

Suggested Procedure

1. Before the lesson, use the recording in conjunction with the audioscript to decide at which points you want to break the listening. This may come at a significant stage in the development of the meaning of the text or after a particular language point. Leave some time for listeners to get used to the speakers' voices before the first break and do not include too many pauses or have them in close proximity, because the constant stop/start will disorientate learners.
2. Decide whether you want to present the traditional prelistening stage, which includes setting the context and preteaching vocabulary. Field (2009) argues that a significant amount of real-world listening happens when we have little preparation for what we are going to hear: Imagine hearing a song for the first ever time. Many listening experiences activate schemata—in a scenario where a stranger stops you on the street, for example, you are almost certainly going to hear a request for directions—but by treating all listening as predictable, we may be misinforming learners. In other words, overpreparing listening can be underteaching the skill (also see Chapter 1 for more on the prelistening phase of listening instruction).
3. Alert students that you are going to stop the recording at different points. When you stop it, students need to write down the last 10 words they heard and compare with a partner. The figure 10 is arbitrary, and it could be more or less

according to the level and capabilities of the class. However, it should be long enough so that students are recalling a text at utterance rather than word or phrase level.

4. Stop the recording the first time. Give students time to write down what they last heard individually and then in pairs.
5. Ask students some general comprehension questions up to this point. (Do not do this before they write because working memory is limited.)
6. Invite a student to write what they last heard on the board. Ask students to correct or fill in information before you confirm with the audioscript.
7. Tell students to parse the sentence. Check this as a class and then ask students whether the grammar caused any problems and why.
8. Restart the recording, go to the next break, and repeat the procedure.
9. At the end of the listening, you could ask the standard global listening comprehension questions.

Notes

- This task is represented as a variation on a textbook exercise, on the rationale that most teachers centre their lessons around textbooks. However, it could be successfully applied to a wide range of external listening texts, such as YouTube videos and TED Talks. If the text is very long and linguistically/cognitively challenging, you may flip the classroom and ask learners to listen the first time before the lesson. This is legitimate and efficient because the task focus is not on general comprehension, although this needs to be established.
- The writing and editing of the portion of text could be facilitated by using a collaborative writing tool, such as Google Docs, on mobile devices. Google Docs lets the teacher monitor and correct multiple texts online, so it allows feedback, and privacy, for individual students.

A misinterpretation of skills-based approaches to instruction is that a student's language knowledge is secondary to learning strategies. An evaluation of parsing shows that grammar is both a resource and a strategy because a developed grammar allows listeners to build meaning. As demonstrated, parsing thus lends itself to listening activities which are pedagogically principled and fully engaging.

References

Abrahams, D. J. (2017). Communication beginnings: An introductory listening and speaking text for English language learners. *PDXOpen: Open Educational Resources, 18*.

Bever, T. G. (1970). The cognitive basis for linguistic structure. In J. R. Hayes (Ed.), *Cognitive development of language* (pp. 279–362). Wiley Blackwell.

Biber, D., Johansson, S., Leech, G., Conrad, S., & Finegan, E. (1999). *Longman grammar of spoken and written English*. Pearson Education.

Boersma, P., & Weenink, D. (2020). *Praat: doing phonetics by computer* (Version 6.1.16) [Computer program]. http://www.praat.org/

Carter, M., & McCarthy, M. (2006). *Cambridge grammar of English*. Cambridge University Press.

Cauldwell, R. (2014). *Phonology for listening: Teaching the stream of speech*. Speech in Action.

Council of Europe. (2001). *Common European framework for reference of languages: Learning, teaching and assessment*. Cambridge University Press.

Cruttenden, A. (2014). *Gimson's pronunciation of English* (8th ed.). Routledge.

Davies, M. (2008). *The corpus of contemporary American English* (COCA). https://www.english-corpora.org/coca/

Davis, P., & Rinvolucri, M. (1988). *Dictation: New methods, new possibilities*. Cambridge University Press.

Drury, J. E, Baum, S. R., Valeriote, H., & Steinhauer, K. (2016). Punctuation and implicit prosody in silent reading: An ERP study investigating English garden-path sentences. *Frontiers in Psychology, 7*, 1375. https://doi.org/10.3389/fpsyg.2016.01375

Field, J. (2009). *Listening in the language classroom*. Cambridge University Press.

Field. J. (2011). Into the mind of the academic listener. *Journal of English for Academic Purposes, 10*(2), 102–112. https://doi.org/10.1016/j.jeap.2011.04.002

Graham, S., & Santos, D. (2015). *Strategies for second language listening: Current scenarios and improved pedagogy*. Palgrave Macmillan.

Hewings, M. (2017). *Advanced pronunciation in use* (2nd ed.). Cambridge University Press.

Kirkwood, A., & Price, L. (2014). Technology-enhanced learning and teaching in higher education: What is "enhanced" and how do we know? A critical literature review. *Learning, Media and Technology, 39*(1), 6–36. https://doi:10.1080/17439884.2013.770404

Marks, J., & Bowen, T. (2012). *The book of pronunciation*. Delta.

Mills, J. (2020, February 8). *Prosody for all the skills: how to integrate the "music" of language into any lesson* [IATEFL PronSIG webinar]. Available at https://www.youtube.com/watch?v=Kr2J5jDFmQM

Oller. J. W. (1979). *Language tests at school*. Longman.

Quirk, R., Greenbaum, S., Leech, G., & Svartvik, J. (1985). *A comprehensive grammar of the English language*. Longman.

Rimmer, W. (1997). Dictation for teaching and testing pronunciation. *Speak Out! The Newsletter of the IATEFL PronSIG, 21*, 36–38.

Rukthong, A., & Brunfaut, T. (2020). Is anybody listening? The nature of second language listening in integrated listening-to-summarize tasks. *Language Testing, 37*(1), 31–53. https://doi:10.1177/0265532219871470

Simon, P. (1966). Flowers never bend with the rainfall [Recorded by Paul Simon and Art Garfunkel]. On *Parsley, Sage, Rosemary and Thyme*. Columbia.

Srinivasa-Desikan, B. (2018). *Natural language processing and computational linguistics: A practical guide to text analysis with Python, Gensim, SpaCy, and Keras*. Packt.

Sun, K., & Wang, R. (2019). Frequency distributions of punctuation marks in English: Evidence from large-scale corpora. *English Today, 35*(4), 23–35. https://doi:10.1017/S0266078418000512

Thoms, J. J., Arshavskaya, E., & Poole, F. J. (2018). Open educational resources and ESL education: Insights from US educators. *TESL-EJ, 22*(2).

van Gompel, R. P. G. (2013). *Sentence processing*. Taylor & Francis Group.

van Gompel, R. P. G., & Pickering, M. J. (2007). Syntactic parsing. In R. Gomez (Ed.), *The Oxford handbook of psycholinguistics* (pp. 289–307). Oxford University Press.

Wajnryb, R. (1990). *Grammar dictation.* Oxford University Press.

Yeldham, M., & Gruba, P. (2014). Toward an instructional approach to developing interactive second language listening. *Language Teaching Research, 18*(1), 33–53. https://doi:10.1177/1362168813505395

WAYNE RIMMER (EdD) is an English for academic purposes tutor at the University of Manchester in the UK. He is also a volunteer teacher for the Council of Academics at Risk, and his current research explores pedagogical accommodations to the needs of refuge seekers.

CHAPTER 6

MARNIE REED

Sources of Mishearing: Identifying and Addressing Listening Challenges

Listening in Real Life

A student revolt, early in my teaching career, sparked my interest in listening. I was teaching in a private language school in the United States and a cohort of highly verbal, articulate, fluent, and polite students protested with increasing insistence that they could not understand people—including me—outside the classroom. I happen to be a fast talker, and the secretary in this institution had learned to stall students who came to her with requests to switch teachers because their new teacher talked too fast. But these high-intermediate students had been with me for two sessions, and they had become accustomed to the speed of my speech. They could readily discuss a wide variety of topics, from the mundane to their professions, their ambitions, their philosophies, and even the meaning of life. How could it be that students could produce so much language, albeit with varying degrees of accuracy, yet insist they could not understand the people they encountered in person, on the radio or television, or even their teachers conversing with each other between classes?

Hounded by these frustrated students, a colleague and I persuaded the institution's director to offer a dedicated listening class. Shrewd businessman that he was, he decided that the school could offer an extra listening class pro bono, that is, the students—who attended daily from 9 am to 4 pm—would not have to pay additional tuition for this extra class. We thought this quite magnanimous until we realized it also meant that we teachers would not be compensated for teaching the extra class. And to fit this listening class into the already full day, the class would meet from 8 am each morning, a most ambitious start time for students who regarded rigid schedules through the lens of their own cultures' more relaxed time orientations.

Having created the course, my colleague and I realized we needed to create a curriculum—or at least some materials to get us started. Though initially not convinced of the problem, I'd found one recent class exchange so sufficiently puzzling that I wondered if we could address it, too, in our new elective. It occurred after lunch one day when I noticed that a student who had been in attendance in the morning was now absent. My inquiry, "Where's Luis?", prompted this helpful explanation from a classmate, during which he left off the third-person, singular, present tense –*s* ending:

"Teacher, today is Friday. Every Friday Luis go to the bank."

Because we had spent at least some portion of each day for two entire sessions on the simple present tense, with particular attention to the –*s* morpheme, the missing verb ending drew a particularly strong reaction from me. "Luis *go* to the bank?" I asked, emphasizing the error by saying it more loudly, clearly, and with a higher pitch. It was evidently clear from my exaggerated delivery that something was amiss, and the student rightly assumed he'd made an error, which he promptly attempted to fix. Knowing he always made mistakes with prepositions, he tried, "Luis go at the bank" followed by a few more attempts with a variety of prepositions from his repertoire. As I was to learn years later, intonation serves as a navigation guide (Gilbert, 1994). I'd intuitively used a feedback type known as repetition with intonation, but clearly the intonation I intended to signal the locus of the error was not informative to the uninitiated. My signal had gone right over the student's head. Perhaps we could include intonation in our new elective class.

We started with some dictations; the results were startling, humbling, and quite convincing. Here are two samples from our very first class. The first was collected as it appears below from almost all the students:

Listening Sample 1: Teller all meter at the bank.

All students accurately transcribed the preposition phrase *at the bank* and all students vigorously agreed that the sentence made no sense. But all equally vehemently insisted they had faithfully transcribed the sentence I had dictated, "Tell her I'll meet her at the bank."

The second sample was written on the board by a student randomly selected to transcribe one of the dictated sentences, "He looked it up":

Listening Sample 2: He looked up.

When we asked other students what they had written for that particular sentence, they agreed with their classmate's transcription. What could account for this discrepancy? We noted that students' pronunciation of the verb *look* + –*ed* ending as two syllables [lʊk ɛd] seemed to block their ability to hear what was said. Their transcription contained the same number of rhythmic beats as the original sentence, albeit with the glaring omission, of course, of one entire word. So, here a mismatch occurred between the words spoken and students' mental acoustic image of the verb + –*ed* ending, resulting in a mishearing of what was said.

Listening in the Research

Several questions have driven my curiosity ever since that fateful first day of the listening class elective: How do we account for this conundrum whereby our second language (L2) English learners can produce more speech than they can understand, why do they fail to attend to intonation as a signaling device, and what do we do about it? Fortunately, listening has been undergoing a revival of interest in the field, as measured by an increase in the number of empirical studies devoted to it (Vanderplank, 2013), accompanied by an effort to translate research into practice. It is now obvious that my students were not an anomaly. Indeed, learner surveys have confirmed two listening challenges: recognizing known words in rapid speech, and not understanding the message despite understanding the words (Vandergrift & Goh, 2012). The first challenge requires ability to segment a continuous speech stream. Scholars inform us that establishing the boundaries between lexical units requires familiarity with how sounds can be combined in English and with connected speech processes (CSPs; Tyler & Cutler, 2009; Field, 2008). We can think of this sentence parsing as the "Izzybizzy" [ɪziybɪziy] phenomenon. None of the three words in this question ("Is he busy?") is particularly difficult, even for beginning level students. Yet when linked in continuous speech, they don't sound the way they look in dictionaries. Students accustomed only to citation forms will struggle with CSPs, whereby words are linked and contracted, and sounds are deleted, reduced, or altered (also see Chapters 2, 3, 4, 5, and 8 for more on these bottom-up listening challenges).

Learners' approach to listening, research informs us, is to unconsciously apply speech segmentation strategies from their first language to locate L2 word boundaries (Weber & Cutler, 2006). This is problematic, though, as word boundaries differ from language to language (Altenberg, 2005). This adversely impacts how students segment their L2 speech, prompting McAllister (1996) to ascribe a "perpetual foreign accent" to even highly proficient L2 listeners. Learners also substitute known words for unrecognized words, and have difficulty letting go of wrong choices (Broersma & Cutler, 2008).

As applied to Listening Sample 1, I may have inadvertently primed the students, with my reference to the bank, to think of a bank teller, though there are also story tellers and fortune tellers. Students also would be familiar with taxi meters or parking meters. So, they latched on to wrong words, unaware of such connected speech features as deleted sounds and contracted words, all the while fully aware that their transcribed sentence made no sense.

Another source of mishearing, the mismatched acoustic image in Listening Sample 2, has also been addressed extensively in the literature. The conventional thinking, supported by Flege's (1995) speech learning model and reflected in student pronunciation texts and teacher training manuals (see, e.g., Ur, 2008), is that learners need to hear something before they can pronounce it. However, an increasing number of studies explores whether production can actually precede and shape auditory perceptual abilities. Sheldon and Strange (1982) found that Japanese learners of L2 English were better able to produce liquids /l/ and /r/ than to discriminate the two sounds.

Tsukada et al. (2005) found a similar production advantage for Korean children's perception of a number of English vowels. In a series of studies based on problematic sounds for Arabic L2 English students, Linebaugh and Roche (2013, 2015) found that articulatory training in the production of target L2 sounds afforded an advantage that focused listening did not achieve. That is to say, as the students' own production of the target sounds became increasingly like the actual targets, their ability to perceive and distinguish the difficult sounds increased.

This resonates with a personal experience from my years living and teaching English in Japan. As a country gal, I was not familiar with the conventions of riding trains or subways. Because I always commuted during rush hour and could not reliably see the names of passing train stops, my commute consisted of counting stops to get to and from work in the heart of Tokyo. My students one day asked if I'd found an apartment, and when I told them the name of my town, conveniently the same as the name of the train stop, they were at a loss. I pulled out the train pass, and they all exclaimed, saying the town's name, which I insisted I had just told them. To this they replied that my pronunciation was "not even close," and they spent the greater part of the next few classes teaching me to pronounce the name of my train stop. Approaching the station that evening, I suddenly heard one word, clear as a bell, in the unrelenting string of announcements that accompanied my daily commute. It occurred to me they were announcing the names of the stations—how convenient!—and that I didn't have to count any more. And then I wondered, why hadn't I heard the word for the past several weeks? This experience has informed both my teaching and teacher training ever since.

When "repeat after me"—providing external input—doesn't work, changing the instructional focus to convergent production, that is guiding the student's own output to converge with the target sound(s) and allowing that output to serve as input in a closed-circuit auditory feedback loop, improves students' listening. In other words, the alternative to focusing on students listening is to shape their own speech production (Casserly & Pisoni, 2010). Students' increasingly target-like speech production can facilitate their speech perception. In short, speaking helps listening.

The second challenge identified in the surveys is understanding what is meant by what is said. Pickering (2012) defines intonation as the "systematic and linguistically meaningful use of pitch movement at the phrasal or suprasegmental level" (p. 280). Understanding speaker intent requires familiarity with the functions of intonation. These include syntactic functions, like signaling grammatical structure (e.g., falling intonation at sentence boundaries); discourse functions, such as turn-taking cues (also see Chapter 9) and differentiating question types (e.g., rising or falling intonation for yes/no or *wh*–questions, respectively); and emotive functions, including attitude and affect. Most, if not all pronunciation textbooks cover these functions amply. However, as Levis (1999) cautions, the characteristic textbook treatment of intonation is to overemphasize its role in grammatical relations and conveying speakers' attitudes and emotions (p. 37). What is often overlooked or only indirectly addressed is treatment of the pragmatic functions of intonation. A typical classroom exchange reported in Reed and Michaud (2015) captures the problem:

Listening Sample 3

Student: Teacher, can I turn in my assignment late?

Teacher: You *can*.

Student: Okay, thanks!

The proficient listener hears the (unspoken) next word, *but*, that is implied by the pitch change on *can*; the nonnative speaker does not. Tomlinson and Bott (2013) describe the source of the problem: "Often what a speaker intends to say is not directly retrievable from a linguistic form; rather listeners must infer it" (p. 3569). To put it another way, "a speaker *implies* something without necessarily putting it into words . . . Something is left unsaid—perhaps some kind of reservation or implication" (Wells, 2006, p. 27).

In the Listening Sample 3 exchange, the teacher's words are affirmative, but the message is negative. Learners who miss the point may be relying solely on the words in an utterance, unaware of the signaling function of intonation. Wichmann (2005) accounts for this discrepancy by noting that intonation "has the power to reinforce, mitigate, or even undermine the words spoken" (p. 229).

Listening Challenge 1: Understanding What Is Said

Scholars have provided insights into the sources of the challenges facing L2 English learners. We can illustrate the combined effects with two sample sentences.

Listening Sample 4: My boss said he'd fixed all the problems.

To decode this sentence requires knowledge of CSPs, which occur when words are linked in continuous speech. Listening Sample 4 exhibits the following:

- linked words (said he'd; fixed all)
- contracted words (he'd)
- deleted sounds (~~h~~)
- grammar sounds (fix + past participle *–ed* is one syllable)

For students whose native language has a more restricted syllable structure than English, inflectional noun and verb endings pose articulatory challenges (also see Chapter 3 for more on listening for affixes). The word *fix* [fɪks] contains two consonant sounds in final position; this is the maximum number allowed in languages like Spanish. Adding the *–ed* morpheme (the allomorph [t]) requires exceeding that language's syllable structure. Therefore, when teaching, we must give our students time to do the articulatory movements needed to produce three consonant sounds in the coda of a syllable. Now, let's consider the knowledge required to decode another sample sentence.

Listening Challenge 2: Understanding What Is Meant by What Is Said

> *Listening Sample 5:* My boss *said* he'd fixed all the problems.

These are the exact same words in the exact same order as Sample 4; however, unlike Sample 4, this is not a case of reported speech. The implicational fall-rise pitch contour (Wells, 2006), represented by italics on the written page, alerts proficient listeners to infer that the speaker does not believe the problems have been fixed. To succeed at inference, students must notice the marked (unusual) intonation that differs from the neutral, unmarked intonation of everyday speech. To assist learners with this listening challenge, we would do well to provide instruction that, in the words of Allen (1971), "teaches the student to think in terms of the speaker's intention in any given situation" (p. 73). The following observation by Paunović and Savić (2008) captures both the student's dilemma and the pedagogical challenge:

> Students often do not have a clear idea of why exactly 'the melody of speech' should be important for communication, and therefore seem to lack the motivation to master it, while teachers do not seem to be theoretically or practically well-equipped to explain and illustrate its significance. (pp. 72–73)

Given the identified listening challenges our learners face and the recommendations from the research, it appears that a two-pronged instructional focus is called for: Teach CSPs and grammar sounds so students understand the message content, and teach stress and intonation so students understand the message meaning.

Listening in the Classroom

Establish the Scope of the Task

Speaking and listening are two of the four integrated skills that are often taught together. Instructors seeking guidance in addressing listening may turn to their institution's curricular guidelines, only to find objectives reminiscent of reading goals (e.g., "Students will understand main ideas and significant details") that offer few particulars on how to go about the task. Textbooks often offer a starting point (e.g., "Teach note-taking skills"), which presupposes that students can process the aural input and merely need assistance organizing it. There can be value, certainly, in teaching the sound of transitional phrases. For example, *First of all* contains an r-colored vowel (a rare sound [underlined in the following description] that occurs in under one percent of the world's languages) plus the consonant sound /v/, substituted with /b/ in Japanese, causing one of my students to complain that my usual lecture opener contained a word not found in his dictionary, *fustobal.* As previously mentioned, when teaching note-taking is equated with teaching listening, the potential focus is the product, not the process of comprehension (see, however, Chapter 10 for more on note-taking). As described by Mendelsohn (2006), "Much of what is traditionally mis-named *teaching* listening should in fact be called *testing* listening" (p. 75).

An alternative is to truly integrate listening and speaking. Considering mishearings such as those discussed previously, this invites the integration of pronunciation instruction into the curriculum. Students tend to assume their problems in this domain are troublesome consonant or vowel sounds. North American English has 29 of the former and roughly 15 of the latter; we refer to these consonant and vowel sounds as segmentals. Fortunately, as I often assured my students, no one has 44 pronunciation problems. The task is to identify just those sounds in the students' field-specific lexicon that must be addressed. For example, a Japanese neurosurgeon preparing to deliver a conference talk in English on brain lesions in different brain regions must be able to differentiate either word-initial consonants /l/ and /r/ or the word-medial consonants /ʒ/ from /dʒ/, both highly problematic for Japanese speakers.

CSPs, such as linked and contracted words and deleted, reduced, and altered sounds are relevant for teaching in English as a second language (ESL)—or English-speaking—settings. As Jenkins (2000) points out, these are less relevant in settings where nonnative speakers are more likely to be speaking in English with other nonnative English speakers. CSPs are best differentiated in the ESL classroom as helpful for listening, but not essential for speaking. Inform students that practice producing them *in* class will benefit them *out of class*, where CSPs are abundant in the external input. As a former student once related, he felt defeated within moments of his arrival in the United States when someone in the taxi line at the airport turned and asked, "Do you mind if I smoke?" to which he wanted to reply if only he knew what a [mayndıfay] was.

In addition to segmentals are the suprasegmental features, those that ride above the level of the individual consonants and vowels. These are the prosodic elements that include stress and intonation. Often, errors with word stress combine with segmental errors, producing challenges for even proficient listeners (also see Chapter 2 for strategies for teaching phonemic awareness and word stress). A seasoned writing instructor reported being baffled when a student seeking help revising her essay's thesis statement stated, "It is [ə kɝd]" (*occurred*) until it became clear the statement was *awkward*. Missing glide /w/ in the syllable onset cluster and wrong lexical stress combined to obscure the student's intended word.

Finally, students from a wide variety of language backgrounds tend to either entirely omit or to mispronounce inflectional endings on regular nouns and verbs. I think of this as the "Everybody understand me" phenomenon. In social interactions, it would be rude to correct these errors; in the ESL classroom, these are often considered strictly grammar errors. The students know and can recite the rules or pass a grammar test; they are just so focused on their message that they "forget" to include the endings. If this is so, how do we account for the read aloud situation where students omit the *–s* or *–ed* endings that appear on the page they are reading? These grammar errors have a phonological source, are stigmatizing, and are teachable (see Reed, 2012, for an instructional intervention).

Establishing the four components that make up the scope of the task (CSPs, segmentals, suprasegmentals, and grammar sounds) is in keeping with Hancock (2012), who advocates that we treat pronunciation as a listening skill.

Take Action Steps

Having identified both learner and instructional challenges, it remains to propose an approach that applies research to pedagogy. Inspired by Horwitz (1987), it seems wise to investigate our students' beliefs and their listening strategies. As Nix and Tseng (2014) point out, "learner beliefs affect the language learning strategies employed and also affect the motivation to learn, thereby indirectly influencing L2 learning outcomes" (p. 114). Three action steps are suggested:

1. Determine beliefs
2. Identify strategies
3. Assess skills

If these align, no intervention is required. If not, a realignment is needed. The following activities provide instructors some direction in integrating this realignment into lessons.

Understanding Message Content

To understand what students believe about their own listening practices, it is helpful to administer a short survey. This survey probes learner beliefs and metacognitive strategies.

Preinstruction Survey to Assess Understanding Message Content

Directions: Circle T or F to Indicate True or False

1. Native speakers speak too fast. If they didn't speak so fast, I could understand them. T/F
2. When listening, I pay attention to the content words. The little words aren't important. T/F

Let's examine the results of a study reported by Lacroix et al. (2016) in which the subjects (n = 14 high-intermediate to advanced-level students in an academically oriented intensive English program) had uniformly responded True to both survey questions. Listening skills were assessed using a three-sentence introduction to a podcast from an episode of *This American Life* by host Ira Glass (2010) entitled "Parent Trap." The results of the assessment were used to establish preinstruction baseline data. Students received a cloze passage; of the 64 words, all 46 content words were supplied. There were 18 blanks for the "little" function words. For the purpose of prelistening background building, the context and background information were supplied. ("You are about to hear a brief introduction to a story about a young man named Dave and what happened to Dave during the worldwide financial crisis of 2008.") Students were given directions to fill in the blanks as they listened to the podcast introduction. Following is the sample passage (Figure 1), numbered for ease of reference, with one blank per word.

The failure rate for the students in this Speaking and Listening elective class was 100%. Some students wrote occasional words in the margins; no students filled in any

Dave was [1] ____ ____ late 20s, and it would not be accurate to say that [2] ____ ____ living at home [3] ____ ____ parents, but only because half the time [4] ____ ____ staying [5] ____ ____ sister's house. [6] ____ ____ playing in a band, doing some writing, not making much money, [7] ____ ____ parents were worried. And one day, [8] ____ ____ hanging out [9] ____ ____ mom.

Figure 1. Cloze passage from *This American Life* podcast.

blanks. Even in the face of this lack of success, many students confidently parroted what they'd been taught in their TOEFL Prep classes: "Focus on the content words; the little words aren't important." None could answer the accompanying comprehension questions. However, very likely a proficient English listener would be able to fill in the blanks without even listening. How is that possible?

Three Variables for Processing Listening Input

Similar to reading, listening utilizes three kinds of information. For both skills, when students are provided with a title or context, background knowledge can be activated, initiating top-down processing. For reading, assuming students possess the ability to decode orthographic script (i.e., literacy), bottom-up processing can also be activated. For listening, where spoken input replaces orthographic input, the activation of bottom-up processing involves decoding the acoustic information, matching sounds with words, and finally matching words to meaning. As summarized by Voss (1979):

> If the perception of speech is determined by the three variables of content information, linguistic information and acoustic information . . . then the non-native speaker because of his imperfect command of the language (i.e. deficient generative system [=linguistic information] is less likely to make accurate linguistic predictions in his reconstruction attempts. He will therefore have to depend more heavily on the acoustic information. (p. 130)

In other words, proficient listeners rely on what they know about English grammar and syntax to fill in the gaps that occur in speech when the "little" words are reduced. However, English learners' limited command of English grammar and syntax means that they have fewer tools at their disposal when listening, and they revert to trying to make sense of the aural unput. As we discovered, CSPs distort the acoustic signal. Now what?

Implement Strategies to Process Listening Input for Message Content

To assist students with segmenting connected speech in ways that make sense, it is helpful to explicitly teach strategies for incorporating bottom-up and top-down processing while listening.

Listening Strategy 1: Use Three Kinds of Information to Process Message Content

1. *Context information*: what you already know about the topic of conversation (background knowledge, world knowledge, content knowledge)
2. *Language information*: what you already know about how the English language works (the grammar, the vocabulary, and the sound system)
3. *Acoustic information*: the sounds that you actually hear someone saying

To implement these three strategies, direct students to use three steps to decode what was said.

Use Three Steps to Decode Message Content

Step 1: What did you hear? Write down what it sounded like.

Step 2: Does it make sense? Reread what you wrote.

Step 3: What was really said? Use the three kinds of information to decode what you heard.

Figure 2 captures the strategies in practice.

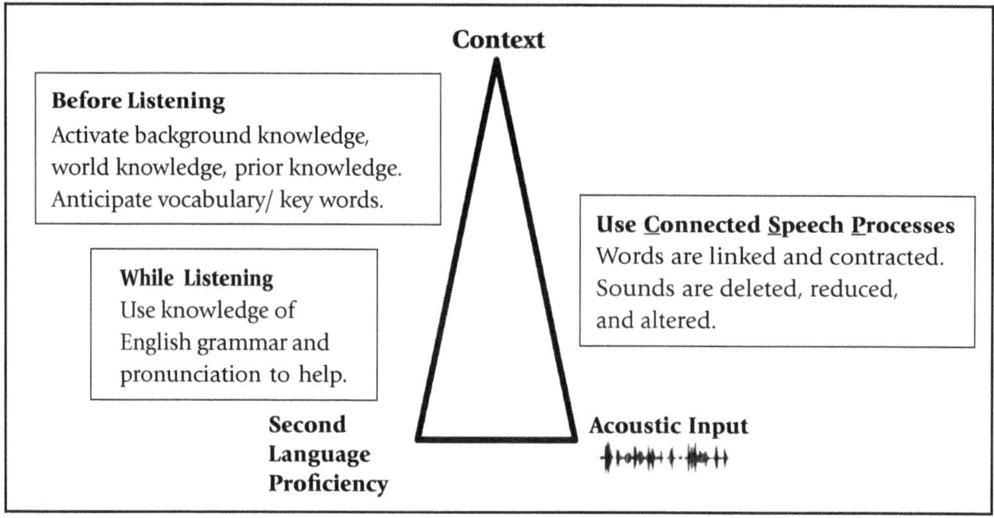

Figure 2. Three strategies to decode aural input.

In tests of language proficiency, reading and listening instruments typically consist of obscure passages that deliberately reduce the likelihood of test takers answering the comprehension questions based on their prior knowledge. Regardless of whether they are deprived of a context or dependent on a misleading context, as in Listening Sample 1 with the inclusion of the preposition phrase *at the bank*, or when they are provided a context as in the podcast passage in Figure 1, students seem to rely on surface-level processing of the listening input, completely bypassing the language variable—the information a proficient listener uses to successfully fill in the blanks without hearing the passage.

We all use these three types of information to process listening input in our first languages; students need to be made aware of the importance of relying on language information in processing their L2. Once this has been introduced, you can form a triangle with your hands to serve as a reminder.

Sample Instructional Debrief 1: Use Three Kinds of Information to Process Message Content

In light of the challenges posed by CSPs, it is helpful to explicitly demonstrate examples of these strategies in use. Here is an example of a think-aloud you might demonstrate for the class. For instance, to illustrate Listening Strategy 1 in action, we'll use the three kinds of information to debrief the incorrect transcription in Listening Sample 1, "Tell her I'll meet her . . .":

1. Use **context information**
   - minimal context was provided; back ground information cannot be activated
2. Use **language information**
   - Every English sentence needs a verb. Isolate possible verbs: *tell* and *meet.*
   - Every verb needs a subject. In a command, the subject is understood to be *you.*
   - Most sentences use a subject-verb-object pattern; this sentence has two clauses. [(Will you please) Tell her (that) I'll meet her.]
3. Use **acoustic information**
   - Words are linked: *Tell her* becomes *Tellher*; *meet her* becomes *meether*
   - Sounds are deleted: the /h/ is deleted in the words *~~h~~e, ~~h~~er, ~~h~~is, ~~h~~im,* except:
     - when it's the first word in a sentence or a clause
     - when it's stressed for emphasis
     - when *his* functions as a possessive pronoun
   - Words are contracted: *I will* becomes *I'll*

As you explicitly demonstrate these strategies, learners will be able to see how a sentence like "(Will you please) Tell ~~h~~er (that) I'll meet ~~h~~er" can sound like "Tell~~h~~er I'll meet~~h~~er." (See the Appendix for a list of select CSPs with illustrative examples.)

Sample Instructional Debrief 2: Use Checklists to Pronounce Noun and Verb Endings

One possible explanation for learners' failure to detect and accurately interpret noun and verb endings when listening may be their failure to produce and accurately pronounce these endings in their own speech. To address the mispronunciation of regular noun or verb endings, checklists offer several advantages. They concisely illustrate the logic of the various pronunciations of endings, such as [t], [d], and [ɪd] for regular verb *–ed* endings and [s], [z], and [ɪz] for *-s* endings. They offer succinct mnemonics to assist students' rule internalization for self-monitoring, and they streamline instructor feedback to provide metalinguistic error correction. To increase students' metacognitive strategy use, make the language of instruction for introducing a new rule or concept match the language of corrective feedback. This, in turn, becomes the same language students use to self-monitor and self-correct.

Remember that producing the *-ed* verb ending may require adding more consonant sounds to the end of words than the native language allows. Therefore, allow students time for the requisite articulatory manipulation, and alert them that fluency will temporarily slow as pronunciation accuracy increases. Figure 3 illustrates a see-at-a-glance checklist for the pronunciation of regular noun and verb endings.

In its most succinct form, student mispronunciation of *looked* as two syllables [lʊk ɛd] would elicit this peer student- or instructor-initiated prompt: No /t/ or /d/ (final sound); no extra syllable (ending).

Student Learning Outcomes

It is always beneficial to use formative assessments during the semester with listening in mind. To this end, you should redirect instructional objectives to a primary focus on the listening skills processes, with passage comprehension as a by-product of successful listening skills implementation. In other words, lesson activities and plans should broaden the focus of listening from strictly comprehension tasks that test learners to include bottom-up skill building as well. At the semester end, use post-instruction summative assessments and repeat pre-instruction surveys to ascertain whether learners' beliefs and/or strategies have changed. To assess skill progress, use a cloze passage of comparable length to the pre-instruction passage, and to ensure there is no new vocabulary or idiomatic usage in the post-instruction passage, thus ensuring face validity.

Sample (Correct) Postinstruction Responses, Listening Challenge 1: Understanding Message Content

1. Native speakers speak too fast. If they didn't speak so fast, I could understand them. T/F

   False: The problem isn't the speed of speech; the problem is connected speech processes.

2. When listening, I pay attention to the content words. The little words aren't important. T/F

   False: I use three kinds of information (context, language, acoustic) to process input.

Keep in mind that metalinguistic awareness often precedes procedural automatization. That is, students might know more about grammar or syntax and the importance of using bottom-up and top-down processing than they can deploy such processing

Checklist: How do you pronounce noun and verb endings?						
	For an *-ed* ending . . . (regular past tense/past participle verbs)			**For an *-s* ending . . .** (regular 3rd person singular verbs, regular count noun plurals, possessive nouns)		
say it with an **extra syllable** if:	the final sound of the verb is **/t/ or /d/**	Say it: [ɪd] *examples:* insisted, conceded		the final sound of the verb/ noun is a **hissing sound***	Say it: [ɪz] *examples:* approaches, uses	
say it with **no extra syllable** if:	the final sound of the verb is **anything *other* than /t/ or /d/**	Say it: [t] the final sound is voiceless ⅄ *example:* looked	Say it: [d] the final sound is voiced *example:* used	the final sound of the verb/ noun is ***not* a hissing sound or 2-part consonant***	Say it: [s]. *example:* insists	Say it: [z]. *example*: concedes
⅄Voiceless sounds are: /k/, /p/, /f/, /s/, /ʃ/, /tʃ/				*Hissing sounds: /s/ at the end of *ace*, /ʃ/ at the end of *wish*, /tʃ/ at the end of *teach*, /z/ at the end of *use*, /dʒ/ at the end of *acknowledge*		

Figure 3. Checklist to pronounce regular *-ed* and *-s* noun and verb endings.

consistently in real time. Learning advances from explicit declarative knowledge to implicit procedural accuracy in stages, and takes time. Therefore, changes in metalinguistic awareness and metacognitive strategy use, even in the absence of consistent accuracy, is still progress.

Understanding Speaker Intent

To assess student beliefs, strategies, and skills, administer a short survey, similar to the one suggested for assessing understanding message content.

Preinstruction Survey to Assess Understanding Message Meaning

Circle the best response:

1. If I can understand all the words in a sentence, I can understand the meaning of the sentence.

   AGREE NOT SURE DISAGREE

2. English intonation is merely decorative; intonation cannot change the meaning of the sentence.

   AGREE NOT SURE DISAGREE

3. I notice English intonation and I use it to interpret speakers' meaning.

   AGREE NOT SURE DISAGREE

4. Listen and circle the correct answer (italics represent the rise-fall intonation contour):

   "The *teacher* didn't grade your exams."

   Have the exams been graded? Yes / No

Where realignment is necessary, address metalinguistic awareness that intonation signals speaker intent, adjust strategies at the metacognitive level, and reassess skills at the procedural level. Following the diagnostic needs assessment, direct learners in the instruction phase to use a three-step strategy to process speaker intent.

Use Three Steps to Decode Message Meaning

Step 1: Detect the intonation signal.

Step 2: Locate the intonation signal.

Step 3: Interpret the signal: Emphasis? Contrast or correction? Implication?

Step 1. Detect the intonation signal. Listen and circle the correct answer (italics represent intonation):

a. She's not a *teacher*.
b. *She's* not a teacher

Do the two sentences sound the same? or different? (Sample correct response: "Different")

Step 2. Locate the extra intonation. Listen to the two sentences again and respond.

1. Which word has extra intonation in Sentence (a)? _________
2. Which word has extra intonation in Sentence (b)? _________

Explain the difference. (Sample correct response: "In (a), *teacher* has extra intonation")

Step 3. Interpret the intonation signal. Circle the correct answer (italics represent the intonation):

a. She's not a *teacher*,
   i. she's an engineer.
   ii. he's a teacher.
b. *She's* not a teacher,
   i. she's an engineer
   ii. he's a teacher.

(Sample response: "In (a), *teacher* has extra intonation; she's something else, like an engineer")

Sample Postinstruction Responses, Listening Challenge 2: Understanding Message Meaning
For the postinstruction summative assessment, students listen to the preinstruction sentences and demonstrate any acquired skills: For example, students listen to the following sentences:

a. The teacher didn't grade your exams.
b. The *teacher* didn't grade your exams.

Evidence of improved postinstruction awareness would be ability to label the sentences as different, to state that (b) had extra intonation on the word *teacher*, and to answer that yes, the exams had been graded, but not by the teacher. The extra intonation implied what the listener must infer: Someone else graded the exams.

This chapter has introduced two listening challenges: understanding what is said and understanding what is meant by what is said. Approaches, strategies, and checklists have been offered to assist learners with parsing continuous speech and recognizing known words in connected speech to access utterance content and with detecting, locating, and interpreting marked intonation to access message meaning.

References

Allen, V. (1971). Teaching intonation, from theory to practice. *TESOL Quarterly, 5*(1), 73–81. https://doi.org/10.2307/3586113

Altenberg, E. P. (2005). The judgement, perception, and production of consonant clusters in a second language. *International Review of Applied Linguistics, 43*, 53–80. http://doi.org/10.1515/iral.2005.43.1.53

Broersma, M., & Cutler, A. (2008). Phantom word activation in L2. *System, 36*(1), 22–34. https://doi.org/10.1016/j.system.2007.11.08.003

Casserly, E. D., & Pisoni, D. B. (2010). Speech perception and production. *Wiley Interdisciplinary Reviews: Cognitive Science, 1*(5), 629–647. https://doi.org/10.1002/wcs.63

Field, J. (2008). *Listening in the language classroom.* Cambridge University Press.

Flege, J. E. (1995). Second language speech learning: Theory, findings, and problems. In W. Strange (Ed.), *Speech perception and linguistic experience: Issues in cross-language research* (pp. 233–277). York Press.

Gilbert, J. B. (1994). Intonation: A navigation guide for the listener (and gadgets to help teach it). In J. Morley (Ed.), *Pronunciation pedagogy and theory: New views, new directions* (pp. 38–48). TESOL Press.

Glass, I. (Host). (2010, February 19). Parent trap (No. 401) [Audio podcast episode]. In *This American life*. WBEZ Chicago. https://www.thisamericanlife.org/401/parent-trap

Hancock, M. (2012). *Pronunciation as a listening skill.* Hancock McDonald. http://hancockmcdonald.com/ideas/pronunciation-listening-skill

Horwitz, E. (1987). Surveying student beliefs about language learning. In A. L. Wenden & J. Rubin (Eds.), *Learner strategies in language learning* (pp. 119–129). Prentice-Hall.

Jenkins, J. (2000). *The phonology of English as an international language.* Oxford University Press.

Lacroix, J., Reed, M., & Harbaugh, A. (2016). The effect of metacognitive strategy instruction on L2 learner beliefs and listening skills. In J. Levis, H. Le, I. Lucic, E. Simpson, & S. Vo (Eds.), *Proceedings of the 7th annual pronunciation in second language learning and teaching conference* (pp. 76–87). Iowa State University.

Levis, J. (1999). Intonation in theory and practice, revisited. *TESOL Quarterly, 33*(1), 37–63. https://doi.org/10.2307/3588190

Linebaugh, G., & Roche, T. (2013). Learning to hear by learning to speak: The effect of articulatory training in Arab learners' English phonemic discrimination. *Australian Review of Applied Linguistics, 36*(2), 146–159. https://doi.org/10.1075/aral.36.2.02lin

Linebaugh, G., & Roche, T. (2015). Evidence that L2 production training can enhance perception. *Journal of Academic Language & Learning, 9*(1), A1–A17.

McAllister, R. (1996). Perceptual foreign accent: L2 users' comprehension ability. In A. R. James & J. H. Leather (Eds.), *Second-language speech* (pp. 119–132). Mouton de Gruyter.

Mendelsohn, D. (2006). Learning how to listen using learning strategies. In P. Gorden (Ed.), *Current trends in the development and teaching of the four language skills* (pp. 75–89). Mouton de Gruyter.

Nix, J-M. L., & Tseng, W-T. (2014). Towards the measurement of EFL listening beliefs with item response theory methods. *The International Journal of Listening, 28*, 112–130. https://doi.org/10.1080/10904018.2013.872990

Paunović, T., & Savić, M. (2008). Discourse intonation—Making it work. In S. Komar & U. Mozetić (Eds.), *As you write it: Issues in literature, language, and translation in the context of Europe in the 21st century, V*(1–2), 57–75.

Pickering, L. (2012). Intonation. In K. Malmkjaer (Ed.), *The Routledge linguistics encyclopedia* (3rd ed., pp. 280–286). Routledge.

Reed, M. (2012). The effect of metacognitive feedback on second language morphophonology. In J. Levis & K. LeVelle (Eds.), *Proceedings of the 3rd annual pronunciation in second language learning and teaching conference* (pp. 168–177). Iowa State University.

Reed, M., & Michaud, C. (2015). Intonation in research and practice: The importance of metacognition. In M. Reed & J. Levis (Eds.), *The handbook of English pronunciation* (pp. 454–470). Wiley Blackwell.

Sheldon, A., & Strange, W. (1982). The acquisition of /r/ and /l/ by Japanese learners of English: Evidence that speech production can precede speech perception. *Applied Psycholinguistics, 3*(03), 243–261. https://doi.org/10.1017/S0142716400001417

Tomlinson, J. M., & Bott, L. (2013). How intonation constrains pragmatic inferences. In M. Knauff, M. Pauen, N. Sebanz, & I. Wachsmuth (Eds.), *Proceedings of the annual meeting of the Cognitive Science Society, 35* (pp. 3569–3574). Cognitive Science Society.

Tsukada, K., Birdsong, D., Bialystok, E., Mack, M., Sung, H., & Flege, J. (2005). A developmental study of English vowel production and perception by native Korean adults and children. *Journal of Phonetics, 33*(3), 263–290. https://doi.org/10.1016/j.wocn.2004.10.002

Tyler, M. D., & Cutler, A. (2009). Cross-language differences in cue use for speech segmentation. *Journal of the Acoustical Society of America, 126*, 367–376.

Ur, P. (2008). *A course in language teaching: Practice and theory.* Cambridge University Press.

Vandergrift, L., & Goh, C. (2012). *Teaching and learning second language listening: Metacognition in action*. Routledge.

Vanderplank, R. (2013). Listening and understanding. In P. Driscoll, E. Macaro, & A. Swarbrick (Eds.), *Debates in modern languages education* (pp. 53–65). Routledge.

Voss, B. (1979). Hesitation phenomena as sources of perceptual errors for non-native speakers. *Language and Speech, 22*(2), 129–144. https://doi.org/10.1177/002383097902200203

Weber, A., & Cutler, A. (2006). First language phonotactics in second-language listening. *Journal of the Acoustical Society of America, 119*(1), 597–607. https://doi.org/10.1121/1.2141003

Wells, J. C. (2006). *English intonation: An introduction.* Cambridge University Press.

Wichmann, A. (2005). The role of intonation in the expression of attitudinal meaning. *English Language and Linguistics, 9*(2), 229–253. https://doi.org/10.1017/S1360674305001632

MARNIE REED is professor of education and affiliated faculty in the Program in Linguistics at Boston University. She is also director of the graduate program in Teaching English to Speakers of Other Languages (TESOL) in the College of Education, where she teaches courses in linguistics, second language acquisition, and applied phonology.

Appendix: Connected Speech Processes

Connected Speech Processes: *English doesn't sound the way it looks.*
(important for listening comprehension; not necessary for speaking)

ɪzzybɪzzyy } ***How many words? Where are the word boundaries?***
Words don't sound like their dictionary entries.

Sounds are linked

Consonants to consonants	(same place of articulation: *sit down, last time, some more*)
Consonants to consonants	(different place of articulation: *last page, social media*)
Consonants to vowels	(*take on, talk about*)
Vowels to vowels	(*key issue; go around*)

Sounds *are* deleted

/h/ in *he, her, his,* and *him*	***Except:*** Sentence-initial: *He's late.*
E.g. *Is he busy? → Is ~~h~~e busy?*	Stressed: *I don't mean him; I mean her.*
Sounds like: *[ɪziybɪziy]?*	Pronouns: *his/hers: That's not his; it's hers.*

Sounds are reduced

can → kn	I can do it → *I kn do it.*
and → n	Law and Order → *Law 'n Order;* wait and see → *wait 'n see*
an → n	US units (mph) miles per hour → *miles an hour* → *miles 'n hour*
of → ɘ	a lot of time → *a lotta time*
or → r	right or wrong → *right 'r wrong*

Sounds are altered

you → yl	See you later → *See ya later.*
After /d/ → dʒə	Would you? → *Would ja?* Could you? → *Could ja?* Did you? → *Did ja?*
After /t/ → ʃtə	Can't you? → *Can 'tcha?* Won't you? → *Won 'tcha?*
to → tɘ	have to → *hafta*
/t/ → d	*letter → leDer, better → beDer, water → waDer*
you're/your → yer	You're right. → *yer right.* It's on your right. → *It's on yer right.*
After /d/ → dʒər	You did your homework? → *You di djer homework?*
After /t/ → ʃtər	Put your hat on. → *Pu tcher] hat on.*
got to → gotta	
want to → wanna	
going to → gonna	

Words're contracted

(Negative) not → n't: *isn't, aren't, doesn't, don't, won't, can't, shouldn't,* etc.
(Auxiliaries): I am → *I'm,* I will → *I'll,* I have → *I've,* I would/had → *I'd,* I would have → *I'd've*
you are → *you're,* you have → *you've,* you will → *you'll,* you would/had → *you'd*
(s)he/it/they → he's, she's, he'll, she'll, it'll, he'd, she'd, it'd, they're, they'll, they've, they'd
(Modals): could have → *could 've,* would have → *would 've,* should have → *should've, etc.*
(Existential Pronouns): there is a → *there's a;* there are → *there're*
(Proper Nouns): Jane will ... → *Jane'll;* Bob will → *Bob'll ...*
(Common Nouns): the judge will ... → *the judge'll ...*

Adapted from "Listening Skills Instruction," by M. Reed, 2019, *PSLLT Conference Proceedings* (pp. 401–412). Iowa University Press.

CHAPTER 7

FREDDIE GAY

Paying Attention to Weak Forms

Listening in Real Life

"We can't understand you very well teacher. Can you speak more slowly?" I had just started training a group of intermediate-level English teachers in Malaysia. I did not think I was speaking quickly. As I was tasked with moving this group of learners to an advanced level of English and therefore surmounting the intermediate-plateau, I discussed their listening challenges with them. They found it easy to understand other Malaysian English speakers. However, listening to native speakers was difficult owing to "speed" and "accent." One listening strategy that I had been promoting to help learners who had difficulty listening was to "listen for content words." After some reflection, I realised that use of this strategy may hinder progress beyond the intermediate level.

When communicating in English, many of these teachers would often either omit grammatical morphemes or produce them with the duration, intensity, and pitch peak consistent with stressed syllables in English content words. I realized that this tendency must be affecting my students' ability to score highly on speaking proficiency tests, but it also led me to consider their listening ability. Did they have difficulty decoding these words when listening? Had they stored only the strong form (the dictionary citation form of many grammatical words, e.g., determiners, prepositions, and auxiliary verbs) in their mental lexicon? If so, this might be causing an inability to recognize weak forms (the reduced form of such words, whose vowels are represented by the International Phonetic Alphabet [IPA] symbol for the unstressed midcentral vowel schwa, /ə/, which is similar to the vowel sound /ʌ/ in words like *but* or *of*).

To investigate, I set up a nonword dictation (Field, 2008). I told learners that I would say a mixture of real words and invented words and they should guess how to spell unknown words. The nonword phrases were dictated twice at a natural pace. Following are some illustrative responses. The phonemic chart captures variable U.S. and U.K. pronunciations.

Phonemic Chart Representation	English Orthographic Interpretation	Learner Response
UK /ˈniytʃfəˈfowp/ US /ˈniytʃfɚrˈfowp/	neech for fope	*neat phone*
/wiykənˈdætʃ/	we can datch	*weekend that*
/ˈglæphəzˈheyd/	glap has hade	*clap at eight*

The responses revealed that learners found weak forms difficult to decode accurately. Consistent with Field (2004), it also showed that learners were reluctant to guess non-words and instead tended to inaccurately match them to known words that shared some sounds in common with the nonwords.

I then created an online multiple-choice quiz that asked learners to select the most common pronunciation of several words. Learners saw the written form and were presented with audio of a strong and weak version of the word to choose from, for example *to*: /tuw/ vs. /tə/. There was a tendency to state that the strong form pronunciation was more common. Furthermore, such incorrect judgements were commonly accompanied with quite high degrees of certainty.

Instructing learners to listen for content words diverts their attention away from weak forms. This is problematic because it can prevent learners from engaging with an important layer of meaning that such forms help convey. Hence, it seems fair to question the value of promoting the strategy of "listening for the content words" without ensuring that we devote sufficient time to addressing the decoding of weak forms, too.

Listening in the Research

There is evidence that learners' first language has a profound effect on how they perceive phonemes. Escudero (2007) argues that second language (L2) sounds in late learners are originally perceived through a filter organised and entrenched around perceptual categories that are represented in the learners' first language (L1), leading to interference in the processing of the L2. Given that the English schwa sound is inherent in a preponderance of weak function words, it is crucial for teachers to provide perception training for groups of learners whose first language does not contain weak forms. Even if the sound of the weak form is represented in a language's phoneme inventory, it may be difficult to recognize because of differences in rhythm or phonotactics (permissible sound combinations or syllable placement). For example, Malay has the midcentral unrounded vowel, but final syllables tend to be lengthened and words of two syllables receive stress on the final syllable (Clynes & Deterding, 2011). This could have been a factor contributing to the tendency to prefer strong forms in the previously described activities.

The nature of a learners' L1 alphabet system may also contribute toward inaccurate mental representation of phonological form, especially in the case of a highly transparent alphabet where there is a one-to-one relationship between a sound and its spelling (also see Chapter 2 for a discussion about the implications the weak English sound-spelling correspondence has on L2 listeners). According to Bassetti (2008), orthographic input processed while reading may be interpreted using L1 phonological rules. Furthermore, she suggests that the L1 rules applied when reading activate during L2 listening. The spoken input is interpreted using these L1-based rules, "leading to non-targetlike phonological representations of L2 phonemes, syllables and words" (Bassetti, 2008, p. 199). Going back to my Malay learners, it is likely that because of the transparency of the Malay alphabet, when reading aloud, they "[tended] to give English auxiliary verbs, prepositions etc. their full 'written' pronunciation" (Yong, 2001, p. 282). Without explicit intervention linking the more common spoken form to the spelling pattern, the mental representation of such words is likely to approximate a strong form rather than a weak form.

L1 interference in processing weak forms occurs at a suprasegmental level, too. The strategies that are used to segment and recognise words in a stream of speech vary across languages because they are attuned to the prosodic features of the language (Cutler, 2000). English native speakers have been evidenced to use a strategy that assumes new word beginnings when hearing full-quality stressed syllables (Cutler & Norris, 1988) and is sensitive to prosodic units known as feet, which are broadly defined as consisting of a strong syllable and any weak syllables that may immediately follow. This strategy helps native listeners to effortlessly process connected speech effects, such as cliticization, where weak function words attach to stressed content words to form feet across word boundaries (see Figure 1).

The rhythm of English is often described as "stress-timed" because there is usually equal time duration between each stressed word. To accommodate words into this rhythm, widespread use of weak forms is made (see Figure 2).

The ability to recognise the function words is therefore crucial to accurate decoding and encouraging a proficient segmentation routine. Native English speakers are adept at recognising high-frequency function words. Over time, "acoustic templates" for common weak syllables or strings of weak syllables are stored in long-term memory, leading to enhanced recognition (Grosjean & Gee, 1987). Moreover, Field (2008) demonstrated that there is a correlation between level of L2 English proficiency and the percentage of words accurately transcribed. For example, accurate rates of recognition for *a* and *of* rose

S	W	S	W
"want	to	tell	her"
UK /ˈwɑn(t)ə	ˈtel(h)ə/		
US /ˈwɑn(t)ə	ˈtel(h)ɚ/		

Figure 1. Cliticization in English.

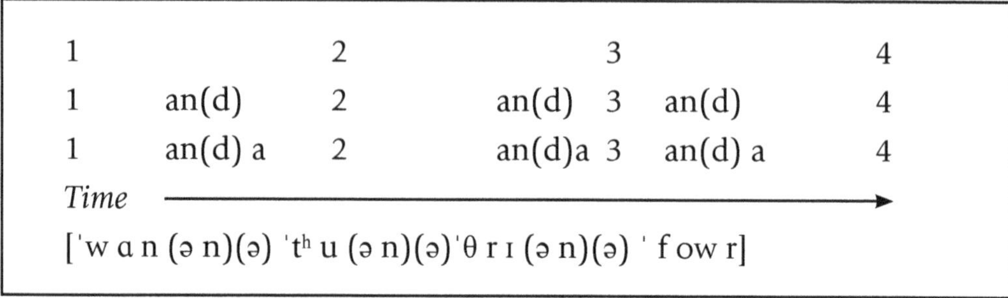

Figure 2. Stress timing in English.

from an average that was lower than 20% in intermediate levels to approximately 75% for advanced levels. For native speakers, the recognition level was close to 100%.

Constructing templates of weak form patterns is complicated by the fact that their perception can be made more challenging by other connected speech features (also see Chapter 6 for more on connected speech processes). One such feature highlighted in Figure 1 is elision, where /t/ in *to* and /h/ in *her* might be dropped completely. Another feature is resyllabification, where a final consonant in a word jumps over to join onto a vowel from a following word to form a new syllable. Combined, in British English these processes can turn "want to tell her" into [wɑ nə 'tɛ lə] with the /l/ being lengthened to serve as both the end of *tell* and the beginning of, what in orthographic form, is *her*.

Variability in pronunciation caused by dialects can also be challenging for the L2 listener; for example, American English speakers will usually pronounce *r* at the end of weak forms *her, for, your,* and *were,* whereas British speakers tend to omit it completely. Furthermore, some weak forms are homophonous; for example, a single schwa sound may represent: *a, are,* or *her*. Homophony (words with unrelated meanings sharing the same phonological form) in weak forms might occur because of frequent interaction with other connected speech processes; for example, *and* will often lose /d/ when it occurs before a word with a consonant (as illustrated in Figure 2) and is, therefore, often realised as /ən/, a form shared with *an*.

So far, I have established that

a. weak forms also have a full-quality strong form which is used in certain contexts,

b. a number of weak forms are homophonous, and

c. learners who read such words before hearing their weak forms may assume an incorrect pronunciation (possibly governed by the phonology of their first language).

The first two of these factors could lead to the psychological phenomenon of blocking (Ellis et al., 2014, p. 549). The theory of blocking implies that learning the citation form before the weak form could impede learning that the weak form is a common (but less salient) cue to the same word. This situation may be compounded by the fact that learners from languages which have transparent alphabets are more likely to assume a strong form as representing the spoken form of the word. Therefore learning /kʊd/ = *could* might inhibit further learning that /kəd/ and /kə/ also = *could*.

As well as decoding, it is important to focus on meaning-building processes in L2 listening instruction (Field, 2008). Linking weak forms to their meanings can pose problems, as not all weak forms convey basic meanings. For example, English Vocabulary Profile (www.englishprofile.org/wordlists; Cambridge University Press, 2015) lists a number of senses of prepositions, modal verbs, determiners, and conjunctions realised through weak forms at B2–C1 level of the Common European Framework of Reference for Languages (CEFR; Council of Europe, 2001). These all have homonym senses at lower levels and as a result might be confused with other, more basic meanings. Tyler (2012) highlights that many grammar words are polysemous: For example, *to* has seven different meanings which have developed from a basic meaning (facing a goal). Tyler (2012) argues that explicit instruction highlighting these meaning connections can aid acquisition of the full range of senses associated with a form. In listening, learners will often need to be able to identify the correct sense of such words under considerable time constraints and would likely benefit from instruction that practises this process.

Learners of some languages may find aspects of the meaning of articles difficult to grasp. Snape and Yusa (2013) provided explicit training in perceiving and understanding the meanings of articles to Japanese learners of English. Learners evidenced improved perception and understanding of meanings indicating specificity or nonspecificity, but they still struggled to understand meanings that indicated genericity (e.g., "the lion will become extinct soon," "a beaver builds dams") immediately after the intervention. Larsen (2018) conducted longitudinal classroom-based research aimed at improving learners' ability to understand short bursts of fast speech, and comments "students were likely to mishear the same grammatical forms they were having difficulty with due to the structure of their L1" (Larsen, 2018, p. 31). His investigation involved targeted dictations focusing on commonly omitted weak forms and found that perception improved. His intervention did not include training on the meaning of articles but did combine dictation with awareness-raising of the concept of theme, the part of the sentence which introduces a new topic, and rheme, which provides further information about the topic. There was a focus on teaching the importance of the former in comprehending the most essential part of the meaning of sentences, under the premise that improved perception combined with grammatical awareness can lead to better listening comprehension.

This section has brought to light a range of challenges that learners face when attempting to decode and understand weak forms. I will now outline practical activities to address these issues in the classroom.

Listening in the Classroom

Raising Awareness of Forms

In many contexts, raising awareness of the pronunciation of weak forms is an important first step for helping learners address their perception. It is argued that the analysis of sounds when listening to English projects onto syllables rather than phonemes. Cutler (1997) argues that even though English segmentation is based on stress, the minimum allowable word is a syllable-sized unit. This gives the syllable significance because it "has a fundamental relationship with the very unit that listeners seek in speech" (Cutler, 1997, p. 843). Furthermore, syllables provide a more reliable unit than phonemes as variations caused by connected speech processes would be easier to track, and they account for a much smaller subset (Field, 2008, p. 167).

Therefore, it makes sense to develop an awareness of the schwa sound's centrality to weak forms through exposure in a word context. Weak forms can be directly contrasted with their strong forms in pronunciation perception games in which students get to choose their own path based on which sound they hear, similar to "Pronunciation Journey" (Hancock, 1995), which involves using a map that branches four times, leading to 16 different cities.

In order to play this kind of game, you need to make a pronunciation pyramid template like the one shown in Figure 3 (replace the letters with the names of cities) and display it or give each student a copy.

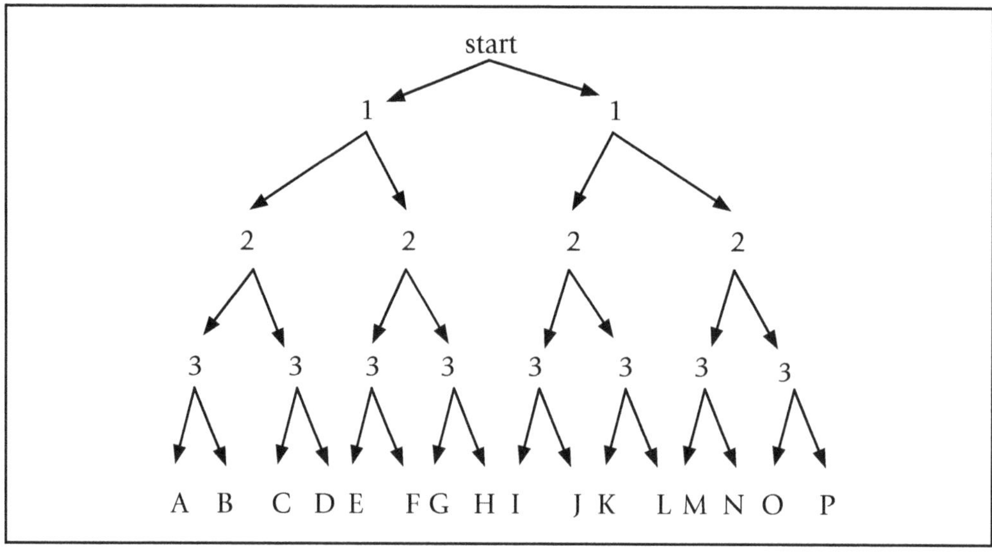

Figure 3. Pronunciation perception pyramid template

Once the pyramid is handed out or displayed to learners, write the following on the board, with the chosen form you wish to target in the middle:

Left		Right
weak form	**some**	*strong form*

If you say the weak form of the target word, the learners move to the left on their map, and to the right if you say the strong form. After the fourth time, learners can quickly compare if they are in the same city before you confirm and choose a new weak form to focus on. A variation of this task is to list four weak forms on one side and their corresponding strong forms written in the phonemic chart on the other. The following example is with modal auxiliary verbs:

	Left	Right
1.	/kən/	/ˈkæn/
2.	/kə(d)/	/ˈkʊ(d)/
3.	/ʃə(d)/	/ˈʃʊ(d)/
4.	/məs(t)/	/ˈmʌs(t)/

You can lead students on several different journeys until satisfied that the class is able to discriminate between the strong and weak forms.

After the main activity, review the weak and strong forms by saying them again and encourage learners to pay attention to your lips as each word is spoken, as there is evidence that accurate speech perception is facilitated by visual facial cues, such as lip movements (Hardison, 2007). This can form part of a multisensory approach that also incorporates movement and touch. Model a gesture that the learners should do every time you say one of the weak forms that reflects their reduced nature (e.g., a gentle flick of the hand). Conversely, the gesture for the strong forms should be a movement that represents their stressed nature (e.g., a bang on the table). This combination of the auditory, visual, and tactile is argued to "feed the brain with diversified input to reinforce the cognitive processing, internalisation and retention of new sounds in long-term memory" (Odisho, 2007, p. 7).

Although more time-consuming to prepare, the activity could also be done by prerecording several different voices saying target weak and strong forms, possibly incorporating different accents. This means the activity would follow an empirically proven method for improving perception of sounds known as high variability pronunciation training (Thomson, 2018). The combination of exposure to different voices combined with a forced decision between two sounds is key to this approach.

Make sure that learners receive pronunciation practice of the target weak forms immediately after you have modelled their pronunciation. Numerous studies have shown there is a link between the accurate perception of a sound and its accurate production (Isbell, 2016; also see Chapter 6). Potential confounding effects from written forms on learners' pronunciation are reduced when a spoken model is provided as a prompt for learners to repeat (Bassetti & Atkinson, 2015). These findings suggest a strong interplay between perception and production. A learner who receives immediate feedback on inaccurate production of a weak form and is able to refine their production to achieve greater accuracy may well improve their ability to hear the weak form at the same time.

A logical follow-up step after perception training of individual weak forms involves playing extended listening passages (e.g., listening passages from course books) and asking learners to identify all the weak forms they hear. Learners should be primed to hear the forms they have been focusing on, perhaps with a list on the board or in a handout, making them easier to discriminate. As well, you should consider slowing the playback speed down if possible, so that the reduced forms become more salient (tools and methods for doing this will be discussed in more detail) and pausing between phrases. Such a task gives an opportunity for learners to hear the forms in context, which is important because the environment in which a word occurs can affect how it is pronounced. It also provides an opportunity for awareness-raising of the prevalence of the weak form over the strong form. Learners can mingle to compare and discuss their answers and you can then elicit the correct answers and write them on the board, grouping the weak forms according to grammatical category (Figure 4).

Weak forms

Modal verbs
can /kən/
could /kə(d)/
should /ʃə(d)/

Determiners
some /səm/
her /hər/,/hər/ /ə/
the /ðə/
a /ə/

Prepositions
to /tə/
at /ət/
for /fə/, /fər/

Conjunctions
but /bət/
and /ənd/, /ən/
as /əz/

Pronouns
us /əs/
them /ðəm/
her /hər/,/hə/, /ə/

Auxiliary verbs
are /ə/, /ər/
was /wəz/
have /həv/, /əv/

Figure 4. Weak forms grouped by grammatical category.

This activity promotes the use of a cognitive strategy "for controlling the processing of L2 information" (Oxford & Schramm, 2013, p. 50). After the activity has finished, provide pairs of students' discussion questions that encourage metacognition:

- How many weak forms were used?
- How many did you identify correctly?
- Which weak forms were difficult to hear? Why?
- Did you confuse any of the weak forms for different words? Why do you think this happened?
- How useful do you think this activity is? Do you think doing it regularly will help you to improve your listening skills? Why/why not?

There is evidence that many learners with high proficiency in listening apply both cognitive and metacognitive strategies to improve their learning (Macaro et al., 2013; also see Chapter 1). Ideally learners would go on to apply such strategies independently should they feel it is beneficial for their development, so they should be encouraged to do this activity with different listening passages outside classroom time. It has recently been argued that a goal of strategy training should be to encourage learners to adopt strategies that are promoted by the teacher and that they see value in, and move from being an "other-regulated" (teacher-dependent) strategy user to a "self-regulated" (autonomous) user (Thomas & Rose, 2018).

Dictation-Based Approaches

Dictation has increasingly gained currency as a way of providing targeted bottom-up listening practice (Davis & Rinvolucri, 2002; Field, 2008; Kazazoğlu; 2013). There are not a great deal of dictation activities in published textbooks that focus specifically on weak forms, but there may be opportunities for teachers to exploit pronunciation and grammar activities for this purpose. Let's consider the following example dictation gap-fill exercise. It comes from a pronunciation resource book which focuses on weak forms (answers provided in parenthesis).

1. He gave .... (the) plate .... (to) me.
2. Steve .... (and) John .... (have) gone.
3. It's .... (a) present .... (from) Steve.
4. You .... (should) give him .... (a) call.

(Adapted from Hewings, 2004, p. 98)

It is imperative that, before listening, you encourage learners to consider the grammar context that the missing words occur in. Knowledge of grammar helps listeners to hear weak forms, and learners will benefit from having time to think about the missing grammar words. It is important to note that, in many cases, more than one answer is possible. Make learners aware of this and instruct them to write down all the weak forms they think are possible for each gap. Allow the learners to discuss their hypotheses in pairs and small groups. This discussion provides an opportunity for peer learning but, more importantly, it encourages learners to externalise the thought processes behind their reasoning.

You play a critical role during the discussion in monitoring, assessing, and providing feedback and explanations. Scaffold learners by careful use of questioning. (e.g., "What *kind* of word is *gone*?", "What type of word usually goes before a past participle?", "Is the subject singular or plural?") Guide learners, but be careful not to confirm any answers before learners listen. Being aware of the meaning of function words and collocations they occur in will help learners to process them when listening. Furthermore, it will encourage learners to use knowledge of syntax and co-text to aid with decoding, thus accounting for the insight that effective listening involves "a kind of negotiation, where the listener weighs a number of pieces of evidence for deciding what the input is" (Field, 2008, p. 133).

The dictation activity itself can be enhanced using technology. Several applications and plugins for online learning management systems allow learners to slow down playback of audio files (e.g., the Slow Fast Slow app [www.studioneat.com/products/slowfast] for smartphones or the H5P Dictation activity [h5p.org/dictation], which can be used on Moodle, Canvas, and WordPress, among others publishing systems). Using these resources, you can record the dictation sentences before class and make them available via a website or social messaging app, putting the learner in control of playback. Being able to slow down the audio can help learners process the inherently degraded quality of weak forms. Slowing fast speech down maintains the prosodic features of continuous speech, whereas these may be lost when speech is deliberately articulated slowly and carefully. Be sure you make learners aware it is these very processes that complicate accurate decoding more than the pace of speech itself. It is, therefore, imperative that you monitor and draw learners' attention to features of connected speech, weak forms, and stress patterns that cause decoding difficulties. Ask questions that elicit examples of such features from learners, and use the board to highlight and discuss the ways in which speech deviates from citation forms.

If you are in control of the audio, you can make use of the ability to control playback speed when providing practice decoding sentences or chunks with weak forms. Start by playing the whole speech at full speed. On further plays, gradually slow down playback (e.g., 90%–80%–75%). Finally, write the sentence or chunk on the board for learners to check. Ask them if any of the words were changed or dropped and try to elicit correct answers. Annotate the written form or use the phonemic chart to highlight deviations from the citation forms. You could also start with slow playback and gradually speed up to add variation to the technique.

If possible, try to obtain examples of sentences or chunks being used by diverse speakers, from a range of different accents. It is often the case that learners are exposed to one accent variety (often the teacher's one) when learning English, especially if they are also using a published course book from the teacher's own country. However, outside of the classroom, learners are likely to hear a range of accents through the different media sources they use. It is quite a common complaint for learners to say they struggle to understand an accent that they are not accustomed to. Hence, it might be a good idea to play the same sentence or chunk spoken in different accents. Learners should guess which accent each sample corresponds to, and you can facilitate discussion of differences in pronunciation and accent that occur. A useful tool for finding phrases spoken in U.S., U.K., and Australian accents is YouGlish (youglish.com), which instantly locates examples of words or phrases being used in YouTube videos with an option to filter them by accent.

Dictation approaches targeting weak forms can be integrated into work that raises awareness of grammatical structure. As mentioned earlier, Larsen (2018) focused on developing understanding of the position and function of theme and rheme, with a view to helping learners understand the importance of the theme in orientating the listener to "what the message is concerned with" (Halliday, 1994, p. 38). Such grammar awareness-raising activities were combined with listening "gap-fill exercises which omitted the start of the clause" (Larsen, 2018, 31). Figure 5 shows a handout for an activity that adopts this approach. The idea is to explain the concepts of theme and rheme, have learners predict the missing words from the target themes drawing on their knowledge of grammar and collocation, and then dictate the sentences for them to fill in the gaps.

(Noun Phrase) Theme	**Rheme**
More ..... (and) more students	*want to study English.*
..... (The) president ..... (of) ..... (the) United States ..... (of) America	*will address the nation shortly.*
..... (A) decent pair ..... (of) shoes	*costs at least $60.*

(Adverb Phrase) Theme	**Rheme**
In ..... (a) week ..... (or) two,	*I'll take a break from work.*
In case ..... (of) ..... (an) emergency,	*dial 911.*
..... (At) ..... (the) end ..... (of) ..... (the) day,	*it doesn't matter very much.*

(Imperative) Theme	**Rheme**
Take ..... (a) break	*for about 20 minutes.*
Cut ..... (the) onions ..... (and) carrots	*and then wash them.*
Tell ..... (them)	*to wait as we missed our train and so are running late.*

Figure 5. Sample sentences for addressing difficulties in decoding sentence themes.

Explaining the concept of theme and rheme and teaching different structures that themes occur in may lead learners to pay attention to and better understand the most important information in a sentence, learning that might be enhanced upon further listening exposure. At the same time, learners receive practice decoding weak forms that form common semifixed patterns of language (the following are a subset):

- at + the + (start/end) + of + the + (noun)
- article + (noun) + of + article + (noun)
- in + article + (time/place)
- (action verb) + article + noun
- (imperative verb) + object pronoun

Building upon this, you can make learners aware of such schematic patterns and encourage them to record them in their notebooks. This could then lead into the modeling of a strategy whereby you play an extended listening passage, pause after any example of one of the patterns being used, and write down exactly what was said as an illustrating example.

Discovery Listening

Dictogloss is another well-known type of dictation that can be used to improve understanding of the form and meaning of weak forms (see also Chapter 5 for another way to use dictogloss to promote listening skill development). Wilson (2003) advocates an adaptation of dictogloss that has a focus on sound or word recognition and guides learners to "discover the reasons for their listening difficulties" (p. 337). This approach, which he calls "discovery listening," involves playing a short listening passage to learners at normal speed (no note-taking allowed) and asking them to work in small groups to reconstruct it. There is then a discovery stage where learners compare their reconstruction with a transcript of the listening, attempt to classify the mistakes they made, and reflect on their relative importance. One advantage of this approach over other kinds of dictation activity is that there is more context for learners to work with, and this can encourage them to use a balance of top-down and bottom-up processing. Wilson (2003) points out, however, that it is important that the chosen texts for discovery listening are graded to avoid being too difficult and forcing learners to overrely on "top-down contextual guesswork" (Wilson, 2003, p. 341).

From the perspective of weak forms, using the aforementioned approach is likely to make learners discuss any forms that they found difficult to perceive or understand during the reconstruction stage, and there is a chance for noticing the source of the difficulty and reflecting upon it during the discovery stage (also see Chapter 12 for an examination of the benefits of the metacognitive approach). This will happen alongside a range of difficulties unrelated to weak forms, but it is possible to adapt this activity to put a more intense focus upon weak forms. Begin by telling learners that they are not going to be able to copy down every word as they listen because they will not have time. They need to copy down key words (content words) and leave gaps for functional words (e.g., articles, conjunctions), which they will have time to add in later. Model this by saying one sentence and writing down only the key words and the gaps on the board. Follow the same stages (listening, reconstruction, discovery) for the content words only. In the discovery stage, display the content words and the correct number of gaps. The following is an example I used with a group of intermediate English for academic purposes learners:

> [1]……… ……… **Shard** [2]……… **London** [3]……… ……… **Burj Khalifa** [4]……… **Dubai, concrete** [5]……… ……… **ubiquitous material now** [6] ……… ……… ……… **usage** [7] ……… **Roman times** [8]……… **today, engineers** [9] ……… **had** [10]……… ……… ……… **little bit crafty** [11]……… **enable** [12]……… ……… **build taller bigger** [13]……… **stronger structures.** [14]……… **first** [15]……… **all, what** [16]……… **concrete?**

Now that students have done the three stages with a focus on content words, it is time to repeat the stages for the function words. Knowing the number of gaps and the content words will support them.

> [1]*From the* **Shard** [2]in **London** [3]*to the* **Burj Khalifa** [4]*in* **Dubai, concrete** [5]*is a* **ubiquitous material now** [6]*but from its* **usage** [7]in **Roman times** [8]*to* **today, engineers** [9]*have* **had** [10]*to be a* **little bit crafty** [11]*to* **enable** [12]*us to* **build taller bigger** [13]*and* **stronger structures.** [14]*But* **first** [15]of **all, what** [16]is **concrete**?

During the discovery phase, you can ask learners questions similar to those outlined on page 101 to encourage them to think about the missing words, although in this case *weak form* should be changed to *grammar or function word*. This is because not all grammar words have weak forms (e.g., *in, be, its,* and *is* in the preceding sample passage).

Addressing Polysemy

Most weak forms are polysemous (have many meanings), and there are a number of meanings judged to be at B2 CEFR level and even some at C1 level. It is uncommon for course books to focus on the higher level meaning of these weak forms explicitly, and, during listening, learners may match the meaning incorrectly with one they have already learnt for that form. The following approach takes weak forms that have meaning at B2 level, according to English Vocabulary Profile (Cambridge University Press, 2015). The Cambridge and Oxford Online Learner Dictionaries (Cambridge University Press, 2021) also list the level of many words according to the CEFR.

Begin by writing down the weak forms underlined in the sentences shown in Figure 6 on the board. Ask learners to work in groups and write down the meanings they know for these forms. Tell learners you will read a sentence that contains one of the forms. After you have finished saying the sentence, ask them which form was used. Monitor the pronunciation and make sure they accurately repeat it; model it if necessary. Now, ask learners to look at the meanings they brainstormed and say which one was used. If they did not write down the corresponding meaning, ask them to create one that matches

Sentence	Meaning of Target Weak Form
1. I voted for the Green Party at the last election.	in support of
2. You could tell she wasn't lying from the fear in her voice.	introduce reason
3. She can be really rude at times.	how someone behaves
4. When my parents were away, my grandmother would take care of me.	repeated action in the past
5. The book was written in the sixties.	introduce a period of time

Figure 6. Sample sentences for addressing polysemy. (Sentences from Cambridge Learner Dictionary/English Vocabulary Profile; Cambridge University Press, 2021, 2015)

the sense in the context of the sentence. Monitor and provide guidance until a group explains the correct meaning. Repeat the process for the other sentences.

Now that learners have a list of meanings with corresponding weak forms, their polysemous nature will become clear and you can play extended listening passages, pause every time one of the weak forms is said, and ask learners to identify the correct meaning. There are many occasions when weak forms form part of idioms, too (e.g., "at face value," "at that," "at it again"), and you can raise awareness of this, should any arise, when playing the listening passage. Once again, you are modeling a strategy that learners can be encouraged to adopt independently.

Weak forms pose challenges for learners to decode accurately. It is essential for teachers to ensure they integrate activities that improve learners' ability to perceive them. Teachers can combine this bottom-up approach with a top-down one that encourages learners to use their knowledge of grammar and context before listening to help them process the weak forms they will hear in the activity or passage. Given that this is an important area that is often neglected by textbooks, teachers will need to regularly supplement and adapt materials to ensure sufficient coverage is given. Teachers can also model strategies that learners can use for helping them to process weak forms and encourage learners to apply the strategies autonomously when they see value in them. Finally, it should not be taken for granted that learners will understand the meaning of all weak forms once they have been accurately perceived. Teachers should identify meanings that their learners may find difficult in advance and be sure that learners are given practice associating them with their corresponding spoken forms.

References

Bassetti, B. (2008). Orthographic input and second language phonology. In T. Piske & M. Young-Scholten (Eds.), *Input matters in SLA* (pp. 191–206). Multilingual Matters.

Bassetti, B., & Atkinson, N. (2015). Effects of orthographic forms on pronunciation in experienced instructed second language learners. *Applied Psycholinguistics, 36*(1), 67–91. https://doi.org/10.1017/s0142716414000435

Cambridge University Press. (2015). English vocabulary profile. http://vocabulary.englishprofile.org/

Cambridge University Press. (2021). Cambridge learner dictionary. https://dictionary.cambridge.org/dictionary/learner-english/

Clynes, A., & Deterding, D. (2011). Standard Malay (Brunei). *Journal of the International Phonetic Association, 41*, 259–268. https://doi.org/10.1017/s002510031100017x

Council of Europe. (2001). *Common European framework for reference of languages: Learning, teaching and assessment*. Cambridge University Press.

Cutler, A. (1997) The syllable's role in the segmentation of stress languages. *Language and Cognitive Processes, 12*(5–6), 839–846. https://doi.org/10.1080/016909697386718

Cutler, A. (2000). Listening to a second language through the ears of a first. *Interpreting, 5*(1), 1–23. https://doi.org/10.1075/intp.5.1.02cut

Cutler, A., & Norris, D. (1988). The role of strong syllables in segmentation for lexical access. *Journal of Experimental Psychology: Human Perception and Performance, 14*(1), 113–121. https://doi.org/10.1037/0096-1523.14.1.113

Davis, P., & Rinvolucri, M. (2002). *Dictation. New methods, new possibilities.* Cambridge University Press.

Ellis, N., Hafeez, K., Martin, K., Chen, L., Boland, J., & Sagarra, N. (2014). An eye-tracking study of learned attention in second language acquisition. *Applied Psycholinguistics, 35*(3), 547–579. https://doi.org/10.1017/s0142716412000501

Escudero, P. (2007). Second language phonology: The role of perception. In M. Pennington (Ed.), *Phonology in context* (pp. 109–134). Palgrave.

Field, J. (2004). An insight into listeners' problems: Too much bottom-up or too much top-down? *System, 32*(3), 363–377. https://doi.org/10.1016/j.system.2004.05.002

Field, J. (2008). *Listening in the language classroom.* Cambridge University Press.

Grosjean, F., & Gee, J. P. (1987). Prosodic structure and spoken word recognition. *Cognition, 25*(1–2) 135–155. https://doi.org/10.1016/0010-0277(87)90007-2

Halliday, M. (1994). *An introduction to functional grammar* (2nd ed.). Edward Arnold.

Hancock, M. (1995). *Pronunciation games.* Cambridge University Press.

Hardison, D. (2007). The visual element in phonological perception and learning. In M. Pennington (Ed.), *Phonology in context* (pp.135–158). Palgrave MacMillan.

Hewings, M. (2004). *Pronunciation practice activities.* Cambridge University Press.

Isbell, D. (2016). The perception-production link in L2 phonology. *MSU Working Papers in Second Language Studies, 7*, 57–67.

Kazazoğlu, S. (2013). Dictation as a language learning tool. *Procedia—Social and Behavioral Sciences, 70*, 1338–1346. https://doi.org/10.1016/j.sbspro.2013.01.195

Larsen, G. (2018). Exploring the effects of raising metacognitive and grammatical awareness on students' ability to listen to short bursts of speech. *Cambridge Assessment English Research Notes, 69*, 28–36.

Macaro, E., Graham, S., & Vanderplank, R. (2013). A review of listening strategies: Focus on sources of knowledge and success. In A. Cohen & E. Macaro (Eds.), *Language learner strategies* (pp. 165–185). Oxford University Press.

Odisho, E. (2007). A multisensory, multicognitive approach to teaching pronunciation. *Revista de Estudos Linguísticos da Universidade do Porto, 2*, 3–28.

Oxford, R., & Schramm, K. (2013). Bridging the gap between psychological and sociocultural perspectives on L2 learner strategies. In A. Cohen & E. Macaro (Eds.), *Language learner strategies* (pp. 47–68). Oxford University Press.

Snape, N., & Yusa, N. (2013). Explicit article instruction in definiteness, specificity, genericity and perception. In M. Whong, K. Gil, & H. Marsden (Eds.), *Universal grammar and the second language classroom* (pp. 161–183). Springer.

Thomas, N., & Rose, H. (2018). Do language learning strategies need to be self-directed? Disentangling strategies from self-regulated learning. *TESOL Quarterly, 53*(1), 248–257. https://doi.org/10.1002/tesq.473

Thomson, R. (2018) High variability [pronunciation] training (HVPT): A proven technique about which every language teacher and learner ought to know. *Journal of Second Language Pronunciation, 4*(2), 208–231. https://doi.org/10.1075/jslp.17038.tho

Tyler, A. (2012). *Cognitive linguistics and second language learning.* Routledge.

Wilson, M. (2003). Discovery listening—improving perceptual processing, *ELT Journal, 57*(4), 335–343. https://doi.org/10.1093/elt/57.4.335

Yong, J. (2001). Malay/Indonesian speakers. In M. Swan & B. Smith (Eds.), *Learner English* (2nd ed., pp. 279–295). Cambridge University Press.

FREDDIE GAY is currently a freelance English teacher and teacher trainer. He has worked in teaching and teacher training positions in several countries and holds the DELTA and MPhil in English language and applied linguistics from the University of Cambridge.

CHAPTER 8

MARK McANDREWS

Listening for Thought Groups

Listening in Real Life

About 4 years ago, when I was teaching at a university-based intensive English program in the United States, I had a student from China who was particularly eager to experience local culture and make American friends. Having previously lived in China myself, I was happy to talk with him after class about some of the similarities and differences that I perceived between the two countries, particularly concerning social etiquette. On one occasion, he asked me if I had any advice for visiting Americans' homes, because he had been invited to a small gathering. I explained that some Americans leave their shoes on in their house or apartment, and generally do not turn on the TV while guests are visiting unless they specifically intend to watch something. As a final piece of advice, I told him: "When you visit Americans, bring something for everyone to eat or drink."

The following week, I asked him how the gathering had gone. He said that everyone had enjoyed themselves, and that he had made several new friends. He was confused, however, about the advice I had given him. He said that he felt slightly embarrassed because all of the guests except him had brought food or beverages to share at the gathering. I was taken aback because I specifically remembered telling him about the American custom of bringing something to share when one is invited to another's home. Being an English teacher, I was determined to figure out where the miscommunication had occurred between me and the student. After several minutes of back and forth, we pinpointed the source of confusion. It had been my telling him that:

> "When you visit Americans, bring something for everyone to eat or drink."

When my student had listened to that sentence the week before, he understood the word *Americans* to be the subject of the verb *bring*, rather than the direct object of the verb *visit*. He heard:

"When you visit, Americans bring something for everyone to eat or drink."

In written English, the distinction between the two sentences is made clear with a comma. In spoken English, however, other means must be used. The spoken equivalent of a comma is a thought group boundary—a shift in prosody that marks the boundary between groups of words—and though my student had understood each word in the sentence, he misheard where the thought group boundary was. The result was that, instead of bringing food or drinks to the party, as I had suggested, he expected his hosts to provide all the refreshments. This incident provided a rich teaching opportunity at the time, and also sparked my interest in teaching learners to listen for thought groups.

Listening in the Research

In everyday speech, words are pronounced in groups whose boundaries are expressed *prosodically*, that is, through changes in pitch, volume, word duration, and pausing. In the field of English language teaching, this characteristic of speech is often referred to as *thought groups*. Linguists have developed several different formal descriptions of this phenomenon, which they refer to in a technical sense as *prosodic structure* (Cooper & Paccia-Cooper, 1980; Ferreira, 1988; Selkirk, 1984; 2011; Truckenbrodt, 1999). Though the individual descriptions differ somewhat in their details, there is general agreement about the close relationship between thought groups/prosodic structure and syntax: speakers tend to produce acoustically salient thought group boundaries at the edges of major syntactic constituents, such as clauses. This can be illustrated by returning to the previous example about visiting Americans' homes:

1. When you visit Americans, bring something for everyone to eat or drink.
2. When you visit, Americans bring something for everyone to eat or drink.

The sentence in (1) includes two clauses: *when you visit Americans* and *bring something for everyone to eat or drink*. Clauses are major syntactic constituents, and speakers tend to use prosody to mark the boundaries between them. In English, this is accomplished using pitch movement, word lengthening, and sometimes silent pauses (Anderson & Carlson, 2010; Kjelgaard & Speer, 1999; Speer et al., 2011). For example, for the sentence in (1), the word *Americans*, which is the final word in a clause, might be spoken with rising pitch, and could be followed by a short, silent pause. The same is true for the word *visit* in (2). The word *Americans* would also be slightly longer in (1), because it is at the end of a clause, than in (2), where it is at the beginning of a clause. It is important to note that speakers do not produce silent pauses at each thought group boundary in everyday connected speech. Often, the first sound after a thought group boundary follows directly after the previous sound, without intervening silence, in the same way that words within clauses tend not to be separated by silent pauses (Goldman-Eisler, 1972). For example, in casual, rapid speech, speakers might produce the sentence in (2) without any silent pause whatsoever between *visit* and *Americans*; in this case, the /t/ sound at the end of "visit" resyllabifies as the onset of the first syllable in *Americans* (i.e., a consonant-vowel linking process).

Speakers also produce thought group boundaries at lower levels of syntactic structure, but the boundaries are much less perceptually salient below the level of clauses. Consider a hypothetical example:

3. Amy saw the man with binoculars.

The sentence in (3) is ambiguous: Either Amy used binoculars to see the man, or she saw a man who had binoculars. To understand the intended meaning of this sentence, the listener would need to know whether *the man with binoculars* is one noun phrase, or *with binoculars* is a separate adverbial phrase. In the same way that speakers use prosody to mark the boundaries between clauses, they tend to do the same for syntactic phrases. However, the prosodic cues of pitch movement and word lengthening are much less perceptually salient at the level of phrasal boundaries, compared to clausal boundaries (Speer et al., 2011). For the sentence in (3), if the speaker's intended meaning was that Amy used binoculars to see the man, there would be a very subtle thought group boundary after *man*. If the speaker's intended meaning was that Amy saw a man who had binoculars, the words *the man with binoculars* would be pronounced as a single thought group. Even highly proficient listeners might struggle to hear the acoustically subtle prosodic differences between the two possible meanings of the sentence in (3).

A large body of research attests to the fact that, for highly proficient listeners, such as native speakers, listening for clausal thought groups is a regular part of the repertoire of cognitive processes that allow them to comprehend speech fluently. One study that investigated this listening ability was Schafer et al. (2000). To test the extent to which native speakers produce and comprehend thought groups, the researchers recorded the interactions between participants as they played a specially designed cooperative board game. The game consisted of two players communicating with each other to move shapes, such as squares, towards certain goals on the game board. The rules of the game were designed such that they elicited players to repeatedly speak sentences such as:

4. When that moves the square, it should land in a good spot.
5. When that moves, the square will encounter a cookie.

For pairs of sentences such as (4) and (5), the first five words are the same, but the syntactic structures are different. In (4), the first clause is *When that moves the square*. In (5), the first clause is *When that moves*. The native speakers playing the game were unaware that the researchers were interested in how they expressed thought groups. The researchers made audio recordings of the sentences spoken by the players, and then edited them such that they were cut off after the fifth word. Using the example from (4) and (5), the edited recordings consisted of the words *When that moves the square*. The researchers then asked a different group of native speakers to listen to the edited recordings and choose what they thought the speaker would say next. For example, the native listeners heard "When that moves the square" and had to choose either "it should land in a good spot" or "will encounter a cookie."

The researchers found that native listeners chose the correct continuation 74% of the time (this accuracy rate might have been even higher if not for hesitations in the recordings, which listeners could have interpreted as thought group boundaries). The only explanation for this result is that the native listeners were listening for thought group boundaries and used the boundaries they heard to comprehend where one clause ended and the next one began. Several other psycholinguistic research studies have found similar results in terms of native speakers listening for thought groups (e.g., Anderson & Carlson, 2010; Clifton et al., 2002; Kjelgaard & Speer, 1999). More recently, researchers using brain imaging technologies have come to the same conclusion: Highly proficient listeners regularly make use of thought group boundaries as they comprehend speech (e.g., Bögels et al., 2013; Holzgrefe-Lang et al., 2018).

In a recent study, McAndrews (2020) compared native speakers and English as a second language (ESL) learners in terms of their ability to listen for thought groups. The ESL learners had recently arrived in the United States from China, where they had been studying English for an average of 11 years. For the thought group listening test, participants first listened to sentences that had been cut off after a few words, and then had to choose what the speaker would say next out of two possible continuations. Here are two examples of items from the thought groups listening test:

6. *Participants heard*: "After Jim practiced"

   What did he say next?

   (a) ". . . Matthew tested him."

   (b) ". . . math, he took a break."

7. *Participants heard*: "Anne decided to walk"

   What did he say next?

   (a) ". . . The bus was too crowded."

   (b) ". . . the dog after dinner."

For each item on the test, one of the possible answers continued the original clause that learners heard, and the other answer began a new clause. For example, (6b) ". . . math, he took a break" continues the original clause (6) "After Jim practiced." The other possible answer, (6a) ". . . Matthew tested him," is a new clause. The correct answer was determined by whether there was a thought group boundary at the end of the audio clip. For (6), the speaker produced a thought group boundary after *practiced*, meaning he had reached the end of the clause. The correct answer was therefore (6a). For (7), the speaker did not produce a thought group boundary after *walk* in "Anne decided to walk," meaning the clause was not finished. The correct answer was therefore (7b) ". . . the dog after dinner." On the test as a whole, ESL learners scored only 54% (i.e., slightly above the score achieved by random guessing), compared to 78% for native speakers. Even after an average of 11 years of studying English, these learners demonstrated very little ability to hear thought groups, highlighting the need to teach this listening skill.

Listening in the Classroom

In this section, I present an instructional sequence for teaching ESL learners how to listen for thought groups. The instructional sequence has been designed around the tenets of skill acquisition theory (Anderson, 1987; DeKeyser, 2007). Instruction begins with explicit teaching and tightly controlled exercises that facilitate learners' acquisition of accurate declarative knowledge about the acoustic form and syntactic function of thought groups. This is followed by progressively more open-ended activities designed to facilitate fluent performance of this listening microskill. The pedagogical phases described are as follows:

a. Presentation
b. Accuracy Practice
c. Fluency Practice

Presentation

The purpose of the Presentation phase of instruction is to introduce to learners in a clear and memorable way the acoustic form and syntactic function of thought groups. By its nature, spoken language is fleeting, and in most authentic listening situations, there is no tangible or lasting record of what was said. The fleeting nature of spoken language makes it more difficult for teachers and learners alike to focus their attention on specific linguistic elements in the stream of speech. For this reason, when you introduce the concept of thought groups to learners, you may want to begin with written examples.

The closest counterpart to thought group boundaries in written English is punctuation. For learners who have at least some experience with written English, introducing thought groups as a kind of spoken punctuation could be an easier conceptual jump to make, rather than starting with more abstract descriptions. A memorable example (also described in the Introduction) that you can use to introduce the syntactic function of commas (and thought groups) is the following:

8. Let's eat, grandma!
9. Let's eat grandma!

You could begin the Presentation phase by writing these two sentences on the board and asking learners to think about what they mean. After a few moments, expect to hear some scattered chuckles from the class! The sentence in (8) is directed at grandma, enjoining her to eat a meal with the person who is speaking, her grandchild. The sentence in (9) is directed at someone other than grandma, suggesting that the two of them eat grandma! Another example that you could use to introduce the concept comes from the title of a grammar book by Truss (2009), *Eats, Shoots and Leaves*. Truss (2009) writes:

> A panda walks into a cafe. He orders a sandwich, eats it, then draws a gun and fires two shots in the air. "Why?" asks the confused waiter, as the panda makes towards the exit. The panda produces a badly punctuated wildlife manual and

> tosses it over his shoulder. "I'm a panda," he says, at the door. "Look it up." The waiter turns to the relevant entry and, sure enough, finds an explanation. "Panda. Large black-and-white bear-like mammal, native to China. Eats, shoots and leaves." (p. i)

In both of these examples, a single comma changes the meaning of the sentence dramatically. After explaining or eliciting the differences in meaning, and depending on the level of the learners, you may want to draw on some metalinguistic terminology to describe the syntactic function of commas in these examples. Technically speaking, the comma in (8) indicates that the preceding word (i.e., *eat*) is the last word in a clause. For some learners, the terms *phrase* or *thought* or *idea* might be more accessible than *clause*.

Having established the syntactic function of commas (which is likely a review for many learners), you could now begin to make a connection between punctuation and spoken thought group boundaries. For example, you could say: "When we read, commas and periods are helpful because they tell us when one clause is finished and the next one will begin. But what about when we listen?" It is likely that some learners will suggest that speakers use silent pauses where commas and periods would go in the written form. Though it is true that speakers sometimes leave silence between clauses, that is not always the case. It is important, therefore, to help learners become aware of two additional acoustic cues to thought group boundaries: pitch movement and word lengthening.

As discussed previously, the last word in a clause is typically spoken with pitch movement of some kind, and its duration is slightly longer than it would be if it were in a different syntactic position. For example, in (8), the word *eat* might be spoken with rising, falling, or falling-then-rising pitch movement. In (9), *eat* would typically be spoken with relatively flat pitch. Further, when (8) is spoken at a normal conversational pace, the word *eat* might last approximately 200 milliseconds, compared to 150 milliseconds in (9). (See Anderson & Carlson, 2010, for more information on the relationship between syntactic position and word duration). Initially, you could repeat the contrastive example sentences (e.g., [8] and [9]) multiple times and ask learners to notice how the pronunciation is different, making sure that the class eventually lands on the pitch movement and word lengthening cues that accompany the optional silent pause. Share the insight that the three acoustic cues to thought groups (i.e., pitch movement, word lengthening, and optional silent pauses) are not very perceptually salient; that is, they are not easy to detect unless you know what to listen for. Arming learners with metalinguistic awareness of the three cues can improve student attitudes and increase motivation for the substantial amount of practice needed to develop accurate perceptual abilities.

Accuracy Practice

Once learners have developed declarative knowledge of the form and function of thought groups during the Presentation phrase, move on to facilitating the Accuracy Practice phase. The purpose of this phase of instruction is to help learners develop the ability to hear thought groups accurately before moving on to the listening Fluency Practice phase.

As we have seen, thought groups help listeners process the syntax of spoken English, specifically in identifying boundaries between clauses. Therefore, the ultimate goal of this sequence of pedagogical activities is to improve learners' syntactic processing by listening for thought groups. Before the syntactic function of thought groups can be practiced, however, learners need to be able to distinguish between the acoustic cues that express thought group boundaries, versus the absence of those cues. Perceiving prosodic cues, including pitch changes, can be challenging for many learners (see Chapter 6). As an analogy, the form-function distinction for thought groups is similar to listening for rising versus falling pitch at the end of sentences. Before learners can become proficient in comprehending the grammatical function expressed by that pitch distinction (e.g., asking a question versus making a statement), they must first be able to hear the difference between rising pitch and falling pitch. In the same way, before learners can comprehend the syntactic function of thought groups, they must be able to accurately perceive the acoustic cues that express thought groups. In a technical sense, learners must first develop accurate phonological categories.

One straightforward way to practice perception of thought groups is to provide learners with pairs of written sentences that differ only in comma placement. You would then speak one of the sentences and ask learners to identify which sentence was spoken. Returning to the first example from this chapter, one pair of sentences could be:

1. When you visit Americans, bring something for everyone to eat or drink.
2. When you visit, Americans bring something for everyone to eat or drink.

Ask learners to "listen for the comma." Then, speak either (1) or (2) and ask learners to decide which one you said. Learners could hold up one or two fingers, providing you with immediate feedback. Again, providing written versions of the sentences, including punctuation, gives learners something tangible with which to associate the acoustic cues of thought groups. This scaffold can be removed as learners move through the progression of practice activities.

Given the subtlety of the acoustic cues that express thought group boundaries, learners will likely need copious practice items. How can you come up with pairs of sentences like (1) and (2), which differ only in comma placement? First, you will want to make use of verbs such as *visit* and *eat* that can be either transitive or intransitive. In other words, choose verbs that can either take a direct object or not. These include *leave, ask, call,* and *watch,* among others. Next, design pairs of sentences that include either imperative verbs or vocative nouns. The sentence in (1) includes the imperative form of the verb *bring*. Another example of an imperative verb:

10. When you call your parents, ask about the weather.

The other sentence in this pair would be:

11. When you call, your parents ask about the weather.

For the sentence in (10), *call* has a direct object (*your parents*), and the verb *ask* is imperative. In (11), *call* does not have a direct object, and *your parents* is the subject of *ask*. An example of a sentence with a vocative noun is:

12. You should watch, Ben.

In (12), *Ben* is a vocative noun: The speaker is addressing someone named Ben. The other sentence in this pair would be:

13. You should watch Ben.

In (13), *Ben* is the direct object of the verb *watch*. By exploiting these syntactic ambiguities, you can design pairs of sentences that differ only in comma placement, which are an ideal starting point for learners who are developing the ability to perceive the acoustic form of thought groups. More pairs of sentences for this activity can be found in Appendix A.

Once you have multiple pairs of sentences, listening practice can begin. Initially, you will probably want to speak slowly and exaggerate the thought group boundaries; it would likely be too difficult for learners to jump right into perceiving naturalistic speech. For example, having directed learners' attention to the sentences in (12) and (13) written on the board or a handout, you would say either "You should watch, Ben" or "You should watch Ben," speaking slowly and exaggerating your pitch movements. You would ask the class which sentence you had spoken, providing feedback on the accuracy of learners' answers and highlighting the difference in pronunciation between the two sentences (e.g., by using gestures, as in the "conductor's baton" technique; Gregersen, 2019) before moving on to the next pair.

As an additional step in this process, you could ask students to chorally repeat the sentences after you. Once learners are able to perceive the exaggerated acoustic cues for thought groups, you can gradually make your speech more naturalistic. Again, the acoustic cues for thought groups in authentic connected speech are typically not very perceptually salient; it may take going through the pairs of sentences multiple times to build up learners' perceptual skills.

Once learners have developed the ability to accurately perceive thought group boundaries, the next step is to practice the syntactic function that thought groups fulfill in the mental processes of highly proficient listeners. As discussed previously, research has shown that highly proficient listeners, such as native speakers, use thought groups to help them process boundaries between clauses. The goal of the next practice activity, then, is to help learners develop the ability to use thought groups to identify clause boundaries.

For this activity, speak incomplete sentences (referred to hereafter as *stems*), and then have learners select the correct sentence continuation out of two written options. The correct sentence continuation will depend on the location of thought group boundaries in the stem. One example of this type of practice item is:

Oral stem: After James left$_{(,)}$ the party$_{(,)}$ . . .
Written continuation 1: . . . he drove home.
Written continuation 2: . . . got boring.

Keep in mind that the stem is not presented to learners in written format; you would speak it or play it over a speaker. For this example, if you produce a thought group boundary after the word *left*, then the correct continuation is Continuation 2. The complete sentence would be "After James left, the party got boring." On the other hand, if there is a thought group boundary after *party*, learners should choose Continuation 1. The complete sentence would be "After James left the party, he drove home." In this way, learners make a connection between thought groups and syntax as they listen. They must "listen" for clause boundaries, just as highly proficient listeners do.

You will find that it is easier to come up with items for this activity than the previous one, because only part of the sentences must be the same. As with the previous activity, verbs that take an optional direct object (e.g., *leave, call*) will be useful for designing items. Another example of an item for this activity is:

Oral stem: Tim called$_{(.)}$ H/his brother$_{(.)}$ . . .
Written continuation 1: . . . It was his birthday yesterday.
Written continuation 2: . . . is getting married.

Unlike previous examples, which begin with a subordinate clause followed by a main clause, this item consists of two independent clauses. In this case, the written equivalent of the thought group boundary would be a period, rather than a comma. If you produce a thought group boundary after *called*, the correct continuation would be Continuation 2, and the complete sentences would be "Tim called. His brother is getting married." If the thought group boundary occurred after *brother*, learners should select Continuation 1. In this case, the complete sentences would be "Tim called his brother. It was his birthday yesterday." More items for this activity can be found in Appendix B.

As with the previous activity, you could speak slowly and exaggerate your prosodic cues for the first few items, and gradually build up to more naturalistic speech as learners become more accurate. After each item, you can speak both versions of the complete sentences so that learners can compare them. Once learners have achieved a good level of accuracy in using thought groups to identify clause boundaries, instruction can move on to practice that targets the development of fluency in this listening microskill.

Fluency Practice

The term *fluency* is often associated with the speed and fluidity of spoken productions, but the same underlying principles can be used to describe all cognitive abilities, including listening comprehension. When we listen in everyday situations, there is no time to stop and think about each word or grammatical structure we hear; people normally speak too quickly for that to be an option. This being the case, proficient listeners must develop some degree of automaticity in processing different elements in the stream of speech.

When a skill is performed automatically, it is done quickly, accurately, and with little effort or conscious attention (Segalowitz, 2003; 2010). The purpose of the Fluency Practice phase is to help learners develop automaticity in comprehending thought groups.

Nation and Newton (2009) describe characteristics of activities that target fluency. First, learners' attention should mostly be on message-level meaning, rather than the language itself. Second, learners must have previous experience with the language items or skills being practiced. Finally, learners should be encouraged to perform faster than they would without time pressure. The following homework activity was designed with these characteristics in mind.

Begin by describing the phenomenon of finishing someone else's sentence. This happens in conversations when someone begins a sentence, and their interlocutor anticipates what is coming next. For example, imagine a classroom situation in which a learner says, "He talk." The teacher then says, "When the subject is *he*, you have to . . . ," and before she can finish the sentence, the student interjects with "use *s*. I know!" For the upcoming homework activity, learners' job will be to finish the sentences of others. The sentences will not be random, however; they will include the same kinds of syntactic ambiguities as previous practice activities, which will require learners to listen for thought groups. The sentence stems in Appendix B can also be used for this activity. An example is:

Oral stem: When I call$_{(')}$ my mother$_{(')}$ . . .

After listening to (and not reading) the stem, learners must finish the sentence orally. Unlike the previous activities that develop accuracy, sentence continuations are not provided. Learners must generate their own continuations, based on the content of the stem. This should direct most of their attention to message-level meaning, rather than solely on comprehending thought group boundaries, which fulfills the first characteristic of fluency-developing activities described previously. For this particular item, if the thought group boundary is after the word *call*, a logical continuation could be "wants to talk for hours." If the boundary is after *mother*, a possible continuation is "she asks if I'm eating enough." Learners are free to come up with any interesting or humorous sentence continuation as long as it fits the meaning and thought group pattern of the stem.

In many other pedagogical situations, fluency practice would be conducted in a pair work format, but this might not be possible in the case of listening for thought groups. The spoken input that students receive must include consistently accurate acoustic cues for thought groups, which learners might not be able to produce. A whole class plenary format might not be the best option, either, because only one learner at a time would have an opportunity to finish your sentences. The best format for this type of practice could be individual homework. Supply learners with an audio file of recorded stems, and learners could record themselves finishing the sentences. The audio file could be manipulated such that the time between items becomes progressively shorter. At the beginning of the homework activity, learners would have more time to think of sentence continuations as they get used to the activity format, and then gradually come under increasing time pressure. By directing learners' attention to message-level meaning, conducting the activity after a good amount of accuracy practice, and adding an element of time pressure, this activity should help learners develop automaticity in comprehending thought groups.

Other Pedagogical Considerations

The sequence of instructional activities described in this chapter was designed to help learners understand the acoustic form and syntactic function of thought groups (Presentation phase), develop the ability to perceive thought groups and use them to identify clause boundaries (Accuracy Practice phase), and develop automaticity in performing this listening microskill (Fluency Practice).

You might want to keep in mind three additional pedagogical considerations. First, when designing your own items, keep the vocabulary simple and the scenarios familiar, which will allow learners to focus their attention on thought groups (during Accuracy Practice) and formulating their sentence continuations (during Fluency Practice). Second, you might want to enlist your colleagues or other proficient speakers to record audio stimuli, including sentence stems. This is one of the defining characteristics of high variability phonetic training (Bradlow et al., 1999; Thomson, 2018), which maintains that learners develop more robust target phonological categories when training input is produced by a range of different speakers, rather than a single speaker. Further, listening for thought groups practice should be distributed over multiple sessions, rather than massed together in a single day. The activities described in this chapter could be broken up into 10- to 15-minute chunks and recycled over weeks and months. These recommendations are consistent with research in instructed second language acquisition, and learning science in general, which suggests that learning is more effective when instruction is distributed over time (Donovan & Radosevich, 1999; Rogers, 2015). Finally, given that listening instruction in many contexts consists of one set of listening passages and comprehension questions after another (Graham et al., 2014; Siegel, 2014), following the pedagogical sequence described in this chapter will allow students to finally answer the question: "What did you learn in (listening) class today?" Listening for thought groups!

References

Anderson, C., & Carlson, K. (2010). Syntactic structure guides prosody in temporarily ambiguous sentences. *Language and Speech, 53*(4), 472–493. https://doi.org/10.1177/0023830910372497

Anderson, J. R. (1987). Skill acquisition: Compilation of weak-method problem situations. *Psychological Review, 94*(2), 192–210. https://doi.org/10.1037/0033-295X.94.2.192

Bögels, S., Schriefers, H., Vonk, W., Chwilla, D. J., & Kerkhofs, R. (2013). Processing consequences of superfluous and missing prosodic breaks in auditory sentence comprehension. *Neuropsychologia, 51*(13), 2715–2728. https://doi.org/10.1016/j.neuropsychologia.2013.09.008

Bradlow, A. R., Akahane-Yamada, R., Pisoni, D. B., & Tohkura, Y. I. (1999). Training Japanese listeners to identify English /r/and/l: Long-term retention of learning in perception and production. *Perception & Psychophysics, 61*(5), 977–985. https://doi.org/10.3758/BF03206911

Clifton C., Carlson, K., & Frazier, L. (2002). Informative prosodic boundaries. *Language and Speech, 45*(2), 87–114. https://doi.org/10.1177/00238309020450020101

Cooper, W. E., & Paccia-Cooper, J. (1980). *Syntax and speech*. Harvard University Press.

DeKeyser, R. (2007). Skill acquisition theory. In B. VanPatten & J. Williams (Eds.), *Theories in second language acquisition: An introduction* (2nd ed., pp. 97–113). Routledge.

Donovan, J. J., & Radosevich, D. J. (1999). A meta-analytic review of the distribution of practice effect: Now you see it, now you don't. *Journal of Applied Psychology, 84*(5), 795–805. https://psycnet.apa.org/doi/10.1037/0021-9010.84.5.795

Ferreira, F. (1988). *Planning and timing in sentence production: The syntax-to-phonology conversion* [Unpublished doctoral dissertation]. University of Massachusetts.

Goldman-Eisler, F. (1972). Pauses, clauses, sentences. *Language and Speech, 15*(2), 103–113. https://doi.org/10.1177/002383097201500201

Graham, S., Santos, D., & Francis-Brophy, E. (2014). Teacher beliefs about listening in a foreign

language. *Teaching and Teacher Education, 40*, 44–60. https://doi.org/10.1016/j.tate.2014.01.007

Gregersen, T. (2019). Teaching English prosodic features. In J. I. Liontas (Ed.), *The TESOL encyclopedia of English language teaching*. Wiley Blackwell.

Holzgrefe-Lang, J., Wellmann, C., Höhle, B., & Wartenburger, I. (2018). Infants' processing of prosodic cues: Electrophysiological evidence for boundary perception beyond pause detection. *Language and Speech, 61*(1), 153–169. https://doi.org/10.1177/0023830917730590

Kjelgaard, M. M., & Speer, S. R. (1999). Prosodic facilitation and interference in the resolution of temporary syntactic closure ambiguity. *Journal of Memory and Language, 40*(2), 153–194. https://doi.org/10.1177/0023830917730590

McAndrews, M. (2020). *Prosody instruction for ESL listening comprehension* (ProQuest document ID #2409697421) [Doctoral dissertation, Northern Arizona University].

Nation, I. S. P., & Newton, J. (2009). *Teaching ESL/EFL listening and speaking*. Routledge.

Rogers, J. (2015). Learning second language syntax under massed and distributed conditions. *TESOL Quarterly, 49*(4), 857–866. https://doi.org/10.1002/tesq.252

Schafer, A. J., Speer, S. R., Warren, P., & White, S. D. (2000). Intonational disambiguation in sentence production and comprehension. *Journal of Psycholinguistic Research, 29*(2), 169–182. https://doi.org/10.1023/A:1005192911512

Segalowitz, N. (2003). Automaticity and second languages. In C. Doughty & M. Long (Eds.), *The handbook of second language acquisition* (pp. 382–408). Wiley Blackwell.

Segalowitz, N. (2010). *Cognitive bases of second language fluency*. Routledge.

Selkirk, E. O. (1984). *Phonology and syntax: The relation between sound and structure.* MIT Press.

Selkirk, E. O. (2011). The syntax-phonology interface. In J. A. Goldsmith, J. Riggle, & C. L. Alan (Eds.), *The handbook of phonological theory* (pp. 435–483). Wiley Blackwell.

Siegel, J. (2014). Exploring L2 listening instruction: examinations of practice. *ELT Journal, 68*(1), 22–30. https://doi.org/10.1093/elt/cct058

Speer, S. R., Warren, P., & Schafer, A. J. (2011). Situationally independent prosodic phrasing. *Laboratory Phonology, 2*(1), 35–98. https://doi.org/10.1515/labphon.2011.002

Thomson, R. I. (2018). High variability [pronunciation] training (HVPT): A proven technique about which every language teacher and learner ought to know. *Journal of Second Language Pronunciation, 4*(2), 208–231. . https://doi.org/10.1075/jslp.17038.tho

Truckenbrodt, H. (1999). On the relation between syntactic phrases and phonological phrases. *Linguistic Inquiry, 30*(2), 219–255. https://doi.org/10.1162/002438999554048

Truss, L. (2009). *Eats, shoots and leaves*. Harper Collins.

MARK McANDREWS is an assistant professor in the Department of English at Western Kentucky University, where he teaches courses in linguistics and TESOL. Previously, he taught ESL and English for academic purposes at Northern Arizona University, and EFL at Shantou University (China).

Appendix A: Sentence Pairs for Accuracy Practice Activity

Imperative verb items

If the boss calls you, answer the phone / If the boss calls, you answer the phone

When he asks his friends, listen to him / When he asks, his friends listen to him

When they leave you, call me / When they leave, you call me

After you visit your grandparents, clean up / After you visit, your grandparents clean up

If you're not watching the kids, get some ice cream /

If you're not watching, the kids get some ice cream

Vocative noun items

Why don't you call, Mom / Why don't you call Mom

They'll ask, Dad / They'll ask Dad

She left, buddy / She left Buddy

I'm going to go visit, Lucy / I'm going to go visit Lucy

I can't watch, Brianne / I can't watch Brianne

Appendix B: Oral Stems and Continuations for Accuracy Practice Activity and Fluency Practice Activity

Subordinate-main clause items

When I call$_{(')}$ Dad$_{(')}$ . . . he asks about my job / sounds really happy

If he's cooking$_{(')}$ the food$_{(')}$ . . . everyone will love it / will taste great

If your friends join$_{(')}$ you$_{(')}$ . . . it will be more fun / can chat with them

When you leave$_{(')}$ the house$_{(')}$ . . . you should lock the door / is dark

Before you eat$_{(')}$ the food$_{(')}$ . . . make sure it's hot / must be prepared

Independent clause items

My friend called$_{(.)}$ T/the doctor$_{(.)}$ . . . He was feeling sick / told him to stay home

My Dad loves cooking$_{(.)}$ H/his potatoes$_{(.)}$ . . . He grows them himself / are really delicious

She wants to join$_{(.)}$ T/the club$_{(.)}$ . . . It looks like a lot of fun / is looking for new members

You shouldn't leave$_{(.)}$ T/the kitchen$_{(.)}$ . . . The stove is still on / still needs to be cleaned up

I didn't want to drink$_{(.)}$ T/the water$_{(.)}$ . . . There was something in it / was too warm

CHAPTER 9

JONATHON RYAN

Listening in Interaction: Understanding Projection

Listening in Real Life

Most English as a second language students I teach go on to further study, where they often face difficulties participating in discussions dominated by native speakers. In many cases, they struggle not because they are shy or unable to express their ideas, but because they miss the opportunities to speak: One classmate finishes and another starts in an apparently seamless flow of talk. Knowing not to interrupt, the international student waits patiently. But by the time an opportunity arises, the topic has moved on and the opportunity is lost. At stake here are issues of equity and participation, and to make matters worse, there is often a perception that international students do not contribute enough—particularly galling if grades are awarded for class participation.

I have also witnessed the opposite outcome from a similar underlying cause. In one group discussion among doctoral students, the local (native-English-speaking) student happened to be rather shy and quiet and the two international students more extroverted and talkative. The local student took a back seat in the conversation and when a question was eventually put to her, she was keen to answer. She provided a few words before momentarily pausing to plan her response, the other two students jumped in, cutting off what would have been her main contribution.

Not long before, I had become aware of an approach to interaction—conversation analysis—which provided profound insights into what was happening. Applications of conversation analysis to language teaching were scant, and as a (then) new book by Wong and Waring (now in its second edition, 2021) argued, "of the many aspects of spoken English, turn-taking is perhaps the least tackled in pedagogical materials and classroom instruction, perhaps because it is the least understood" (2021, p. 21).

Later, I found connections with other problems that second language users reported. For instance, my colleague—a highly proficient nonnative English speaker—spoke of her acute embarrassment in the following situation: During a friendly conversation, a neighbour had asked her to look after their cat while they were away, to which she happily agreed. The neighbour then asked, "Do you like cats?" to which she replied, "No, not really." The neighbour's face dropped. My colleague immediately recognised the neighbour's discomfort at having seemingly imposed a burden. As she came to realise, her neighbour expected a response somewhere between "I don't mind them" and "I love them," and so her unexpected negative answer ought to have been softened.

In a final example, just yesterday (at the time of writing) I told my class an anecdote, which was going well until I got to the end . . . when I got no response at all. My punchline hung awkwardly in the air. Perhaps they didn't get it, or didn't care, but I suspect that the issue was either not recognising I had finished or being unsure how to respond (surprise, concern, or laughter?).

Although seemingly disparate, the four preceding incidents are all linked by the concept of *projection*, which concerns the probable trajectories of a current speaker's turn. As the examples illustrate, it is fundamental to listening within social interaction yet remains little known within the English language teaching (ELT) community. However, the related listening skills are very teachable, and students are typically receptive to the associated teaching practices.

Listening in the Research

Before focusing on projection, it is worth briefly considering the nature of listening in interaction (L-in-I). Interactions include such events as ordinary conversations or chatting, discussions, service encounters, meetings, and so on, which collectively account for the majority of most people's day-to-day listening. Interactions are fundamentally participatory, and so the terms *speaker* and *listener* are understood not as predetermined or otherwise fixed roles, but as temporary statuses, subject to momentary back and forth change. Even when listening to a longer turn (e.g., a story), an interactant will have certain rights and responsibilities to respond. They will, for example, have some rights to query the storyteller (e.g., to seek clarification or challenge certain claims) and will be expected to display their attentiveness, such as through using continuers (*Mhm; Uhuh*).

This contrasts with the rather different behaviours occurring in (largely) noninteractional listening. These include contexts like lectures, speeches, and sermons, where listener participation is highly constrained, and contexts involving structurally one-way communication, such as train departure announcements, radio, and television. Although listeners may act on the information they hear (e.g., take lecture notes; move to a train platform), they have little or no power to shape what will be said next.

Although some complexities have been glossed over here (see Ryan, in press), it should be clear that L-in-I is far more commonplace and fundamental to daily life and that noninteractional listening is subsidiary. It is, then, somewhat curious that noninteractive frameworks dominate the teaching of listening (at least as a separate subskill). This holds true even when listening to dialogues, where students are inevitably cast in the role of eavesdroppers. However, as this chapter aims to show, this oversight can be readily addressed, in part through a focus on *projection*.

The concept of projection contrasts with that of *retrospection*. Retrospection, which typically accounts for virtually all classroom listening-focused activities, involves looking back and relates to an understanding of what has been said till now. It is the focus of all manner of tasks, including comprehension checking, note-taking, and most listener-response approaches. Its overlooked counterpart, projection, involves looking forward and relates to anticipating subsequent actions; it is not to be conflated with the related ELT terms *prediction* (a strategy applied prior to listening for identifying content; e.g., Graham & Santos, 2015) and *anticipation* (predictions made during pauses in listening texts; see Field, 2008, pp. 262–264).

Projection encompasses three major phenomena:

1. anticipating what action (speech act) is underway,
2. anticipating likely completion points, and
3. identifying expectations around responses (Deppermann & Günthner, 2015).

All three phenomena enable interactants to jointly manage the direction of the interaction (rather than simply respond to stimuli). Unlike the focus of conventional listening activities in ELT, which are fundamentally concerned with the meanings of words and clauses, projection also involves reacting to units that are semantically light or even empty, such as fillers and minimal responses (e.g., *uh, well*), gestures, and micropauses measurable in tenths of seconds (e.g., Streeck, 1995).

Projecting Actions Underway

Action projections are based on an understanding of how turns are normally sequenced. One fundamental way this occurs is in adjacency pairs, in which one action sets up a "slot" in the next turn for a limited range of response types. For instance, an offer creates a slot to be filled—though not always immediately—by either an acceptance or decline (Sacks, 1995).

In the second slot, indications of a problem in progressing the action are signaled very early on. For instance, in declining an invitation, there will usually be cues at the beginning of the turn, such as signs of hesitation (e.g., pause, *uh, we:::ll*) and perhaps the start of other talk (e.g., an explanation). Thus, competent language users will typically get a sense of the direction of a turn based on how it begins. These first moments allow the listener to adjust their expectations before the actual decline is made.

Adjacency pairs can also be extended in various ways. Consider, for example, delicate situations in which people make "big" requests or significant invitations or deliver bad news. Speakers usually avoid simply dropping such information by providing forewarning (*I've got a favour to ask; Have you got any plans tomorrow night?; I have some bad news;* Sacks, 1995, p. 529). Because these turns foreshadow the speaker's intended actions, they allow the listener time to formulate an interpersonally appropriate response. For instance, hearing "Have you got any plans tomorrow night?" allows the addressee an opportunity to plan a face-saving excuse or to steer the talk in another direction. There are also ways in which action projection operates in larger stretches of talk, such as the openings and closings of interactions (Wong & Waring, 2021), and certain forms of institutional interaction, such as doctor visits, where interactants mutually perform certain actions in a certain sequence (Robinson, 2013).

It should be clear, then, that listening in interaction is not merely a matter of understanding the semantic meaning of an utterance (as normally practiced in ELT listening), but of interpreting and responding to the action(s) it projects. Thus, for an utterance such as "Have you got any plans tomorrow night?", rather than focusing on the details (e.g., cloze tests), we might usefully ask students "Why did he ask?" and "What's probably going to happen next?"

Projecting Turn Completion or Continuation

In ELT's neglect of projection, perhaps the most readily observable consequences are learner difficulties with turn-taking, with international students often reporting trouble identifying points of entry into group discussions (Ryan & Forrest, 2021). Enfield's (2017) synthesis of recent studies gives a sense of the problem: In ordinary conversation, the gap between speakers is most commonly 0.2 seconds (about the length of time it takes to blink an eye), yet the length of time that it takes to turn a simple idea into speech is 0.6 seconds. Clearly, listeners "must be gearing up to speak well before the other person has finished" (Enfield, 2017, p. 43). To do so, they anticipate the end of the speaker's turn through a combination of prosody, grammar, and action resolution (e.g., the way a punchline completes a joke).

For instance, the approaching end of a turn may coincide with certain pitch movements (e.g., high falling or high rising), trailing off (decreasing pitch, volume, and speed), and completion of the utterance-level grammatical unit (e.g., the sentence stem *She put* is unlikely to be complete until a "what" and a "where" have been mentioned). Perhaps most reliably, turn endings may be detected when an action (e.g., question, story, compliment) is noticeably complete. Such signals provide somewhat unreliable evidence when taken in isolation, but there is greater certainty when multiple signals coincide (Ford & Thompson, 1996).

Expected Responses

The third aspect of projection involves recognising how the speaker is framing their talk, and therefore what kind of responses they will find most acceptable. For instance, a speaker will use specific cues to indicate they are about to share their personal concerns or troubles (Jefferson, 2015). For instance, in response to "How are you?", anything weaker than "Fine" (e.g., "Oh, okay I guess" in a less than chirpy tone) should alert us to the possibility of a problem, and raise the expectation that we show concern and be attentive. Failure to do so will likely cause further distress. Similarly, when a speaker signals the telling of a joke or funny anecdote, the expected response to the punchline will be either appreciation (e.g., laughter) or a groan; failure to provide such a response is likely to result in either an explanation of the humour or a feeling of embarrassment or confusion, as suggested by my own aforementioned anecdote.

Projection in Language Teaching

As such examples suggest, projection represents a fundamental aspect of listening in interaction, and as illustrated in the introduction, it can prove highly problematic for second language speakers. However, to date there remain few attempts to address it in language teaching (though see Ryan, in press; Ryan & Forrest, 2021; Wong & Waring, 2021). At this point, we might also acknowledge two potential objections to explicitly addressing projection in listening activities. A first objection could be that projection in listening will be addressed through ordinary classroom discourse, especially within communicative teaching approaches. However, such discourse will almost certainly be very limited in scope, with students receiving little exposure to the broad range of interactional phenomena that characterise everyday life. A second objection might be that because participating in an interaction involves being both a listener *and* a speaker, it may be inauthentic to isolate such listening. But from a pedagogical standpoint, it still makes sense to distinguish subskills that can be taught and practiced independently without overcomplication, just as we might distinguish spelling from writing. A specific L-in-I strand allows for tightly focused attention on subskills that may otherwise be overlooked.

As taken up in the following sections (see also Ryan, in press), teachers wishing to incorporate a L-in-I focus must navigate several challenges posed by pedagogical convention and current textbook design. These include the positioning of students as overhearers rather than as interactants (see also Flowerdew & Miller, 2005) and emphasis on the "comprehension approach," with its focus on determining a single correct answer (Field, 2008). Further, as many have commented (e.g., Wong, 2007), textbook dialogues typically stray far from interactional authenticity, and many of the missing elements (such as hesitations and dysfluencies) are ones which play a pivotal role in projection. Addressing such issues in L-in-I requires some rethinking the design of listening texts and activities.

Listening in the Classroom

Projection relates to a varied set of phenomena, for which only some relevant activities can be presented here. Following is a discussion of a few very general principles and pedagogical approaches, followed by two activity types for each of the aforementioned projection types.

Authenticity

A crucial consideration is the authenticity of listening texts in terms of how they model interaction. There are two concerns in particular. Firstly, as numerous researchers have concluded, textbook dialogues tend to present highly idealised representations of ordinary speech, avoiding so-called "performance variables" such as overlapping speech and hesitations, which are crucial to the conduct of interactions, as will be illustrated in this chapter. Secondly, to simplify texts and embed preselected linguistic and thematic content, listening texts are nearly always tightly scripted, rehearsed, and performed. The trouble is that people tend to have low self-awareness of the pragmatic rules they abide by. For example, when asked how they would give a compliment in a certain situation, people's answers often diverge substantially from real life (Golato, 2003). Unsurprisingly, then, both textbook dialogues (Wong, 2007) and movie dialogues (Ryan & Granville, 2020) tend to diverge from the pragmatics of ordinary interaction.

With this in mind, there are three main possibilities for sourcing authentic texts. One possibility is the use of recordings of naturally occurring conversation. In some cases, it may be feasible to record conversations with willing collaborators, making note of when certain target actions arise. These could be then edited into short, usable texts. The obvious problem, of course, is that this may be rather time-consuming or in other ways impractical (e.g., sound quality). A second option is to work with preselected episodes from the research literature, using transcript data as the basis of recordings; in some cases, conversation analysts (e.g., Emmanuel Schegloff) make available the original recordings that they discuss (though the sound quality may be low). An interesting example of working with such transcript data is presented by Waring (2018). A third option is to script and record sequences of speech with careful attention to the patterns established in the literature. Though potentially requiring more initial planning time, this approach ultimately allows for a great deal of flexibility and freedom (see, e.g., Ryan et al., 2019).

Selecting Texts

Aside from general principles of text selection (language complexity, speed, etc.), there are several further considerations in selecting texts suitable for focusing on projection:

- Suitable texts will nearly always include genuine interactions between two or more speakers.
- Generally, the more interactants, the more complex the task will be.
- Working with projections will likely be a very new type of activity for students. Thus, although I have found students very receptive, it may be advisable to introduce it gradually in brief activities.
- Suitable text lengths can be very short, because relevant activities typically involve intensive turn-by-turn listening: For projecting actions, a useful recording might involve several projections in as little as 15 seconds.

Basic Teaching Sequence

The most basic and flexible teaching approach is captured in the following sequence, upon which many further activities can be developed.

1. Provide any particularly relevant details about the context and relationships between the interactants, focusing particularly on a) how well they know each other and b) whether it is a social, work, or other context.
2. As a general rule, play the sequence turn by turn. It might be appropriate to break up longer turns into smaller units.[1]
3. It is very often helpful to replay a turn (either in isolation or with the preceding utterances).
4. After each turn, ask learners to guess what will come next. There is a delicate balance to be reached between providing feedback on these guesses and opening up space for further guesses.

Embedding an Expectation of Contingency

A further challenge is to shift expectations of there being a single right answer. For interactants, projection is experienced as the link between the present moment, and what has come just before, and what *may* follow. But it is often the case that a planned direction does not actually come to pass, because speakers take into account new information and adapt their plans. For instance, an enquiry that projects an invitation ("Any plans tonight?") might get a response that discourages it ("Yes, dinner with friends"), and so the speaker may abandon the invitation before it is ever articulated. Nevertheless, although the invitation was never made, it was still projected. At other times, the action projection of a turn may be interpreted in more than one way, such as "Are you busy tonight?" potentially leading to an invitation or a request ("Could you babysit the kids?").

Rather than a "right" answer, then, the focus should be on identifying the range of most plausible next turns. At its most basic, in a projection-focused lesson, the students do not preview the (entire) recording. When a recording is played through, its trajectory is established and the outcome becomes fixed. Instead, the recording is played (and replayed) in small sections (usually turn by turn).

Though most language learners respond well to the notion of projecting turns, some evidently prefer the certainties of a definitive answer that is validated in the text. A useful initial step is to introduce an expectation of contingency early on. In the following subsections, I introduce step-by-step instructions for some basic teaching activities focusing on projection.

Projecting Actions

Identifying Presequences

As noted previously, some utterances project a particular action by preparing the way for its occurrence. For instance, "Have you got any dinner plans for Saturday?" is recognizable as potentially leading to an invitation (or perhaps an offer). Before actually

[1] See Wong & Waring, 2021, for the notion of turn constructional units.

making the invitation, the speaker is checking the addressee's availability through use of a preinvitation. Other well-examined presequences include prerequests, preoffers and preannouncements (Schegloff, 2007).

1. Prepare a recording that illustrates the use of a presequence.
2. Introduce the context. For instance, "two classmates chatting after class has finished for the day."
3. Play the recording turn by turn. After each turn, students work first in pairs and then together as a class in responding to the following questions:
    a. "What did they say?" (ensuring accurate listening)
    b. [Some turns only] "Why?"
    c. "What is the other person going to say?" (encouraging any plausible answers)
4. After hearing the full sequence, it is often beneficial to examine a transcription of the turn by turn elements in more depth.

The following illustrates a suitable dialogue. Even brief interactions such as this can be usefully unpacked in considerable depth.

Offer sequence
A: How are you getting home?
B: I was going to call my brother.
A: Well, I can drop you off.
B: Oh, are you sure?
A: Yeah, no problem.
B: Thanks.

(Ryan, et al., 2019, p. 23, modified)

Note that although this turns out to be an offer sequence, this is only confirmed in the third line; prior to this, other possibilities existed, including Speaker A making a request ("Can I get a ride with you?").

Following the listening, it may be useful to have pairs or groups focus on the details of key turns, perhaps directing them to notice interesting grammar or vocabulary and guess its purpose. For example, in the first turn, Speaker B uses *was* rather than *is*, thereby indicating contingency and avoiding the implication that this is a confirmed arrangement (cf. "My brother's coming"). These suggest B's openness to receiving A's projected offer.

Listening and Responding to Inferences

One practice when identifying a speaker's course of action involves—in a sense—jumping ahead rather than expecting the speaker to go through the motions of fully articulating it. Consider, for example, the following scenarios, where the (a) versions appear less cooperative:

1(a)
A: Are you using that pen?
B: Nope.
A: Can I borrow it?
B: Sure.

1(b)
A: Are you using that pen?
B: [Hands over the pen]

2(a)
A: Did you go to the lecture?
B: Yeah.
A: Did you take notes?
B: Yep.
A: Can I see them?
B: Sure.

2(b)
A: Did you go to the lecture?
B: Yeah, you wanna see my notes?
A: Thanks.

In these examples, Speaker A's first turn is designed to establish whether the preconditions for what they want have been met: it is pointless (and troublesome) requesting B's lecture notes if they don't exist. In the (b) versions, Speaker B successfully identifies what Speaker A actually wants and acts accordingly prior to the request.

To practice these, a general approach that is readily adaptable for full-class and self-study options, is as follows:

1. Record a collection of such dialogues, perhaps around a particular theme (e.g., phone calls), and for each write the actual response and one or more uncooperative responses. These can be presented in a handout, slideshow, or one of many online interactive media options.
2. Explain that Speaker A wants something. This can be represented by drawing an arrow between a starting point and end point. Speaker B's objective is to help A get to the end point as efficiently as possible.
3. Students listen to the first turn and then work in pairs or groups to select the best response from two or more options.
4. Listen to check the answer. Provide transcripts for review as required.

Projecting Turn Completion or Continuation

Counting and Listing Games

Counting games provide a useful way to sensitise learners to the prosodic patterns that project both turn continuation and completion. In its basic form (see Ryan & Forrest, 2015), the activity involves students listening to the teacher's sequence and competing to provide the next item. For instance, you might start counting "1, 2, 3, 4, 5, 6," and then stop, with students competing to be the first to recognise the opportunity to take a turn and say "7." A good way to conduct this is to have a group of three students standing, with the first one to successfully provide the next number (without interrupting) getting to sit down and a new student standing.

Despite being very simple, with some modifications, the activity provides a way of modeling nearly any conceivable prosodic pattern that projects turn continuation or completion. In the original Ryan and Forrest (2015) article, the patterns were essentially examples of "listing" intonation used when counting (e.g., a series of level tones or slight rises, falls or fall-rise followed by a final sharp pitch movement). But in fact, with a little practice, a much wider variety of prosodic contours can be produced. These can be easily varied by substituting the numbers with longer noun phrases or clauses, such as:

> *For my birthday, I want to get a great big desk for my computer and a dog with floppy ears and a bike.*

These patterns can easily be accompanied by other resources relevant to turn-taking, such as attention to gaze, body language, and gesture, and to prosodic features beyond intonation, such as in-breath (signaling speaker continuation) and trailing off (a combination of decreasing pitch, volume, and speed signaling turn completion). Once students have come to grips with the basic patterns, the patterns can be combined to include a more complex combination of features.

Snippets

Another very versatile activity for turn-taking is also presented in its simplest form in Ryan and Forrest (2015). It can be used to draw attention to a wide variety of auditory (and when done with video, visual) phenomena and—with simple variations—can be used for practice, diagnostic testing, or metacognition. It can be used to draw attention to phonological patterns, grammatical units, or actions.

The core of the activity is as follows:

- Preteach the concepts of prosodic, grammatical, and action completion.
- Using recordings of naturally occurring speech and audio-editing software (e.g., Audacity; www.audacityteam.org), pre-prepare (1) short snippets of naturally occurring talk and (2) longer versions of each snippet revealing what actually happened next. Some will involve speaker continuation and some speaker transition.
- The students' task (either in pairs or small groups) is to listen and decide whether "the speaker is probably finished" or "probably continuing."
- Students analyse and discuss the relevant cues they noticed.

In planning such activities, it is important to be cognizant of the complexity involved, where a certain feature (e.g., pitch drop) might coincide with turn completion in one instance but not in the next, in which another feature (e.g., action completion) provides the most relevant cue. I have therefore found it important to use fairly clear-cut examples (pre-tested on other proficient English users) and to use naturally occurring speech, which may be far richer in auditory (and/or visual) signals than the scripted speech of textbooks and films.

Identifying Expected Responses

The Best Response: Proceed or Game Over?

Minimal responses, such as *uhuh, mm, mhm, okay, oh, right,* and *yeah,* are much more interesting than most teachers would assume. Their use varies substantially across languages and cultures (Xudon, 2009), and they can pose substantial trouble for learners. To be used appropriately, the listener should have a sense of what the speaker has just done (e.g., presented interesting new information; paused for confirmation) and of what is required to signal willingness to go along with the talk. (E.g., *mm* merely signals understanding or agreement and may be inadequate when the speaker has announced something newsworthy, for which *oh* or *really?* might be appropriate.) The key work in this area is Gardner (2001), who identifies minimal responses used with four key functions:

- continuers (encouraging the speaker to continue)
- acknowledgement tokens (indicating no problem in comprehension)
- newsmarking (responding to prior utterances as announcements/new information)
- change-of-activity tokens (proposing "a readiness to move out of the current topic or activity in the conversation into another"; Gardner, 2001, p. 52).

Each of these functions can be carried out in different ways with subtly different effects; for instance, when used with falling intonation, both *mm* and *yeah* can indicate acknowledgement, but *yeah* is far more likely to foreshadow a further comment from the listener (Gardner, 2001). The use of a particular expression will also depend on its prosodic articulation. (Try saying aloud differing articulations of *oh* and reflect on their uses.)

The following activity is more complex to plan than the others discussed in this chapter, but if managed well, can be particularly rewarding. The design of the activity is inspired by the "choose your adventure" book format.

- Prepare and record a scripted dialogue in which one speaker does the majority of speaking and the other makes a number of appropriate minimal responses. (See the example in Table 1.)
- Using audio editing software, divide the main recording into a number of shorter files, with the cuts occurring immediately prior to the hearer's (minimal response) turns.
- Also record the listener reciting a list of other minimal responses. Use these as a "wrong" response when paired with turns in the original dialogue (i.e., they should be inappropriate or misaligned with the turn before). In doing so, as far as possible, be careful to ensure that the wrong choice is in fact wrong rather than simply an alternative.
- To the end of these wrong turns, add a "game over" sound (e.g., from a computer/arcade game) using audio editing software. Recordings of such sounds can be readily found on YouTube and elsewhere.

- Relabel the audio files in sequence 1, 2a, 2b, 3a, 3b, and so on, where for example 2a represents the right response and 2b the incorrect response to 1. There will thus be a successful sequence of answers progressing through to the end of the dialogue and a number of wrong answers resulting in "game over," as illustrated in Figure 1.
- Optional: In one version of this, suitable for first introducing this activity type, the author recorded the responses of native speaker informants to hearing wrong uses of, for example, *oh*. Recorded reactions included laughter and comments such as "That's so wrong!" These were then added to the audio track after the "game over" sound, providing additional feedback on student choices.
- One way to conduct this activity in class is to embed the recordings into a slideshow. The first slide contains the beginning of the dialogue and the first pair (*a* and *b* options) of responses. After listening to the start of the dialogue, students then collectively decide which response to make. If the wrong answer is chosen, game over. If the right answer is chosen, proceed to the next slide, which will include the whole recording up to now, followed by two further response choices, and so on.

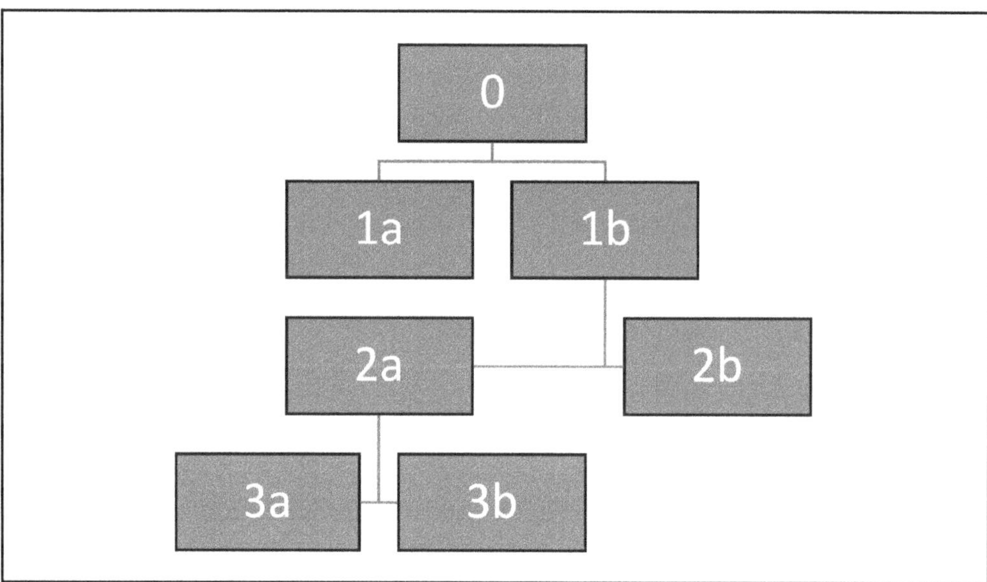

Figure 1. Slide organisation.

Table 1. Proceed or Game Over?

	Full Dialogue With Appropriate Responses	Wrong Responses
0	S1: What've you been doing recently? S2: Um, not much. But I've been watching this series on TV,	
1	S1: Uh-huh, S2: Yeah, *Derry Girls*? S1: Don't know it, S2: Oh, it's sooo funny	S1: Oh.
2	S1: Mm? S2: It's from Northern Ireland and set during the 1980s, I think, during the Troubles,	S1: Is it.
3	S1: Oh, is it? S2: Yeah, it's about a group of girls at a strict Catholic school, one of them— Erin, I think her name is, is the main character, so it kind of follows her more	S1: Oh, great.
4	S1: Mhm S2: And then there's one guy, the cousin of one of the others, and he's the only boy at an all girls' school, so they really give him a hard time,	S1: Oh / I see.
5	S1: Oh really? S2: Yeah, it's so funny. I recommend it.	S1: Yeah.
6	S1: Okay, S2: Apparently it's been really popular in Britain. It's on Netflix if you want to see it.	S1: You're kidding.
7	S1: Great.	S1: Oh.

Explanation of wrong answers:

1. *Oh,* a news receipt discourages further talk on the topic.
2. *Is it*: news receipt; yes/no question with falling intonation discouraging talk.
3. *Oh, great* is an assessment, again discouraging further talk.
4. *Mhm* is a continuer and more appropriate here (where the message seems unfinished) than a news receipt.
5. *Oh really,* a newsmarker, is more appropriate here (for a semipunchline) than *yeah,* which signals receipt of information.
6. *Okay* accepts the recommendation and indicates readiness to move on; *You're kidding* is a newsmarker—inappropriate here when the whole topic was clearly geared toward a recommendation of sorts.
7. Both discourage further talk, but *Great* is an assessment and shows appreciation.

Listening to Conversational Narratives

An unfortunate aspect in the design of many listening tasks (especially when used in assessment, see Field, 2018) is the heavy cognitive demands required by the pen and paper activity, with students often struggling to identify what it is that they are meant to do. This is particularly so for learners with low first-language literacy or otherwise interrupted schooling (Tarone et al., 2009). The following activity type dispenses with pen and paper altogether and maintains a reasonably authentic listening activity. It is based on ideas presented in workshops by Wong (2018) and Forrest (2018).

1. Preteach a small set of relevant minimal responses (e.g., *mhm, oh!*) and use choral repetition practice, focusing particularly on intonation.
2. Preteach responses appropriate to the ending of different types of story, (e.g., "That's so lucky!" for a lucky escape or "You poor thing!" for a troubles-telling; see, e.g., Enfield, 2017, pp. 110–117).
3. Prepare (or have students prepare) a conversational narrative, such as an anecdote; ideally this will have stages likely to elicit distinct emotional reactions (e.g., suspense, relief, surprise, laughter, sympathy).
4. This narrative can be either recorded (video or audio only) or recited live, either by you or by students (e.g., in groups). These options each have rather different effects that are worth experimenting with.
5. Prior to beginning, use questions such as the following to establish the purpose of the activity:

    a. How do you feel if

        i. you tell a sad story but the listener doesn't express sympathy?

        ii. you tell your friends some exciting news but they don't respond?

6. Explain to students that they will hear a narrative and that during pauses, they should respond appropriately with the pretaught minimal responses (e.g., *oh!, mmm*, and *oh, no*).
7. Further explain that at the end of the story, they need to say something that

    a. signals their understanding that it is complete.

    b. shows appreciation of the meaning of the story in a way that validates the teller's feeling (e.g., "That's so lucky!").

8. Play the recording or recite the anecdote, initially leading by example in producing minimal responses (e.g., *mhm*).

Certain turns, particularly at the conclusion of a sequence, provide an excellent way to gauge student understanding of the gist of events.

To conclude, presented in this chapter are just a few of the very many options for focusing on projection, which is itself just one crucial aspect of L-in-I. Projection in ELT listening remains largely unexplored territory, and there is considerable scope for action research exploring its implementation and for a great deal of further materials development in this area.

References

Deppermann, A., & Günthner, S. (2015). Introduction: Temporality in interaction. In A. Deppermann & S. Günthner (Eds.), *Temporality in interaction* (pp. 1–23). John Benjamins.

Enfield, N. J. (2017). *How we talk: The inner workings of conversation*. Basic Books.

Field, J. (2008). *Listening in the language classroom*. Cambridge University Press.

Field, J. (2018). *Rethinking the second language listening test: From theory to practice*: British Council.

Flowerdew, J., & Miller, L. (2005). *Second language listening: Theory and practice*. Cambridge University Press.

Ford, C. E., & Thompson, S. A. (1996). Interactional units in conversation: Syntactic, intonational, and pragmatic resources for the projection of turn completion. In E. Ochs, E. A. Schegloff, & S. A. Thompson (Eds.), *Interaction and grammar* (pp. 134–184). Cambridge University Press.

Forrest, L. (2018, October 5–7). *Storytelling breakdown: Teaching storytelling through a conversation analysis framework* [Paper presentation]. CLESOL, Christchurch, New Zealand.

Gardner, R. (2001). *When listeners talk: Response tokens and listener stance*. John Benjamins.

Golato, A. (2003). Studying compliment responses: A comparison of DCTs and recordings of naturally occurring talk. *Applied Linguistics, 24*(1), 90–121. https://doi.org/10.1093/applin/24.1.90

Graham, S., & Santos, D. (2015). *Strategies for second language listening: Current scenarios and improved pedagogy*. Palgrave Macmillan.

Jefferson, G. (2015). *Talking about troubles in conversation*. Oxford University Press.

Robinson, J. D. (2013). Overall structural organization. In J. Sidnell & T. Stivers (Eds.), *The handbook of conversation analysis* (pp. 257–280). Wiley Blackwell.

Ryan, J. (in press). Listening in interaction: Reconceptualizing a core skill. *ELT Journal*.

Ryan, J., & Forrest, L. (2015). Teaching turn-taking. *Modern English Teacher, 24*(4), 69–71.

Ryan, J., & Forrest, L. (2021). 'No chance to speak': Developing a pedagogical response to turn-taking problems. *Innovation in language learning and teaching, 15*(2), 103–116. https://doi.org/10.1080/17501229.2019.1687709

Ryan, J., & Granville, S. (2020). The suitability of film for modelling the pragmatics of interaction: Exploring authenticity. *System, 89*, 1–13. https://doi.org/10.1016/j.system.2019.102186

Ryan, J., Granville, S., Fisher, M., Haseley, L., & Kemsley, K. (2019). *Adrift: Teacher book*. Alphabet.

Sacks, H. (1995). *Lectures on conversation* (Vol. I & II). Wiley Blackwell.

Schegloff, E. A. (2007). *Sequence organization in interaction: A primer in conversation analysis* (Vol. 1). Cambridge University Press.

Streeck, J. (1995). On projection. In E. N. Goody (Ed.), *Social intelligence and interaction: Expressions and implications of the social bias in human intelligence* (pp. 87–110). Cambridge University Press.

Tarone, E., Bigelow, M., & Hansen, K. (2009). *Literacy and second language oracy*. Oxford University Press.

Waring, H. Z. (2018). Teaching L2 interactional competence: Problems and possibilities. *Classroom Discourse, 9*(1), 57–67. https://doi.org/https://doi.org/10.1080/19463014.2018.1434082

Wong, J. (2007). Answering my call: A look at telephone closings. In H. Bowles & P. Seedhouse (Eds.), *Conversation Analysis and language for specific purposes* (pp. 271–304). Peter Lang.

Wong, J. (2018, July 3). *Focus on action: Insights from conversation analysis for second/foreign language teachers* [Paper presentation]. Wintec Research Series, Hamilton, New Zealand.

Wong, J., & Waring, H. Z. (2021). *Conversation analysis and second language pedagogy: A guide for ESL/EFL teachers* (2nd ed.). Routledge.

Xudong, D. (2009). Listener response. In S. D'hondt, J.-O. Östman, & J. Verschueren (Eds.), *The pragmatics of interaction* (pp. 104–124). John Benjamins.

JONATHON RYAN is an English teacher, researcher, and postgraduate supervisor at Wintec (Te Pūkenga), New Zealand, and is head of materials design for video production company Chasing Time English. His research broadly focuses on oral interaction in ELT, and he is particularly interested developing pedagogy responsive to insights from conversation analysis.

CHAPTER 10

WILLIAM C. COLE-FRENCH

Did You Hear That? Note-Taking in the English for Academic Purposes Classroom

Listening in Real Life

I was baffled by what I saw. There before my eyes were pages of notes taken by my students as we listened to TED Talks. Generally, the notes accurately recorded key information presented and, though there were some gaps, I was certain that a third party—who had not seen the TED Talk—could pick them up, read them, and then develop a relatively clear idea of overall topic. These notes were taken by my students as we listened to TED Talks together in class and yet these very same students, with notes in hand, struggled to answer questions about the core content of these TED Talks. It made no sense to me, especially because I could frequently circle the correct answers to these questions on the very notes they had prepared.

What sort of breakdown was occurring between their listening and their comprehension? As I pondered this gap, a metaphorical insight came to me by means of a math assignment my child was completing at school. There, the teacher had asked my child to compare this equation:

$$\left(7^2 - \frac{96}{2}\right) + \left(2 \times 5 - \sqrt{64}\right)$$

to this equation:

$$(49 - 48) + (10 - 8)$$

And in so doing, my son realized that both were essentially the same as this equation:

But none of the equations were truly complete without calculating the final result, which is, of course, 3.

Reviewing my students' notes, I noticed that some of them were capturing a profound amount of detail as they listened to the TED Talk, whereas others were capturing just the key points. Yet none of them demonstrated making the final calculations to understand the overall import of the message. In short, there was an implicit, analytical skill that they were not utilizing as they listened and took notes.

I observed the nonuse of this skill in other ways as well. Part of my work included accompanying my students to their weekly Anatomy and Physiology classes where the basic design and function of the human body was explored. The professor teaching this class was an immigrant herself and thus sensitive to the challenges of navigating a new culture and language. Built into her lectures were varied supports to help English language learners process the content efficiently. She would even go so far as to sometimes give clues for the next exam, saying "now this is the sort of question I will put on the test to check your understanding." Yet, my students made no notes of such remarks and thus the benefit of them for review at a later date was almost surely lost before they even left the classroom. How was I to understand these missed opportunities by students?

Listening in the Research

In the virtual catalog of English language teaching materials, there is no lack of resources that provide opportunities for students to practice listening and note-taking. Generally speaking, authors of these textbooks prepare a series of brief lectures on contemporary topics that actors then record in a professional studio (Siegel, 2019). These performances are meant to simulate presentations that students hear in a classroom. There is, however, limited guidance within these materials for students and teachers alike on how to develop listening and note-taking skills. Were you to review the scope and sequence of available textbooks, you would likely see a collection of predictable strategies, including listening for keywords, listening for the main ideas and supporting details, using abbreviations and symbols, and using enumeration and bullet points. What you might not realize, however, is that students are primarily asked to develop these strategies simply by using them again and again as they listen. There is little in the form of actual skill training for either students or teachers (Graham, 2017).

In fact, researchers have consistently found that many listening language lessons essentially become cycles of hearing a presentation and then answering comprehension questions about the content (Chen, 2013; Siegel, 2014; Field, 2003). Graham (2017) calls this teaching by testing, explaining that in many classrooms, "learners' comprehension is assessed, rather than there being a focus on the processes they used to achieve that comprehension" (p. 107). According to Goh (2008), this repetitious cycle of practicing and testing essentially communicates to students that they need to try harder, producing anxiety and a tendency to revert to translation and subtitles.

As other chapters in this book have suggested, there is no lack of research literature documenting the unique difficulty that listening presents to English language learners. Siegel (2014) reminds us that though written texts allow a learner to read and reread, listeners essentially hear input once. Moreover, Goh (2008), Graham (2017) and Field (2003) all emphasize the complexity of deciphering form and meaning out of thin air—given that spoken texts do not afford the visual benefits of spaces between words and paragraphs, as is customary in written texts. Thus, listeners struggle to segment words within this sound stream of connected speech (Field, 2003; Goh, 2008; also see Chapters 4 and 6 for more on connected speech). Finally, in spoken texts, there is an additional layer of language that carries meaning. Listeners must not only segment words, but analyze stress, intonation, pace, and pausing to discern communicative intent (Reed, 2006; Vandergrift & Goh, 2012; also see Chapters 6 and 9 for more on understanding the communicative intent of speakers).

Note-taking has its own difficulties. Though vital for academic success, the rate at which students generally can record words is just 10% of the rate at which they can be spoken, pressurizing the process for the listener (Piolat et al., 2005; Boch & Piolat, 2005). This cognitive demand of note-taking is further amplified when students are listening in a second or third language (Barbier & Piolat, 2005). Moreover, there is a simultaneous analytical challenge of needing to decide what should be recorded (Siegel, 2016). Chen (2013), in her study in an English as a foreign language context, found that students tended to rely upon a "word-by-word" strategy to process what they heard and thus experienced difficulties in analyzing the relationship of ideas within a text. These students perceived the rate of speech and unfamiliar vocabulary within presentations as the source of their troubles rather than recognizing the inherent limitations of the "superficial" strategy that they were using.

On the one hand, there are many metacognitive strategies that can be taught to help learners not only recognize specific reasons for comprehension difficulties but also go beyond a lack of understanding and resolve it (Graham & Vanderplank, 2011; also see Chapter 1 for an overview of metacognitive strategies). For example, Field (1998) highlights the value of training learners to "use their knowledge of the context to make intelligent guesses about the ideas which link the sometimes dislocated words which they have been able to recognize" (p. 115). Graham (2017) echoes the influence of this strategy nearly 20 years later as she observes the difficulties that develop when students fail to use their background knowledge while listening. Chen (2013) observed that students who were trained in the use of this and other metacognitive strategies became much less likely to blame their difficulties on external factors, such as rate of speech and unfamiliar vocabulary.

On the other hand, Siegel (2016) recognizes the need to outline pedagogically what helps students take effective notes, calling TESOL educators to emphasize the process of decision-making involved in listening with the hopes of strengthening the product of note-taking. Two strands emerge within the existing research.

First, students need training on how to decide what they should include—and in how much detail—in their notes. Field (1998) introduces the category of "discourse markers" as one of three key areas for targeted instruction in listening skill development. These markers include basic elements such as word repetition, but they also include organizational cues such as *first, second,* and *third.* Boch and Piolat (2005) further observed that effective learners recognize "markers in a speaker's text that signal, more or less explicitly, the importance of what is being said" (p. 102) and use them to make decisions about what they write down. In fact, Song (2011) found that student learning outcomes improved when students were trained to recognize the structure of ideas using these markers and to organize their notes accordingly.

Second, students need to be trained to review their notes after listening for the sake of analyzing how different pieces of a lecture are working together toward a particular purpose. van der Meer (2012) observes that "students do not always appreciate the cognitive value of notetaking . . . as a way of meaning-making and understanding" (pp. 13–14). Boch and Piolat (2005) further explain that some students employ a verbatim—what they term as a "copy-regurgitate"—approach with note-taking whereas other students tend to paraphrase, or use what they call a "reformulation-interpretation" approach (p. 102). Their own review of existing note-taking research suggests that the latter is preferable because it better engages students in reflection, but the main thrust advanced in their work underlines the importance of analysis. That is to say, students work more effectively with the complexity of academic learning when they are trained to return to their notes after listening and to analyze them—highlighting key points and supporting details, summarizing the overall message. The more intensively they engaged in this analysis and reflection, the more measurable the benefits were for their memory and understanding. van der Meer (2012) likewise emphasizes this point, explaining that "notes can play an important part in cognitive processing especially if notes are used effectively in subsequent review processes" (p. 20). Instructors then need to provide targeted instruction and incremental practice that help learners develop the decision-making skills essential for active listening.

Listening in the Classroom

Training Students to Be Mindful of Structural Markers and Elements While Listening

Aristotle's concepts of rhetoric—logos, ethos, and pathos—are, with good reason, enduring tools to analyze the structure of spoken and written communication. Together they provide us with basic discourse strategies that speakers use to help their listeners engage with their presentations. Exploring them for purposes of academic listening has the simultaneous benefit of helping students consider ways to make their own presentations more effective. Let's examine each one and discuss how they can be used to structure incremental steps that train students to listen more effectively. For each of these elements, we will frame their function in terms of how they work to engage listeners with the content of a lecture.

Logos—Answering Questions Listeners Ask: "Is your focus clear?", "Can I follow along?"

One of the first things that can help students recognize the structure of a presentation is the prevalence of keywords. Keywords, terms that are most useful in understanding the ideas that a speaker presents, are easily recognizable because they have several measurable characteristics.

Characteristics of Keywords

Keywords will be

a. repeated multiple times throughout a lecture, though the word form may change (e.g., judge, judgement);
b. paired with synonyms to increase the variety of word choice;
c. labeled explicitly as "important" by speakers; and
d. emphasized through pronunciation changes in pitch and pace.

Each of these characteristics lends itself to incremental practice. One of the first things you can do is to give the students a word or phrase and ask them to listen to a 2- to 3-minute segment of a presentation and simply count the number of times it occurs. For example, in Cuddy's 2012 TED Talk, "Your Body Language May Shape Who You Are," the phrase *body language* is of obvious importance. And to no surprise, Cuddy uses the phrase a total of seven times in the first 2 minutes. A secondary question is whether there are any synonyms used for the phrase *body language*. There are—*nonverbals*—and she uses it twice. Students may not notice that the first time, but, given specific instructions to listen for synonyms a second time, they will likely notice.

Next, give students the transcript of the subsequent 2- to 3-minute segment and ask them to circle words that are repeated several times. You can also create a worksheet that summarizes, section by section, the key points of this segment and then ask students to place the words they've selected under the appropriate key point. By doing so, you highlight for your students the way that the repetition of words shifts as the speaker moves from section to section in a lecture. For example, in Cuddy's (2012) TED Talk, first she talks about judgements and outcomes, then she talks about expressions of power, and related words are repeated in several forms along with some synonyms. One easy way to survey students' ideas about which words are repeated is a web-platform like Mentimeter (www.mentimeter.com). This allows students to submit word choices by phone and then creates a word cloud from their submissions.

Having explored one of the most basic elements of logos—keywords—students are now ready to consider an equally useful complement: cue words. Here we can train students to recognize a fairly predictable set of words that speakers use to cue or signal listeners as to the relative importance of ideas in their presentation.

Functions of Cue Words

Cue words serve several functions in a lecture, such as to

a. help the listeners understand the purpose of a talk,
b. preview the organization of information for listeners, and
c. list details and examples of key points.

Cue words include the following markers:

- enumeration markers: *first, second,* and *third*
- chronological markers: *before, next,* and *after*
- contrast markers: *on the one hand* and *on the other hand*
- example markers: *for instance,* and *such as.*

Depending on the academic focus of our students, there may be other discourse-specific markers utilized, such as cause/effect or sequence/process organizational patterns.

Obviously, the first step when exploring cue words is to make sure that students are actually noticing them. For that reason, you can create an advance organizer table in which the different types of markers are listed as headers for each column. Then, you can present examples of each category in turn, selecting segments from their listening materials and asking students to identify what specific markers are used. At the advanced level, this can mean playing the segment, and at a beginner level, students can review the transcript. Be prepared for the fact that students will likely assume you want them to recount the information presented after the marker rather than simply noting which marker is specifically used.

A second step when exploring cue words is to activate the analytical skills of your students in response to specific cue words. You can do this by selecting specific examples in which a speaker previews the focus for next stage of their presentation. You can then present those examples to students—be it by listening, by transcript, or both—along with a specific analytical question that they need to answer. Goldman, for example, in his 2011 TED Talk, states, "We have this idea that if we drive the people who make mistakes out of medicine, what will we be left with, but a safe system. But there are two problems with that." Thus, we can ask: how many problems does Goldman discuss? Or in Russell's 2006 TED Talk, he concludes by saying, "So my 18 minutes is up. So let me finish up with some good news, and maybe a little bit of bad news." And again, it's only natural to ask: What two things will Russell discuss as he finishes his presentation? Sometimes, in fact, we don't even need to listen to a text; the title alone carries a valuable alert for our students. For example, in Shah's 2013 TED Talk, "3 Reasons We Haven't Gotten Rid of Malaria," students should easily be able to answer this question: During this TED Talk, how many reasons will the speaker present about why we continue to battle malaria? Admittedly, putting these examples into print makes them *seem* painfully obvious—but remember the challenge of listening compared to reading and consider all of the distractions and anxieties that our students bring to the process. They need our help to train this kind of analytical focus into their skillset.

The final phase when working with cue words is to ensure that students have opportunities to practice capturing the essential information that is previewed by them. To do this, you can hand out copies of a transcript containing several of the pretaught cue words and play the recording. Students should annotate the transcript to visually link the cue words to the relevant information, and then, in small groups compare their analysis. For example, in Shah's aforementioned 2013 TED Talk, "3 Reasons We Haven't Gotten Rid of Malaria," you could play the exact two or three sentences where the speaker first identifies each of the three reasons. This activity focuses students' attention on the purpose and variety of cue words in a lecture. This same kind of activity, used with longer segments, would work well to draw students' attention to the way speakers use cue words to transition from topic to topic. This is key to skill development because it equips students to follow the cue words, and thus the content of the lecture, in an organized fashion, strengthening their understand of it.

As students develop their ability to monitor cue words, more advanced forms of their use can be assigned for analysis at home. There are two particular patterns to consider here. First, speakers will use parallel grammar structures to highlight the organization for listeners. A great example of this can be found in Natterson-Horowitz's 2014 TED Talk, "What Veterinarians Know That Physicians Don't," when she asks listeners to consider similarities between animal and human medical problems. You can give students a gapped text in which the first noun phrases and final question of each of the three examples she gives are missing. Students would then listen to the text beginning from her explicit statement of purpose, "Here are a few examples of the kind of exciting connections" and fill in the missing noun phrases that she uses to start each example ("fear-induced heart failure," "self-injury," and "postpartum depression") as well as the repeated words she uses in each question concluding the examples ("Shouldn't this knowledge be put into the hands of . . . ?"). As a follow-up activity, ask students to listen to the lecture again and take notes about the details of each of the health problems.

Another advanced form of such of cues can be conveyed through intonation, specifically what Wells (2006) refers to as the "implicational fall-rise intonation pattern" (p. 27). For example, in her 2014 TED Talk "What Your Doctor Won't Disclose," Wen recounts the results of a research study that she administered. She starts this section by describing the basic methodology and then engaging the audience with the results by asking "What did they find?" She then tells the audience explicitly that her research team found three things, but rather than using enumeration markers, she uses the repetition of a specific word alongside this specialized form of intonation. Here again, you can give students the transcript with the specific words explicitly highlighted. Ask them simply to describe the sort of tone Wen uses when saying these words. Together, these elements list the promised three things without ever using numbers.

In both of these advanced forms, the repetition of the pattern—be it grammar or intonation—signals the organizational connection between the separate bits of information, and drawing their attention to it will expand students' understanding of how tuning into the organization of a lecture can help them take better notes and make better use of the notes they take.

Ethos—Answering Questions Listeners Ask: "Can I trust you?", "Are your ideas credible?", "Are you knowledgeable?"

Once students have demonstrated their ability to process the basic buildings blocks by which speakers organize their ideas and guide their listeners, they are ready for a different set of components that speakers use to establish the validity of their ideas. Most immediately, students and teachers can discuss, and then observe, the different functions of key points and supporting details. Every presentation will employ these, and they are used together in one of two ways. On the one hand, the speaker can present a key point and then a series of supporting details to illustrate its meaning and/or the significance. Less commonly, on the other hand, the speaker may present a series of supporting details before tying them together under the umbrella of a larger key point. The essential element either way is to help students build for themselves a clear understanding of the important interplay between these two components through a scaffolded analysis of several examples.

There are several ways to do this. First, start by investigating different types of supporting details that speakers use, such as historical events, relevant facts, research findings, analogies, and stories. Visual aids, including charts, videos, and photographs, would also be appropriate to survey. Students can then listen to segments while reading the transcripts and then work in pairs to categorize (using some of the specific aforementioned types) the ways in which speakers are supporting their ideas. Students could note the supporting details in chart columns or perhaps by highlighting all of one type of supporting detail in one color directly on the transcript. For example, returning again to Cuddy's (2012) TED Talk, her first key point is that other people judge us based upon our body language (2:03–3:18). She then quickly summarizes the findings of two researchers about the ways nonverbals influence perceptions. When students listen to this segment for themselves, they will likely be unprepared to capture the specifics of the research because she speaks very fast, but they should be able to recognize Cuddy's choice to support her idea using information from research. This is a key task because it asks them to identify the fundamental ways that speakers establish validity. Lower level learners could benefit from this activity if the listening text was level-appropriate and you limit the search for supporting details to one or two kinds. For some struggling listeners, even just identifying the details without the extra step of classifying them will be challenging, so keep this in mind when providing differentiation.

Often, speakers will tell stories to illustrate ideas and support their key points. When students haven't been trained to analyze the interplay of supporting details and key points, they frequently get caught up in trying to capture every last detail. This is an unrealistic goal for anyone, and it frequently leads into a tendency to rely upon the transcript, which is reading rather than listening. So, the next step in ethos training is to teach students to always consider the question of purpose in storytelling. Students need practice listening to stories and answering questions such as "Why does the speaker tell this story?", "What does this story exemplify?", and "What is the speaker communicating by means of this example?" For example, in Goldman's 2011 presentation, he spends 2 minutes discussing baseball batting averages before raising the prevalence of errors in medical practices. To fully appreciate his ideas, students will need to build context for themselves (discussed later in this chapter) but they also need to ask themselves what connection batting averages have with medical errors. At the advanced levels, students could simply discuss this question in small groups. At lower levels, students can be given three or four choices to consider together before choosing one. Whatever the method, when we ask students to answer these questions, we emphasize the true task of academic listening—analyzing ways different pieces of a presentation are working together to communicate important ideas.

These questions can lead to another important insight for any listener: The speaker does not intend for us to retain in exact form every word. One signal of this is the pace at which a speaker presents their ideas. Supporting details, especially when several examples are listed in sequence to illustrate a key point, are frequently rattled off at lightning speed, but key points are put forward at a much slower pace with purposeful emphasis by pausing. These sound cues can help a student decide whether to simply get the gist of a speaker's idea or whether a more detailed encoding of essential information is required.

One example that we explore in my English for academic purposes health care classes comes from Goldman's (2011) TED Talk. In it, Goldman takes an extended period of time to relay the story of Mrs. Drucker, who came to the hospital in a truly critical condition and ultimately died because of his mistakes in her care. In the middle of this detailed story, Goldman abruptly changes his pace as he recounts a nurse's question to him: "Do you remember?" He says each word slowly and methodically. While the full significance of these words does not become clear until later, his pace shift and pauses alert listeners to their importance.

To train students to monitor pace and pausing within a lecture, spend a class session working with a few transcripts. First, have students listen to segments at half-speed and mark each instance that a speaker pauses with a line. Next, have them work in groups to compare their annotations and to look for any patterns of emphasis and grammar to explain why speakers pause when they do. Then, introduce students to the pronunciation category "thought groups" (Gilbert, 2008) and highlight the connection between pausing and grammar (also see Chapters 5 and 8 for more on thought groups), before interpreting a disruption to this predictable pattern as a point of emphasis. Finally, have students review different segments of the transcript and make annotations about where speakers will pause before actually listening to it and evaluating their predictions.

Pathos—Answering Questions Listeners Ask: "Is this something I should care about?", "Do you understand me?"

The final discourse element speakers frequently utilize is pathos, which refers to the ways in which they personalize the topic to engage the feelings and imagination of their listeners. On the one hand, its value is easier for students to understand. It can be readily demonstrated by means of any number of television commercials available on YouTube. A powerful example is produced by Thai Life Insurance. Titled "Unsung Hero," it tells the story of an average man who treats others with kindness in the midst of a monotonous daily schedule and yet somehow empowers and transforms those he meets. This commercial is especially useful as a demonstration of pathos because it is not produced in English; even without subtitles it has consistently inspired my students and left us crying.

In academic settings, students frequently recognize the use of pathos during a lecture when others react by laughing or nodding. Furthermore, speakers often simultaneously use some kind of visual aid to amplify the impact of their spoken pathos element. For example, in the Anatomy and Physiology course my students take, the professor begins the chapter on bones with a photograph of a football player whose leg has clearly bent somewhere between the knee and the ankle, eliciting a dramatic reaction from the class as they wince or look away! For all of these reasons, listeners will likely recognize the use of pathos during a presentation.

On the other hand, however, listeners may struggle to understand why a particular instance of pathos would have the personal impact that it does upon the other members of the audience. This is because elements of pathos are culturally bound, chosen specifically to engage listeners by means of something that is familiar and meaningful to them. For example, in Gawande's 2012 TED Talk, "How Do We Heal Medicine?", he draws heavily upon race cars to relay the significance of his ideas. His examples assume that listeners are immersed in the world of high-speed automobiles, which may not be true of our students. They will recognize the words easily enough but they have little category for what these words mean—and so the personal impact of it is completely lost on them.

The challenge presented by elements of pathos highlights the importance of context in listening. In an academic environment, it's important to emphasize two things for English language learners. First, students will almost always be asked to read materials before they listen to a lecture. This step of preparation is not optional because it will build context about the topic that will be explored during the lecture. It also gives students a chance to study topic-specific terminology that is unknown to them and would otherwise lead to a breakdown in comprehension. Second, students will almost always encounter instances of pathos in which they lack the necessary background to fully understand its relevance. Thus, a key component of listening skill training becomes a mitigation strategy to recognize and resolve the difficulties that result from lack of context.

There are several strategies that students and teachers can use here. As a starting point, you can use a word cloud, generated using a site like Word Sift (wordsift.org), in which the high-frequency words are displayed prominently. Students can then review these words to see whether any are unfamiliar. For example, in Li's 2010 TED Talk, "Can We Eat to Starve Cancer?", the most frequently used word is *angiogenesis*. Because this is readily seen with a word cloud, students can work in groups using their phones to search online for the concept prior to listening, which simulates and reinforces the importance of reading to build background knowledge.

After listening, another activity involves the use of phrases in which each word is known and yet the meaning of them together remains hidden to the student. Onie's 2012 TED Talk, "What if Our Healthcare System Kept Us Healthy," speaks of "March Madness" and NCAA basketball to highlight the passionate dedication of college students. This reference almost always fails to compute in the imagination of university-level international students. This is one instance in which the student can benefit from further study to fully appreciate the significance of what has been said. Students can work in groups to first research the unfamiliar phrase (March Madness) and then to propose some ways it relates to the presentation (or choose a best option from a list). Initially, you could propose search terms for the students to use in these instances and then later ask students to agree together on their own search terms for such difficulties.

Training Students to Be Reflective With Their Notes After Listening

Training students to be mindful of Aristotle's three basic elements of rhetoric—logos, ethos, and pathos—has some immediate applicability to their note-taking. In the case of logos, keywords are definitely words to include in notes, and students can be asked to practice combining keywords together into phrases that summarize the essential information. Likewise, cue words can inform student choices about when to use numeration, columns, indentation, and other visualization strategies in note-taking. In the case of ethos, the task of distinguishing key points and supporting details also reinforces the helpfulness of using these visualization strategies as well as guides decision-making about where one section of a lecture ends and another begins.

The real value of training students to recognize and analyze these three basic elements of rhetoric, however, begins after listening to something. Students should be trained to review their notes to look for gaps in their understanding—and these three elements provide an immediate means by which to evaluate those gaps. For logos, students can review the cue words that they heard to see whether they captured all the information promised by the cue. For example, if a speaker says, "there are three reasons . . . ," students check their notes to ensure that they have three reasons, clearly recorded. Or, if a speaker says "here are some examples of . . . ," students can evaluate whether the information they recorded contains examples as well as to analyze for themselves what they are examples of.

For ethos, students can review their notes and then attempt to distinguish key points from supporting details. Moreover, students can also be trained to adopt the Cornell Note-Taking System of leaving space on the left side of their paper as they take notes. This then becomes space in which the student can create *wh–* questions for themselves by which they are prompted to recall key points and supporting details. (For more details, visit Cornell University's "Learning Strategies Center" website, lsc.cornell.edu.) For example, students could pose a question such as "What are the three reasons that . . . ?" or "What examples of ______ does the speaker present?" In fact, several class sessions should be spent training students to formulate such questions for their notes. Such work will likely need to include reminders (or lessons) about proper question grammar as well as a discussion about the inherent limitations of yes/no questions in prompting us to recall and review information.

When students do identify gaps in their understanding, you can train students to engage analytically with the difficulty. Students frequently rely on the transcript, or even a translation if they have the option, to figure out what they missed. But this does not actually give them transferable strategies for the next time they encounter a difficulty. There are two simple ways to deactivate this tendency. First, allow students time and space to discuss the lecture or presentation with one another after listening. In this way, students can ask questions based on gaps in their own understanding and find some clarity in a cooperative manner. Second, for areas where clarity is illusive, students can work together to formulate questions they could use to ask the presenter to clarify their ideas. Both of these tasks mirror healthy communication strategies for any setting. For my classes, I have formalized this process using a worksheet called "Listening and Problem-Solving." (See Appendix A for this worksheet.)

Beyond an evaluation of their notes to identify gaps in understanding, another way to encourage reflection after listening is to immerse students in the art of curiosity. One of the beautiful dynamics at play in any language is the way in which there are a seemingly endless combination of possibilities in terms of how we piece the building blocks of language together to express something. Pinker credits Chomsky with this insight, stating, "virtually every sentence that a person utters or understands is a brand-new combination of words, appearing for the first time in the history of the universe" (1994, p. 22). Thus, there is enduring value in training students to monitor what they hear for novel ways in which speakers use not only the three elements of logos, ethos, and pathos, but also the pronunciation, grammar, and vocabulary systems of English to communicate ideas. When students have been carefully trained in the process of listening, they notice interesting examples of these elements and systems, and they can begin to consider for themselves the value of these choices (by the speaker for the listener) as well their willingness to make such choices themselves when they present something of their own. In my classes, I formalized this work using worksheets called "Cultivating Curiosity." (See Appendix B for this worksheet.)

In conclusion, the goal in all of this is to engage students with the process of academic listening so that they move beyond a simple quest to understand and remember the words toward a true analysis of the relationship between the components and the content of a presentation.

References

Barbier, M.-L., & Piolat, A. (2005). L1 and L2 cognitive effort of note taking and writing. In L. Allal & B. Schneuwly (Eds.), *Proceedings of the special interest group on writing*. SIG Writing of European Association for Research on Learning and Instruction.

Boch, F., & Piolat, A. (2005). Note taking and learning: A summary of research. *The WAC Journal, 16*, 101–113. https://doi.org/10.37514/WAC-J.2005.16.1.08

Chen, A. (2013). EFL listeners' strategy development and listening problems: A process-based study. *The Journal of Asia TEFL, 10*(3), 81–101. https://doi.org/10.18823/asiatefl.2021.18.1.1.1

Cuddy, A. (2012, June). *Your body language may shape who you are* [Video]. TED Conferences. https://www.ted.com/talks/amy_cuddy_your_body_language_may_shape_who_you_are

Field, J. (1998). Skills and strategies: Towards a new methodology for listening. *ELT Journal, 52*(2), 110–118. https://doi.org/10.1093/elt/52.2.110

Field, J. (2003). Promoting perception: Lexical segmentation in L2 listening. *ELT Journal, 57*(4), 325–334. https://doi.org/10.1093/elt/57.4.325

Gawande, A. (2012, March). *How do we heal medicine?* [Video]. TED Conferences. https://www.ted.com/talks/atul_gawande_how_do_we_heal_medicine

Gilbert, J. (2008). *Teaching pronunciation: The prosody pyramid.* Cambridge University Press.

Goh, C. (2008). Metacognitive instruction for second language listening development: Theory, practice, implications. *RELC Journal, 39*(2), 188–213. https://doi.org/10.1177/0033688208092184

Goldman, B. (2011, November). *Doctors make mistakes. Can we talk about that?* [Video]. TED Conferences. https://www.ted.com/talks/brian_goldman_doctors_make_mistakes_can_we_talk_about_that

Graham, S. (2017). Research into practice: Listening strategies in an instructed classroom setting. *Language Teaching, 50*(1), 107–119. https://doi.org/10.1017/S0261444816000306

Graham, S., & Vanderplank, R. (2011). Exploring the relationship between listening development and strategy use. *Language Teaching Research, 15*(4), 435–456. https://doi.org/10.1177/1362168811412026

Li, W. (2010, February). Can we eat to starve cancer? [Video]. TED Conferences. https://www.ted.com/talks/william_li_can_we_eat_to_starve_cancer

Natterson-Horowitz, B. (2014, September). *What veterinarians know that physicians don't* [Video]. TED Conferences. https://www.ted.com/talks/barbara_natterson_horowitz_what_veterinarians_know_that_physicians_don_t

Onie, R. (2012, April). *What if our health care system kept us healthy?* [Video]. TED Conferences. https://www.ted.com/talks/rebecca_onie_what_if_our_health_care_system_kept_us_healthy

Pinker, S. (1994). *The language instinct.* William Morrow and Company.

Piolat, A., Olive, T., & Kellogg, R. T. (2005). Cognitive effort during note taking. *Applied Cognitive Psychology, 19*(3), 291–312. https://doi.org/10.1002/acp.1086

Reed, M. (2006). Pronunciation, stress and intonation, and communicative listening skills. In T. Jones (Ed.), *Pronunciation in the classroom: The Overlooked essential* (pp. 75–88). TESOL Press.

Russell, A. (2006, February). *The potential of regenerative medicine* [Video]. TED Conferences. https://www.ted.com/talks/alan_russell_the_potential_of_regenerative_medicine

Shah, S. (2013, June). *Three reasons we still haven't gotten rid of malaria* [Video]. TED Conferences. https://www.ted.com/talks/sonia_shah_3_reasons_we_still_haven_t_gotten_rid_of_malaria

Siegel, J. (2014). Exploring L2 listening instruction: Examinations of practice. *ELT Journal, 68*(1), 22–30. https://doi.org/10.1093/elt/cct058

Siegel, J. (2016). A pedagogic cycle for EFL note-taking. *ELT Journal, 70*(3), 275–286. https://doi.org/10.1093/elt/ccv073

Siegel, J. (2019). Teaching lecture notetaking with authentic materials. *ELT Journal, 73*(20), 124–133. https://doi.org/10.1093/elt/ccy031

Song, M. (2011). Note-taking quality and performance on an L2 academic listening test. *Language Testing, 29*(1), 67–89. https://doi.org/10.1177/0265532211415379

Vandergrift, L., & Goh, C. (2012). *Teaching and learning second language listening: Metacognition in action.* Routledge.

van der Meer, J. (2012). Students' note-taking challenges in the twenty-first century: Considerations for teachers and academic staff developers. *Teaching in Higher Education, 17*(1), 13–23. https://doi.org/10.1080/13562517.2011.590974

Wells, J. C. (2006). *English intonation: An introduction.* Cambridge University Press.

Wen, L. (2014, September). *What your doctor won't disclose* [Video]. TED Conferences. https://www.ted.com/talks/leana_wen_what_your_doctor_won_t_disclose

Wiles, S. (2020). *About WordSift.* https://wordsift.org/about.html

WILLIAM G. GOLE-FRENCH currently lives and works in Boston, Massachusetts, USA. He teaches as a full-time instructor of ESL within the School of Arts & Sciences at Massachusetts College of Pharmacy and Health Sciences University. Prior to returning to the United States, William lived and work in Vietnam for nearly 10 years through a partnership between the Ministry of Education and Training of Vietnam and Resource Exchange International Vietnam, a U.S.-based nongovernmental organization. William graduated from Boston University (USA) with his Master of Education in TESOL in 2004.

Appendix A: Listening and Problem-Solving

<table>
<tr><td>SPEAKER:</td><td colspan="2">TITLE:</td></tr>
<tr><td>SOURCE:</td><td colspan="2"></td></tr>
<tr><td colspan="3">Review your notes after listening to the assigned materials and circle and number any sections that were more difficult to understand than others. Then, for each section, answer the questions below in one of the boxes on this page.</td></tr>
<tr><td>DIFFICULTY #1:
(1) What do you think made this section difficult to understand?
(2) If you could ask specific questions to clarify the ideas of this difficult section, what would they be?</td><td colspan="2"></td></tr>
<tr><td>DIFFICULTY #2:
(1) What do you think made this section difficult to understand?
(2) If you could ask specific questions to clarify the ideas of this difficult section, what would they be?</td><td colspan="2"></td></tr>
<tr><td>DIFFICULTY #3:
(1) What do you think made this section difficult to understand?
(2) If you could ask specific questions to clarify the ideas of this difficult section, what would they be?</td><td colspan="2"></td></tr>
</table>

Appendix B: Cultivating Curiosity

Define: curiosity (n) [5:3][1,2]

Interest leading to inquiry and analysis—intellectual curiosity

Example: Her natural curiosity led her to ask more questions.

Define: curious (adj) [3:1]

a. Marked by desire to investigate and learn—a curious person

b. Exciting attention as strange, creative, or unexpected—a curious choice

As you listen to the assigned materials and take notes at home, look for ***one or two*** *specific moments when the speaker uses English* ***in ways that seem unusual or clever to you***.

This might take the form of:

(1) how they choose words and put them together (vocabulary and collocations)
(2) how they structure their sentences and organize their ideas (grammar and logos)
(3) what they sound like (uses of stress, pausing, and intonation)
(4) what they used to exemplify and personalize their ideas for the audience (ethos and pathos)

Make note of these one or two specific moments by writing down what they said (the exact words), how they said it (sound), and when they said it during the talk (the exact time). Then think about how the speaker's choices might impact the audience and support their overall success during the talk. You can use the worksheet on the other side of this page to make notes. Bring these notes to class on a piece of paper that you can give to your teacher.

[1] Merriam-Webster. (n.d.). Curiosity. *In Merriam-Webster.com dictionary*. Retrieved November 3, 2017, from https://www.merriam-webster.com/dictionary/curiosity

[2] In the brackets, the first number is the syllable count and the second number is the stressed syllable.

BEFORE	**watching, review the topics we have discussed so far about speaking, pronunciation, and vocabulary.**
AFTER	**watching, think back over what you HEARD as you listened to the assigned materials. Did you notice[3] one or two moments that seemed particularly strange, creative, or unexpected?**

DESCRIPTION: Give some details about what was said and done at that moment. Describe what the speaker does as specifically as possible. Be sure to make note of the time when it occurred.

What made you curious?
(check all that apply)

- ☐ how they chose words and put them together (vocabulary/collocations)
- ☐ how they structured their sentences and organized their ideas (grammar and logos)
- ☐ what they sounded like (uses of stress, pausing, and intonation)
- ☐ what they used to exemplify and personalize ideas for the audience (ethos and pathos)

ANALYSIS: What purpose might the speaker have in mind by using words, grammar, and/or sounds in this way? Does this relate to anything we have discussed so far during our class?

APPLICATION: Is this something that you would like to be able to do when you make a presentation? Why or why not? What kind of help do you need to develop that ability?

[3] notice (v) [2:1]—To see, hear, and think about while watching and listening to the assigned materials

FRANCISCA MARIA IVONE AND WILLY ARDIAN RENANDYA

Bringing Extensive Listening Into the Second Language Classroom

Listening in Real Life

In the past few years, Francisca has been teaching the same groups of students belonging to the same cohort for two to four consecutive semesters. This has given her opportunities to watch them develop their listening ability in the context of listening courses that aim mostly for successful completion of comprehension exercises. To her dismay, her students' listening ability has grown very slowly over the years, regardless of the fact that they have passed four listening courses.

In Francisca's listening classes, there are times that the lesson did not go the way she'd planned. For example, one day in her advanced listening class, the topic was about the Bosnian war of the early 1990s. After completing some pre-listening activities to activate their background knowledge, the students listened to some people sharing stories of how they survived the war. As they did not find the stories relevant to their lives, they did not respond well to the classroom activities. Moreover, they found the recording difficult to comprehend due to the "foreign" accent of the speakers.

Another day in Francisca's intermediate listening class, a handful of students dominated the class because they knew the answers to the comprehension questions; the others, however, were confused and unable to answer any of the questions. It seemed that the audio recordings were too fast for most of them that day, and they could not catch the native speakers' speech rate. When she offered to play the recordings once more, they all said yes, but even then, the texts were just too challenging for them.

Some days, Francisca's students really enjoyed the lessons. For instance, one day in her elementary class, her students listened to the recordings attentively. They did their worksheet dutifully without too many problems, because the topic was familiar and exciting, and the recordings were clear and slow. The class ended quickly because they enjoyed what they were doing.

These illustrations reveal many points that Francisca has found challenging. Her classes are heterogeneous, and she finds it hard to differentiate instruction, so the same materials are used by learners of various levels. Thus, they do not fit everyone's level of proficiency. Consequently, her students often fail to comprehend spoken texts because the second language (L2) input is beyond their comprehension level as a result of topics that were perceived as irrelevant, unfamiliar topics and and accents, fast speech, or unknown words. The focus of all of the listening courses is on intensive listening practice, so learners have limited exposure to spoken text in the L2 and are required to move very quickly from one topic to another because they have to follow the syllabus. They do not listen to texts that fit their levels, needs, and interests. It is, thus, not surprising that their listening skills and proficiency develop very slowly throughout their study.

Listening in the Research

The word *listening* in L2 learning has commonly been used to refer to listening comprehension. The term *listening comprehension*, according to Richards (2005), often gets translated into an approach to teaching L2 listening that emphasizes the importance of explicit teaching of comprehension skills and strategies. In L2 listening lessons, learners are traditionally trained to learn such listening skills as keywords identification, selective listening, making a prediction, main idea comprehension, detail comprehension, full comprehension, making inferences, and replication (Vandergrift & Goh, 2012; Richards, 2005).

L2 intensive listening activities commonly engage learners to listen to nonconversational and conversational aural texts followed by listening comprehension exercises (Rost, 1990). For task completion purposes, learners are often required to memorize what they hear. Frommer (2006) criticises intensive listening activities that are often not cognitively meaningful and are both unrealistic and unproductive because they expect learners to perform total memorization of input. Unlike when listening in their first language (L1), L2 learners have limited memory space for listening to the L2 because they have to focus on lexico-grammatical processing of the target language of which they have partial knowledge (Lynch, 1998). Accordingly, memorization should not be the goal of listening tasks because L2 learners need to be engaged in more meaningful language learning activities.

In a typical comprehension-based intensive listening lesson, success is often determined by the completion of a set of predetermined listening tasks. We believe that this way of assessing comprehension, though useful, does not fully reflect the whole range of factors that contribute to success in comprehension. Following are a number of factors that the literature has shown to contribute to success (or failure) in listening comprehension:

- The five interrelated factors of text, interlocutor, task, process, and listener characteristics (Rubin, 1994)

- Learners' limited vocabulary and prior knowledge as well as the type of input, speech rate, and speaker's accent (Goh, 1999)
- Learners' learning attitudes, lack of learning strategy knowledge, and limited listening skills (Graham, 2006; Hasan, 2000)
- Poor sound quality, the absence of visual aids, unclear pronunciation or fast speech, boring topics, and long texts (Hasan, 2000).
- For lower proficiency L2 learners' real-time processing of aural texts, speech rate, words and phrases in connected speech, and blurry word boundaries (Renandya & Farrell, 2011; also see Chapters 2, 3, 4, 6, and 7 for more information on these bottom-up processing skills).
- A lack of background knowledge (Krashen, 1996, disapproves rushed switches between topics, especially with beginners of L2, because they need to be able to use their background knowledge to ease comprehension.)

As one of the critical factors in the success of L2 listening, learners need to feel confident and motivated in listening in the target language (Dupuy, 1999; Vandergrift & Goh, 2012). This can be done by minimizing their anxiety level. Graham (2006) maintains that when L2 learners fail to comprehend, the cause may be affective rather than linguistic. It could be the case that they are feeling anxious or have low confidence in their ability. Accordingly, listening activities should include listening to comprehensible L2 input that can lower learners' anxiety and increase their confidence levels. Extensive listening activities that allow L2 learners to listen to highly comprehensible texts can help boost their confidence and motivation. Thus, the use of aural texts that are well within students' linguistic competence can be utilized so that students can listen comfortably with minimal comprehension problems. Texts that are beyond learners' proficiency and comprehension level should not be used in extensive listening activities because they can undermine students' confidence and motivation.

Current scholarship in second language acquisition (e.g., Renandya & Jacobs, 2016; Loewen, 2014) suggests that language teaching approaches that promote the development of implicit (unconscious) knowledge should be given more priority. It is this type of knowledge that enables students to use the target language for authentic and purposeful communication. Moreover, successful listeners do not depend solely on comprehension practices that focus on intensive listening activities; they extend their learning beyond the classroom and acquire substantial implicit knowledge by doing independent extensive listening activities (Ivone & Renandya, 2019). Extensive listening, according to Yeldham (2016), provides ample opportunity for learners to engage in "unstructured practice of all the skills, reinforcing their use" (p. 36). This type of practice is believed to facilitate L2 listening development.

The key findings of research into extensive listening to date seem to suggest that its theoretical basis is quite similar to extensive reading, in that both are informed by the "compelling" input hypothesis suggesting optimal language acquisition requires more than interesting input and motivation to improve; it needs to be so interesting that learners do not feel like they are reading or listening in a foreign language (Krashen et al., 2017). In the context of extensive listening, however, compelling input alone is not enough. Learners need to be exposed to a large amount of comprehensible and enjoyable listening material for an extended period (Mayora, 2017; Renandya & Jacobs, 2016; Waring, 2008) in addition to explicit instruction in top-down and bottom-up skill building.

The extensive listening approach is recommended for L2 learners of beginning and intermediate levels (Krashen, 1996; Renandya & Farrell, 2011; Mayora, 2017) because they are not compelled to perform comprehension tasks that test their understanding. Instead, the extensive listening activities allow them to enjoy listening to topics of their interests which over time would help develop their ability to listen with greater comprehension, fluency, and automaticity (Renandya & Farrell, 2011; Dupuy, 1999; Ridgway, 2000; Waring, 2008; Renandya & Jacobs, 2016). Extensive listening helps fluent listeners easily and automatically process and comprehend aural input and reorganise their knowledge (Chang et al., 2019).

To improve listening fluency, Krashen (1996) and Dupuy (1999) proposed the concept of narrow listening, using texts on one topic, of one genre, or by one author. The benefits are apparent here; students get to hear the same language forms related to a familiar topic. Learners should focus on short recordings of the same topic until they grow familiar with it before moving on to another topic. Tutorial and DIY videos, as well as weblogs of someone sharing their stories, are perfect for extensive listening.

Combined with repeated listening, narrow listening is reported to be beneficial in improving vocabulary retention, listening comprehension, and listening fluency, as well as confidence in listening to texts in L2 (Dupuy, 1999). Dupuy (1999), for example, reported that for her lower proficiency learners, a higher degree of comprehension (95% and above) was possible only after they listened to the same material three or four times. Extensive listening activities do not aim for explicit learning of forms, yet as a result of narrow listening, learners may learn implicitly from repeated use of words, expressions, and grammar structure (Matsuo, 2015).

Text selection also influences the outcome or success of the listening tasks, so learners must be encouraged to choose texts based on their relevance, interest, and enjoyment (Renandya & Farrell, 2011; Krashen, 1996; Mayora, 2017). Listening to texts learners find interesting and relevant is more pleasant and motivating than listening to those they have no interest in. For listening texts to be relevant, they should "relate to learner goals and interests, and involve self-selection and evaluation" (Rost, 2002, p. 123). The implication for L2 listening is that learners are given an active role in the selection of listening texts, or at least in the choice of the topic of interest.

In an L2 learning context, learners need support and feedback from teachers as well as other learners. Learners also need to learn how to motivate themselves, to control and monitor their progress, and to keep on practising listening. "As students practise monitoring their own learning and analysing it with what is expected, they eventually develop the skills to make consistent and reliable interpretations of their learning" (Earl & Katz, 2006, p. 46). Listening diaries/journals/logs, in spoken or written forms, can help

> students learn to monitor and challenge their own understanding, predict the outcomes of their current level of understanding, make reasoned decisions about their progress and difficulties, decide what else they need to know, organize and reorganize ideas, check for consistency between different pieces of information, draw analogies that help them advance their understanding, and set personal goals. (Earl & Katz, 2006, p. 44)

Journals are useful for recording extensive listening activities as well as learners' reflection on their listening experience.

Students' comprehension can be enhanced by allowing them to read the transcript before or during listening. The literature suggests that listening-while-reading makes aural texts more comprehensible and exciting (Chang, 2009; Brown et al., 2008), promotes vocabulary development (Brown et al., 2008), and helps learners concentrate on listening to the texts better (Chang, 2009). Moreover, it may result in more substantial and long-lasting effects on the development of listening competence and acquisition of some linguistic elements, such as sounds, words, phrases, and sentences (Renandya, 2012). However, Yeldham (2016, p. 36) cautions us that listening-while-reading "may have short-term comprehension benefits but runs the risk of learners relying too greatly on the printed text, scaffolding that is absent in real-life listening." To more efficiently improve listening fluency, after listening-while-reading a text, learners should be given a chance to listen to the text once again without the assistance of written text (Chang & Millett, 2014). This way, they will not learn to disregard aural texts or develop over-reliance on written text.

Listening in the Classroom

In this section, we discuss extensive listening activities that can be employed both inside and outside of the classroom as part of an extensive listening program. L2 learners need to be able to extend classroom learning into real-life learning so that what they learn in class can benefit them in real life.

Finding Texts That Suit Learners' Needs and Interests

Today, spoken texts are available over the internet in the form of stories, movies, tutorials, talks, documentaries, videocasts, serials, news and current affairs, TV shows, and video clips, to name a few. They are available in the form of audio recordings and videos accompanied by written texts of many forms. They can be found on many English learning websites. The following are some popular websites that provide listening materials for all grades:

- ELLLO/English Listening Lesson Library Online (www.elllo.org)
- BBC Learning English (www.bbc.co.uk/learningenglish)
- British Council LearnEnglish (learnenglish.britishcouncil.org)
- Breaking News English (breakingnewsenglish.com)

- Randall's ESL Cyber Listening Lab (www.esl-lab.com)
- ManyThings.org (www.manythings.org)

For upper intermediate and preadvanced learners, there are voluminous inspiring and informative talks available on TED (www.ted.com) and TEDEd (ed.ted.com) websites. The varied topics made available on these websites will appeal to many L2 learners.

Audiobooks of graded readers are another popular form of extensive listening material. Because extensive listening is informed by the same theoretical principles as extensive reading, the audiobooks of graded readers are suitable to be used in extensive listening programs (Waring, n.d., Renandya & Farrell, 2011; Ridgway, 2000; Reinders & Cho, 2010; Yonezawa & Ware, 2008; Chang, 2012). However, learners may find aural texts more difficult than written texts because of unclear sounds, blurred word boundaries, unfamiliar accents, and fast speech, among other reasons. As the difficulty level of the audio material is obviously above that of its written counterpart, in extensive listening programs, learners are recommended to listen to materials that are one or two levels below their reading proficiency level (Waring, n.d.).

Unfortunately, most graded readers for extensive listenings are not available free of charge. One website that provides a listening library full of more than 1,000 graded reader audiobooks is the Extensive Reading Central website (www.er-central.com). The graded readers developed and sold by publishers are often accompanied by audio recordings that can be used in extensive listening programs. Every publishing company uses a specific grade-level standard. Websites such as Lit2Go (etc.usf.edu/lit2go) and Readworks (www.readworks.org) offer free graded readers not developed specifically for extensive listenings but potentially useful for extensive listening programs. They also use different levelling standards than those used by commercial graded reader publishers.

When finding listening materials for extensive listening by themselves, learners should begin by finding the appropriate materials for their level. They can easily do this by completing the following simple self-assessment, which is adapted from the extensive reading approach.

1. **The 5-Finger Rule:** Play the middle part of an aural text for 1 minute. As students listen, ask them to hold up a finger for every word they do not know. Use the guidelines presented in Figure 1

   Once the students find their level, they can continue listening at that level until they are ready to move up to the next level.

2. **Pick One Random Level:** Students listen to an aural text and then ask themselves the following questions:

   a. Can I understand about 90% or more of the content (the story or information)?

   b. Can I understand over 95% of the vocabulary and grammar?

   c. Can I listen and understand without having to stop the audio?

(Waring, n.d.)

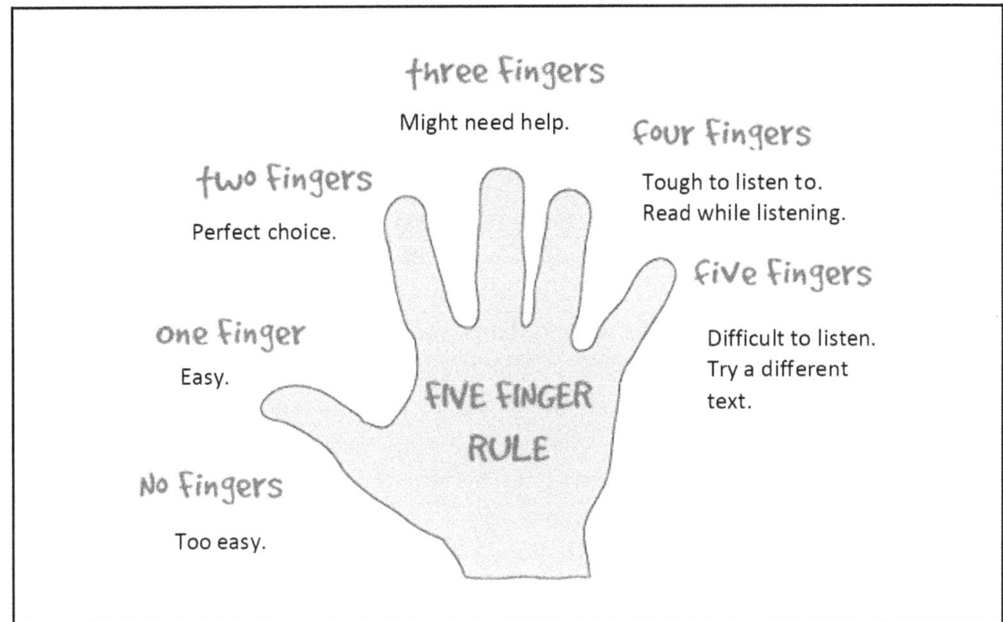

Figure 1. The 5-finger rule guidelines.

> "Yes" answers to the three questions mean they have found extensive listening material that suits their proficiency and comprehension level. If one (or more) of their answers is "no," the text may be too difficult, and they may want to try one level below. If they think the text is too easy or they can understand it 100% without any problems, they may want to try a more difficult text. This self-assessment can be done until they have found the right level that does not make them feel anxious or bored. Once they have found it, they can continue listening to the other texts of the same level.

These two techniques can be applied to materials from English language teaching/learning websites or audiobooks of graded readers. Because different web developers and graded reader publishers use their own labelling and levelling system, it is a good idea to encourage students to do this every time they use a new website or graded reader publisher.

Students should also find topics they are interested in. Let them listen to a text for a minute. If they do not enjoy listening to the text, suggest they find another one.

Narrow and Repeated Listening

Instead of quickly switching from one topic to another, Krashen (1996) and Dupuy (1999) suggest that beginning L2 learners focus on listening to one topic at a time so that they can expand their language competence at their own pace.

Learners should be encouraged to listen to a text as many times as they like and at their leisure, because it enhances comprehension and promotes listening fluency (Chang

& Read, 2007; Nation & Newton, 2009). Nevertheless, low-proficiency learners may need additional support because they lack linguistic competence and experience (Chang & Read, 2006). Krashen (1996) shared his own experience in learning his L2 by listening to the same text repeatedly, which he said made him more interested in the text and gave him the chance to learn something new every time. Depending on the level of the L2 learners, they can listen to texts of one topic, of one genre, or created by the same person. In addition to narrow listening and repeated listening, encouraging learners to listen to a topic from different perspectives is also another way of fostering critical listening.

To implement narrow listening with students, you can encourage your learners to choose some topics they are interested in. After that, they search for short audio recordings or videos on the topic on the web. Encourage them to share the resources they have found with others in the class using your class course management system, other online learning platform, or a cloud storage system. This way, the class can have a collection of resources that everyone can have access to.

Learners can also create their own recordings by interviewing proficient speakers of the language. Have the class work on some questions they will ask the speakers about in advance and then share their interviews with the class so that everyone has access to the narrow topics. Once learners find multiple recordings of the same topic, they can listen to them till they find the topic comprehensible and are ready to move on to another topic.

Listening in Sequences and Series Listening

There is no limit to how long extensive listening materials should be. Should learners find a long text, they can listen in sequences. Because the focus of extensive listening is on enjoyment, learners do not need to finish listening to a text in one seating. Similar to when reading for pleasure, in extensive listening, learners can decide when to stop and when to continue to the next part of a text. Stopping a few times when listening to a long text may trigger their curiosity. To make listening more exciting, you can even encourage them to predict what may happen next to the characters or how a story may flow.

Learners can also listen in sequences to stories presented in the form of series. Series listening resembles real-life listening. L2 learners often watch their favorite TV series in their L1 for months or even years. They follow the plot of the stories and familiarize themselves with the characters in the story. Watching serials is easier because the lexical load of the episodes of the same program is lower than that of unconnected programs (Rodgers & Webb, 2011). Series listening lets learners relate to a story; it makes them curious and want to talk about what will happen to the characters. Using drama series is more advisable because there is more "language" used in the conversation between the characters than that of action movies, for instance.

To give learners the chance to get acquainted and grow with the story, we recommend regular listening or viewing. Encourage your learners to listen to one episode each week and talk about it with other learners. Alternatively, have students write short comments or reflections after listening to the series on the class course management system or other online learning platform, where you and other students can discuss the story online. They can also write it in the form of listening journals. Asking students prediction questions, such as what is going to happen to the main character next week, will get them more involved in the story and allow them to recycle the language used in the series. Reflective questions, such as whom they like best and what scene they like most, and other personal opinions about the story will allow them to relate to the story at a deeper level.

Listening-While-Reading

Though listening extensively to large amounts of comprehensible language is considered a key factor for developing listening skills, previous research has shown that listening without any support can be difficult for beginning L2 learners (Chang & Read, 2006). Research suggests listening can be done simultaneously with reading (Nation & Newton, 2009; Chang & Millett, 2013; Chang, 2009; Brown et al., 2008) to assist aural text comprehension as well as vocabulary building. Beginners and intermediate learners find watching subtitled or captioned videos helps them with vocabulary learning more than when the textual input is not available (Perez et al., 2013; Peters et al., 2016). However, students should be reminded that subtitles and captions may not always be verbatim representations of the spoken words.

Listening-while-reading facilitates low-proficiency listeners in creating the aural–written verification stage that they need to develop auditory discrimination skills (Vandergrift, 2007), and supports high-proficiency listeners in word recognition skills (Vandergrift, 2007; Osada, 2001). It also helps listeners develop an awareness of form-meaning relationships (Osada, 2001). Learners can use transcripts to help them understand aural texts better as well as to confirm words they do not know or could not catch in the recording (Ivone, 2013). After reading and listening to a text, learners should be encouraged to listen to it several times without the transcript to help them focus on the aural input and avoid overreliance on written text (Chang & Millett, 2014).

Ask learners to listen to a text while reading the written script in a low voice or to read it silently. The activity of "reading aloud using the text or script while listening" is called overlapping (Yonezawa & Ware, 2008, p. 1256). It will help learners create a relationship between the written form and the spoken form of words. It can also help with pronunciation and reading speed. Increasingly, learners will be able to read and listen to words and expression at the same speed as the speaker.

Follow-Up Activities in Extensive Listening

The essence of extensive listening is the listening itself; the more listening students do, the more listening benefits they are likely to enjoy. However, when extensive listening is integrated into a formal course, there are questions related to its accountability in terms of assessment. How do you know whether your students are really doing the listening? Mayora (2017) suggests that learners do "comprehension oriented, non-intrusive tasks" (p. 102) to show that they have completed the extensive listening activity. Follow-up activities may take the form of writing or telling an appreciation sentence or paragraph, expressing the main idea, or creating a summary in their native language. More authentic tasks that "reflect real-life listening tasks such as dictation, stimulus-response, note-taking, editing and retelling can also be conducted" (Ivone & Renandya, 2019, p. 249). Depending on the level of proficiency of your learners, you can conduct the follow-up activities in their L1 or in English. Following, we discuss interesting tasks you can assign for learners to show they have responsibly completed the extensive listening activities.

In extensive listening, there are many choices of informal follow-up activities that can be done after the main listening activity. When performing them in class, students can work in pairs, small groups, or as a whole class. Online, students can use social media or the course management system to share and discuss interesting points from the listening materials. The discussion can be typed or recorded and then posted or uploaded as files. Students can also work in small groups, record the discussion, and then upload it online. Other students or groups can listen to each other's postings or recordings and give comments. All of the activities can be completed in spoken and written forms.

1. *Reflect.* Students are given a chance to think about a text after listening to it. Because extensive listening is about listening for pleasure, it is a way of personalising the listening experience. Learners share their opinions about the story/topic or their personal experience concerning the story/topic. After listening, they answer questions, such as
    a. Do you like the story?
    b. Who do you think is the kindest (most evil, strongest, etc.) and why?
    c. If you were to choose a movie star to play the main character part, who would you choose, and why?
2. *Retell.* This follow-up activity gives students the chance to listen to a text and then use their own words to retell it. They can retell both fiction and nonfiction.
3. *Transfer.* Instead of putting their efforts into a verbal summary, students transfer what they have learned from an aural text into other visual formats, such as drawing, pictures, charts, and comic strips, to name a few.
4. *Tweak.* To make the listening experience more personalised and to engage students in thinking about the texts they just listened to, assign them to do some modification to an aural text by changing something, for example a character, the ending, the plot, or the setting.

Progress Monitoring

The use of listening journals in extensive listening can promote listening autonomy because they provide guidance for learners in planning, monitoring, and evaluating their listening activities (Chen, 2017). These journals usually document details of the listener (e.g., name, class), the texts (e.g., title, length, source), the extensive listening activities (e.g., date, length), and the results of any follow-up activities. You can use a structured listening journal template or diary-like journal, and you can guide learners in writing their journals by providing open-ended prompts as pointers of what they should include. The questions can be about the text or the listening experience.

If you need to assign grades to students, you can develop scoring rubrics using prompt questions given to students as assessment criteria. You can give scores based on the completion and quality of their answers. Follow-up activities that result in products or projects can also be assessed using scoring rubrics. To encourage students to regularly listen to aural text in English, set minimum word counts or minimum listening times for students to achieve every week and by the end of the semester. We strongly suggest combined assessment methods to avoid overreliance on the more typical listening comprehension test commonly used in listening courses.

Extensive listening can take place in the language classroom and outside, at a time that is convenient for learners, and through carrying out what they enjoy doing. Moreover, it can be conducted as an individual as well as group or whole-class activity. It gives language learners the chance to learn L2 listening in uplifting, fun, and engaging ways by maximizing exposure to comprehensible and compelling input. Aural texts and multimedia texts that combine audio and visuals to complement each other can be used because listening-while-reading makes aural texts more comprehensible, and multimedia input improves comprehension. By spending an extended period listening to a large amount of comprehensible and enjoyable listening material, learners can learn at their own pace with no intervention from the teacher. They can also listen repeatedly or narrowly, and listening-while-reading can make the aural input more comprehensible. When extensive listening is conducted in class, students can perform nonintrusive tasks after completing activities, such as writing short and simple comments that explain something they appreciated or felt, show the main idea, or a provide a summary or review. We believe that pedagogically sound ideas derived from the research into extensive listening, which we outlined in this chapter, can be productively explored and implemented to make our intensive listening lessons more effective in supporting the development of our students' listening proficiency.

References

Brown, R., Waring, R., & Donkaewbua, S. (2008). Incidental vocabulary acquisition from reading, reading-while-listening, and listening to stories. *Reading in a Foreign Language, 20*(2), 136–63.

Chang, A. C.-S. (2009). Gains to L2 listeners from reading while listening vs. listening only in comprehending short stories. *System, 37*(4), 652–663. https://doi.org/10.1016/j.system.2009.09.009

Chang, C.-S. A. (2012). Gains to L2 Learners from extensive listening: Listening development, vocabulary acquisition and perceptions of the intervention. *Hong Kong Journal of Applied Linguistics, 14*(1), 25–47.

Chang, A. C.-S., & Millett, S. (2013). Improving reading rates and comprehension through timed repeated reading. *Reading in a Foreign Language, 25*(2), 126–148.

Chang, C.-S., & Millett, S. (2014). The effect of extensive listening on developing L2 listening fluency: Some hard evidence. *ELT Journal, 68*(1), 31–40. https://doi.org/10.1093/elt/cct052

Chang, A., Millett, S., & Renandya, W. A. (2019). Developing listening fluency through supported extensive listening practice. *RELC Journal, 50*(3), 422–438. https://doi.org/10.1177/0033688217751468

Chang, A. C.-S., & Read, J. (2006). The effects of listening support on the listening performance of EFL learners. *TESOL Quarterly, 40*, 375–397. https://doi.org/10.2307/40264527

Chang, A. C. S., & Read, J. (2007). Support for foreign language listeners: Its effectiveness and limitations. *RELC Journal: A Journal of Language Teaching and Research, 38*(3), 375–394. https://doi.org/10.1177/0033688207085853

Chen, C. W. Y. (2017). Guided listening with listening journals and curated materials: A metacognitive approach. *Innovation in Language Learning and Teaching, 13*(2), 133–146. https://doi.org/10.1080/17501229.2017.1381104

Dupuy, B. C. (1999). Narrow listening: An alternative way to develop and enhance listening comprehension in students of French as a foreign language. *System, 27*(3), 351–361. https://doi.org/10.1016/S0346-251X(99)00030-5

Earl, L. M., & Katz, S. (2006). *Rethinking classroom assessment with purpose in mind*. Manitoba Education, Citizenship and Youth. http://digitalcollection.gov.mb.ca/awweb/pdfopener?smd=1&did=12503&md=1.

Frommer, J. (2006). Wired for sound: Teaching listening via computers and the world wide web. In R. P. Donaldson & M. A. Haggstrom (Eds.), *Changing language education through CALL* (pp. 67–93). Routledge.

Goh, C. (1999). What learners know about the factors that influence their listening comprehension? *Hong Kong Journal of Applied Linguistics, 4*(1), 17–42.

Graham, S. (2006). Listening comprehension: The learners' perspective. *System, 34*(2), 165–182. https://doi.org/10.1016/j.system.2005.11.001

Hasan, A. S. (2000). Learners' perceptions of listening comprehension problems. *Language, Culture and Curriculum, 13*(2), 137–153. https://doi.org/10.1080/07908310008666595

Ivone, F. M. (2013). *Evaluating English Listening Websites for Independent Study*. School of Languages and Comparative Cultural Studies, The University of Queensland. PhD Thesis.

Ivone, F. M., & Renandya, W. A. (2019). Extensive listening and viewing in ELT. *TEFLIN Journal, 30*(2), 237–256. http://dx.doi.org/10.15639/teflinjournal.v30i2/237-256

Krashen, S. D. (1996). The case for narrow listening. *System, 24*(1), 97–100. https://doi.org/10.1016/0346-251X(95)00054-N

Krashen, S. D., Lee, S. Y., & Lao, C. (2017). *Comprehensible and compelling: The causes and effects of free voluntary reading*. ABC-CLIO, LLC.

Loewen, S. (2014). *Introduction to instructed second language acquisition*. Routledge. https://doi.org/10.4324/9780203117811

Lynch, T. (1998). Theoretical perspectives on listening. *Annual Review of Applied Linguistics, 18*, 3–19. https://doi.org/10.1017/S0267190500003457

Matsuo, S. (2015). Extensive listening inside and outside the classroom. *Kwansei Gakuin University Humanities Review, 20*, 109–115.

Mayora, C. A. (2017). Extensive listening in a Colombian university: Process, product, and perceptions. *HOW, 24*(1), 101–121. https://doi.org/10.19183/how.24.1.311

Nation, I. S. P., & Newton, J. 2009. *Teaching ESL/ EFL listening and speaking*. Routledge.

Osada, N. (2001). What strategy do less proficient learners employ in listening comprehension? A reappraisal of bottom-up and top-down processing. *Journal of the Pan-Pacific Association of Applied Linguistics, 5*, 73–90.

Perez, M. M., van den Noortgate, W., & Desmet, P. (2013). Captioned video for L2 listening and vocabulary learning: A meta-analysis. *System, 41*(3), 720–739. https://doi.org/10.1016/j.system.2013.07.013

Peters, E., Heynen, E., & Puimege, E. (2016). Learning vocabulary through audiovisual input: The differential effect of L1 subtitles and captions. *System, 63*, 134–148. https://doi.org/10.1016/j.system.2016.10.002

Reinders, H., & Cho, M. Y. (2010). Extensive listening practice and input enhancement using mobile phones: Encouraging out-of-class learning with mobile phones. *TESL-EJ, 14*(2), 1–7.

Renandya, W. A. (2012). The tape is too fast. *Modern English Teacher, 21*(3), 5–9.

Renandya, W. A., & Farrell, T. (2011). Teacher, the tape is too fast! Extensive listening in ELT. *ELT Journal, 65*(1), 52–59. https://doi.org/10.1093/elt/ccq015

Renandya, W. A., & Jacobs, G. M. (2016). Extensive reading and listening in the L2 classroom. In W. A. Renandya & H. P. Widodo (Eds.), *English language teaching today: Linking theory and practice* (pp. 97–110). Springer, Cham. https://doi.org/10.1007/978-3-319-38834-2_8

Richards, J. C. (2005). Second thoughts on teaching listening. *RELC Journal, 36*(1), 85–92. https://doi.org/10.1177/0033688205053484

Ridgway, T. (2000). Listening strategies: I beg your pardon? *ELT Journal, 54*(2), 179–185. https://doi.org/10.1093/elt/54.2.179

Rodgers, M. P. H., & Webb, S. (2011). Narrow viewing: The vocabulary in related television programs. *TESOL Quarterly, 45*(4), 689–717. https://doi.org/10.5054/tq.2011.268062

Rost, M. (1990). *Listening in language learning*. Longman Inc.

Rost, M. (2002). *Teaching and researching listening*. Pearson Education Limited.

Rubin, J. (1994). A review of second language listening comprehension research. *Modern Language Journal, 78*(2), 199–221. DOI: 10.2307/329010

Vandergrift, L. (2007). Recent developments in second and foreign language listening comprehension research. *Language Teaching, 40*(2), 191–210. https://doi.org/10.1017/S0261444807004338

Vandergrift, L., & Goh, C. C. M. (2012). *Teaching and learning second language listening: Metacognition in action*. Routledge.

Waring, R. (n.d.). Starting extensive listening. Retrieved from http://www.robwaring.org/er/ER_info/starting_extensive_listening.htm.

Waring, R. (2008). Starting an extensive listening program. *Extensive Reading in Japan: The Journal of the JALT Extensive Reading Special Interest Group, 1*(1) 7–9.

Yeldham, M. (2016). Approaches to L2 listening instruction. *The European Journal of Applied Linguistics and TEFL, 5*(2), 31–42.

Yonezawa, M., & Ware, J. L. (2008). Examining extensive listening. In K. Bradford-Watts, T. Muller, & M. Swanson (Eds.), *JALT2007 Conference Proceedings*. JALT. (pp. 1255–1271).

FRANCISCA MARIA IVONE teaches at the Department of English, Universitas Negeri Malang, Indonesia. She researches English language teaching, technology-enhanced language learning, extensive listening (EL) and viewing (EV), extensive reading (ER), learning autonomy, and collaborative learning. She employed and benefited from ER, EL, and EV during her language learning years. Today, she teaches ER courses and blends ER, EL, and EV programs into the language skill courses she teaches.

DR. WILLY A. RENANDYA is a language teacher educator with extensive teaching experience in Asia. He currently teaches applied linguistics courses at the National Institute of Education, Nanyang Technological University, Singapore. His publications include *Methodology in Language Teaching: An Anthology of Current Practice* (2002, Cambridge University Press) and *Student Centered Cooperative Learning* (2019, Springer International). He maintains a large language teacher professional development forum called Teacher Voices (www.facebook.com/groups/teachervoices).

CHAPTER 12

BETH SHEPPARD

Learning From Mistakes in Listening

Listening in Real Life

In my training to be a language teacher, I was told that listening skills usually develop before speaking, and I came to believe that listening was an "easier" skill than speaking. I doubt that anyone told me this was the case; in my inexperience, I simply inferred one idea from the other.

During my first few semesters as a language teacher, I taught beginning level students (A1–A2 on the Common Framework of References for Languages [CEFR]; Council of Europe, 2001) in Mexico and Peru and didn't question my belief that listening was easier than speaking. On my return to the United States, I began teaching intermediate level (CEFR B1–B2) students. In my speaking/listening classes, I started to notice that students seemed to like the speaking portion better than the listening. Almost all of them scored higher on speaking assessments than on listening assessments. In supposedly interactive small group discussions, students often seemed to take turns speaking without really listening to each other. It seemed that speaking was "easier" than listening for these students.

This surprising realization (remember, I was still quite new to the profession) prompted me to reflect on my own experiences as an intermediate speaker of Spanish. I began to remember how I myself had dominated conversations because I was only able to follow when I mostly had the floor. Using my limited inventory of vocabulary and grammar, including plenty of circumlocutions and grammatical errors, I could express just about any thought to a patient conversation partner. My language knowledge was basically adequate for speaking. When it was time to listen, however, the speaker often didn't rely on the words and structures I happened to be familiar with, and they chose their own speed. Although it seemed I "should" have been able to understand their message, still I often failed to understand their actual speech. I had found listening to be more difficult than speaking at the intermediate level, just like my students.

It seemed that many students experience a kind of "intermediate valley" in listening. On further reflection, it looked to me like intermediate language learners struggle with listening more than any other language skill, and teachers struggle to help them. Why? How can we do better? How do listening skills develop at other levels? I became fascinated with listening instruction. I read everything I could find about this skill, and tried to apply it in my classroom. In this chapter, I would like to tell you about one facet of the answers I am exploring.

Listening in the Research

Listening is an important skill, because most learners use it more frequently than other language skills (Nunan, 1998, as cited in Nation & Newton, 2009, p. 37), and also because listening can unlock many opportunities for language input and further learning (e.g., Vandergrift, 2007). However, listening is also a challenging skill. Many language learners attest that it is their most difficult skill (e.g., Graham, 2006), and that listening makes them anxious (e.g., Kim, 2000; Elkhafaifi, 2005).

Quite a few studies have asked students what makes listening difficult for them. In open-ended interviews (e.g., Liu, 2002; Goh, 1999) and listening journals (e.g., Goh, 2000; Zeng, 2007), students report the following:

- They don't know all the words.
- They can't recognize known words in context.
- They perceive the speech as too fast.
- The sound is "blurred"—they can't separate it into words.
- They have trouble making sense of the grammar.
- They lose concentration or have trouble remembering.
- They feel nervous and anxious.

As language teachers, we need to help students overcome these challenges. However, listening can also be a challenging skill to teach, because it occurs mostly invisibly inside the mind of the student. What teachers hear when they listen to a passage can be quite different from what their students are experiencing (Cauldwell, 2018), so it can be difficult to know how to help. In the face of these challenges, teachers often default to a conventional lesson format which may be familiar to you:

1. Begin with activities that build or activate students' background knowledge about the topic at hand.
2. Read and explain the comprehension questions or other content-related task.
3. Play a recorded audio text one or more times.

4. Students answer the questions or complete the task.
5. Check comprehension questions and explain correct answers.

This plan focuses on producing students' correct answers to comprehension questions, as if understanding the content of a particular text were the goal of the class. When students struggle, teachers may give extra hints in Steps 1 or 2, or extend Step 5 with detailed explanations of the information that students were unable to understand while listening. But how does any of this actually teach students *how* to listen? This style of listening instruction basically boils down to repeated assessment, in which students mostly are not successful. Is there any wonder that many students report that listening is a stressful skill? Comprehension questions and similar tasks provide listening practice as well as assessment, but is this instruction? Can't we do better?

In the last 20 years, many scholars have criticized current listening instruction for its focus on the *product* of listening in the form of correct answers to comprehension questions, rather than on explicit instruction for the *process* of second language (L2) listening. At this point, it can be considered a settled consensus that language instructors must do more than repeatedly test listening skills with audio texts and comprehension questions (e.g., Vandergrift, 2004; Richards, 2005; Field, 2008b; Vandergrift & Goh, 2012; Siegel, 2014). The question is not whether teachers need to teach the listening process, but how they can do so effectively.

Two main approaches emerge from the literature on listening instruction. One calls for a focus on bottom-up listening skills, or decoding of the sound stream into phonemes and words (also see Chapters 2, 3, and 6 for more on these specific aspects of bottom-up listening). The proponents of this approach suggest that students should work intensively with short texts, learning through focused practice in specific areas based on a teacher's diagnosis of their listening challenges (e.g., Cauldwell, 2018; Siegel & Siegel, 2015). The other main approach focuses on developing students' metacognitive skills, or their ability to think about their own listening and learning processes to effectively select and organize strategies for listening success (also see Chapter 1). The proponents of this approach suggest that students should build their skills through student collaboration during repeated, self-directed listening practice in which students develop and apply skills such as planning for listening, monitoring their comprehension, and applying strategies to solve comprehension problems (e.g., Vandergrift & Goh, 2012).

These two approaches may seem to be in tension with one another, but in fact many authors note that they complement each other well. Students need a balance of instruction in both bottom-up and top-down listening skills, although the literature does indicate an imbalance in current instructional practices, with more attention needed on bottom-up processes (e.g., Graham et al., 2014; Siegel, 2014). In fact, learners need a wide variety of tools in order to best improve their listening skills: lots of fluency-building practice, strategies to manage what they don't hear, techniques to diagnose challenges and solve specific decoding problems, and self-awareness to notice and manage all of the above.

In this chapter, I would like to focus on one of the aforementioned needs: a way to diagnose specific decoding problems. Both students and teachers need a better understanding of students' specific listening challenges. This is really quite tricky because, as I mentioned, student listening is much more difficult to observe than their speaking. Listening is fleeting and occurs inside the listener's mind. How can we observe and diagnose its moment-to-moment progress?

One way is to ask learners about their listening experiences. This type of introspection has some advantages, because, after all, the listeners themselves are the only ones who truly know what they are thinking. Studies that use interviews and listening journals, such as Liu (2002), Goh (1999, 2000), and Zeng (2007), rely on delayed introspection. Learners report about their listening experiences significantly after they are finished, and the disadvantage is that their memories may not be completely reliable. However, these studies provide useful information about students' metacognition—how do they *think* they listen? Other studies ask students to reflect more immediately on their listening experiences, usually by pausing a listening text and asking participants what they are thinking (e.g., Vandergrift, 2003) or how confident they are in their comprehension (Ward, 2018). Immediate introspection is more unfiltered and probably more reliable from the standpoint of memory, but it also breaks up the listening experience and may change how students listen because the added task of reporting about listening is an extra mental load. More importantly, what listeners know about their listening is only part of the story. It seems likely that L2 learners may be unaware of important aspects of what they are able and unable to perceive while listening.

Another way to approach the question of what happens inside L2 learners' minds while they listen is to observe what listeners understand as they hear a text, compare this to the speakers' message, and try figure out what's going wrong. Although we can't directly observe the process of aural understanding, we can observe it indirectly by eliciting and then analyzing a response produced in speaking, writing, or other actions. In the literature, these responses have been elicited via a variety of approaches, including dictation, transcription, oral repetition, listening clozes, note-taking, and comprehension questions, each with its advantages and disadvantages (Pemberton, 1995). For example, Cross (2009) asked students to take notes on an authentic news recording and then write out all the information they heard. Cross then analyzed their writing clause by clause to find decoding errors. Emadi (2015) elicited oral repetition of phrases from an audio recording, with feedback from a teacher, and recorded these oral exchanges for analysis. Gao (2014) recorded an entire passage as a series of chunks (three to 11 words in length) and had students transcribe them and then answer a multiple-choice question about challenges after each chunk. Liu (2002) had students follow a gapped transcript while listening and fill in five- to seven-word phrases in the gaps. Field (2008a), Estes (2014), Sheppard and Butler (2017), and Ward (2018) had learners listen to extended texts in which pauses had been inserted at irregular intervals and write the most recent phrase (four to five words) during each pause. Recently, errors in automatic speech recognition (ASR) have also been used as an analog for learners' errors. For example,

Mirzaei et al. (2017) compared ASR errors with mistakes produced by students in partial transcriptions and found that students made mistakes in the same phrases as the ASR system.

Many of these studies include typologies of error types in their results. These include errors related to the following:

- word boundaries (Cross, 2009; Field, 2008a; Liu, 2002; Sheppard & Butler, 2017; also see Chapters 3, 5, and 6)
- phonetic features of individual words, such as number of syllables (Field, 2008a), beginning with a vowel or consonant (Estes, 2014), and mistakes that maintain the correct first phoneme or syllable (Cross, 2009; Ward, 2018; Sheppard & Butler, 2017; also see Chapters 2 and 3 for more on phonetic features of words and the importance of syllables in English listening)
- unknown or infrequent words (Emadi, 2015; Liu, 2002, Sheppard & Butler, 2017, Ward, 2018) or misperceptions of known words (Liu, 2002), and unfamiliar collocations (Emadi, 2015; Sheppard & Butler, 2017; also see Chapter 4 for more on listening and collocations)
- weak forms, especially of function words (Estes, 2014; Field, 2008a; Liu, 2002; Sheppard & Butler, 2017; also see Chapter 7 for more information related to listening to weak forms)

Research that elicits and analyzes student listening errors can provide valuable information about what students actually perceive when they listen. This can be of great use to teachers because, as Cauldwell (2018) put it, "there is a gap between what L1 [first language] and expert-listener teachers believe they hear in the sound substance (tidy forms) and what their students encounter (untidy and for them, undecodable forms)" (p. 24). The "untidiness" of speech is often hidden from proficient listeners with their automatic processing and their focus on meaning. Techniques that allow for analysis of student listening mistakes can help increase teachers' awareness of the acoustic blur, or mushy lack of precision, that characterizes spontaneous speech (Cauldwell, 2018; Liu, 2002).

The teaching suggestions in this chapter focus on a technique used by Field (2004, 2008a), Estes (2014), Sheppard and Butler (2017), and Ward (2018) known as *paused transcription*. In this technique, students are asked to listen to a graded audio text into which pauses have been inserted at irregular intervals. During each pause, subjects write down the last phrase (four to five words) that they heard.

> The rationale for this method is that it taps into a listening process that replicates a real-world one. Subjects listen to the recording with a view to following its meaning, and it is only when a pause occurs that they switch attention to word level. Memory effects are limited by the fact that subjects are asked to transcribe around four or five words—well within the range of Miller's (1956) seven plus or minus two. Furthermore . . . listeners retain verbatim word forms until major clause boundaries and only then "wrap

them up" by replacing them with representations in propositional form. (Field, 2008a, pp. 16–17)

Researchers then analyze the resulting transcriptions, usually by coding each word as correct or incorrect, and asking questions about what kinds of words or contexts led to student errors. Sometimes, the transcribed phrases are also qualitatively analyzed for insights into what students heard.

Error analysis via paused transcription can give the researcher a way to peek inside of students' internal listening process, just a hint of what is going on inside. Of course, it does have some drawbacks because it still depends on students' reproduction of what they heard, even though the delay is very short (Field, 2008a). In addition, students' writing processes can obscure evidence of their comprehension, although, of course, spelling errors are ignored when coding transcriptions if researchers can correctly identify the intended word.

Studies of L2 listening based on paused transcription have found that language learners decode surprisingly few of the words in the input when listening. Table 1 shows results from the four studies, all using graded texts supposedly appropriate to the level of the participating L2 learners. These transcription percentages indicate significant problems with decoding, because other research has estimated that listeners need to decode 95% of the words in audio input for successful comprehension (Van Zeeland & Schmitt, 2012).

In addition, qualitative analysis of students' responses in paused transcription can provide insight into students' strategies when they are unable to successfully decode a word or phrase. Field (2004) discusses three strategies that learners might select when they encounter an unrecognized word in listening. They might take

1. a phonological approach (attempt to transcribe the sounds they heard),
2. a lexical approach (attempt to match approximately to a known word), or
3. a zero approach (no transcription).

Field (2004) found that his subjects selected a lexical approach more frequently than expected, and that lexical matches often were not semantically appropriate. In other words, when students heard a word they didn't correctly recognize, they often transcribed a known word, even if that word didn't make any sense in context. This finding is particularly important in light of evidence (using a different research technique) that L2 listeners are more reluctant than L1 listeners to change their decoding hypotheses when the continuation of the message provides evidence against them (Field, 2008c). In other words, once students have misinterpreted a word, they carry forward that misinterpretation even as it makes the following input more and more confusing.

Improved metacognitive skills can help L2 listeners to better vet their own perceptions. Metacognition means thinking about thinking; for example, when students think about how they listen or when they reflect on their progress in listening, they are practicing metacognition. Vandergrift and Goh (2012) organize metacognitive skills for L2 listening into three categories: planning, monitoring, and evaluation. They note that in

Table 1. Percent Successful Transcription in Paused Transcription Studies

Researcher	Text(s)	Listener Group	% Successfully Transcribed
Field (2008a)	Second language listening comprehension materials	Intermediate ESL undergraduate class, lower placement score	40
		Intermediate ESL undergraduate class, higher placement score	60
Estes (2014)	Unscripted narrative recordings produced by Foreign Language Department for pedagogical purposes	Intermediate Spanish learners (2nd year course at university)	60
		High intermediate Spanish learners (3rd year course at university)	60
		Advanced Spanish learners (4th year course for Spanish majors)	71
Sheppard & Butler (2017)	Textbook (Level 2 of 6 in program)	Preintermediate ESL students (Level 3 of 6 in program)	65
	Textbook (Level 5 of 6 in program)	Intermediate ESL students (Level 6 of 6 in program)	75
Ward (2018)	English for academic purposes coursebook	Midlevel ESL graduate students: in a CEFR B1–B2 course, eliminating students with highest and lowest placement test scores	46

Note: CEFR = Common European Framework of Reference, ESL = English as a second language

think-aloud protocols, "skilled listeners reveal using about twice as many metacognitive strategies as their less-skilled counterparts, primarily comprehension monitoring" (p. 65). Having students check and analyze their own mistakes in paused transcription may be a promising way to build the skill and habit of monitoring their comprehension.

Listening in the Classroom

I love to have an error-friendly classroom. Probably, most teachers try to remind their students that mistakes are an important part of learning, and one of the ways in which this is true is that mistakes help us understand what we still need to do. Certainly, an analysis of errors is central to a diagnostic approach (Field, 2008b) to listening instruction. But beyond just making good use of student errors, if I make it clear that I see every mistake as a gift, if I collect them with joy, I feel it can help reduce my students' listening anxiety.

One meaningful way to elicit students' listening mistakes is through paused transcription as a classroom activity. Bringing this research technique into the classroom can help teachers and learners discover what learners actually hear when they listen to a sample of spoken language. This process of discovery can help diagnose and develop their decoding skills while simultaneously empowering students to increase their self-awareness by analyzing their own listening and checking their progress. In this section, I would like to tell you about students' responses to paused transcription and share step-by-step instructions for implementing this and other techniques of listening error analysis in your own classroom.

I have used paused transcription with both beginning and intermediate English learners. I believe it will also work well with advanced students, given appropriate texts. I found that beginning students struggled with the instructions and often could only transcribe very few of the words. Although they had already heard the textbook audio recordings I used for paused transcription in previous meaning-focused activities, most of them were not able to decode and write enough of the words for a meaningful analysis of individual mistakes, and they seemed discouraged. With beginning students, I prefer to elicit listening mistakes through dictation or gap filling.

With intermediate and advanced students, classroom paused transcription activities can be quite successful. I suggest including this technique on a regular basis, so students have a chance to become very familiar with the activity instructions and the activity becomes easier over time. The first time you present paused transcription, the focus should be entirely on understanding the activity and completing it successfully. Explain the instructions, then give a brief warm-up text with just a couple of pauses as an example. After showing the answers to the warm-up activity, ask students to confirm the instructions with each other in their L1s. When students complete a paused transcription activity, the audio text can be familiar to them (paused transcription activities following meaning-focused activities using the recording) or new to them (a preview for future meaning-oriented activities with that text).

Here are step-by step instructions for creating paused transcription activities:

1. Select an audio text. I prefer to recycle audio texts that also serve another (usually meaning-focused) purpose in the course, perhaps from the textbook. If the text is long, select a 2- to 5-minute excerpt.
2. Listen to the text (don't read the transcript for this step) and scrawl down some good potential target phrases. These should be at the ends of thought units, clauses, or phrases. You can choose by a variety of criteria. These are your listening targets, so what do you want to aim for? Maybe you want fairly clear and easy phrases with known words. Maybe you want to target reduced phrases, or potentially unknown words, or a vocabulary list, or challenging word boundaries. Initially note down a few more target phrases than you really need, along with the approximate time for each phrase. Then, check your list and eliminate a few, making sure that the phrases are irregularly spaced and that the target phrases include mostly unique words (avoid frequent repetition of the same target words).
3. Load the audio file into editing software, such as Audacity (www.audacityteam.org). Locate the end of the first target phrase and insert 10–15 seconds of silence; then, about half a second into the silence, insert a short (e.g., half a second) tone that's just a little bit louder than the audio. Continue with your

selected phrases, and then export your audio. If you aren't able to edit your digital audio file, you can also plan to pause the recording at the end of your target phrases as you play it in class, or read the text yourself with pauses. However, the edited audio file has real advantages, and I encourage you to try it even if you have never edited digital audio before. It's not hard!

4. Make a handout with instructions, spaces for the target phrases, and reflection questions. See example in Appendix A.
5. After students complete the paused transcription, have them check their own work. Give quite specific instructions for correcting the transcriptions: Have them circle every word that they transcribed correctly and write the number of correct words on the side. Students can write the correct words in another color if they wish (Appendix B). Finally, make sure that students reflect on their transcriptions.

You can learn a lot about student listening progress by analyzing paused transcription results, but I suggest that this activity is even more valuable if students develop metacognitive skills by analyzing and reflecting on their own results. This makes it less time-consuming for you, too! In this reflection step, ask students to answer simple questions, such as these:

- Which phrase was difficult?
- Which phrase was easy?
- Which phrase had an interesting mistake?
- Which phrase had an important mistake for your comprehension?
- Why did you hear it that way?

I have been very impressed by students' insights about their listening. They have been able to notice patterns of mistakes, propose reasons for mistakes, and suggest ways to improve their performance. Here are some statements from students' answers to reflection questions after paused transcription:

- The word is singular but I wrote plural. I often take this type of mistake.
- Correct is "a twenty-minute session." I wrote "pretty" instead of "twenty"—both of them have "ty" at the last of these words. It was the reason I mistook.
- The speaker said "this pain relief medicine," but I could catch "medicine" only. Also, I wrote "patients" before "medicine" because I associated the word from the sound [p] of pain maybe.
- The speaker spoke "applies to all" relatively slowly. However the speaker extremely abbreviated the phrase's pronunciation. Additionally, the speaker doesn't put stress on any word!! It sounds like "apply tall." But I didn't catch the word "apply." I think it's because I was too relaxed due to his voice being slow to listen with all ears. I wrote "grammar of all."

- The correct answer is "powered by the sun" but I wrote "power but song." Sun and song have similar pronunciation, but I should write correct answer through the meaning of the speaking.
- The answer is "to take part in a study." I heard "and" instead of "in a." However, I should have think the context, I might know that "in" came after "take part."

Such insights can be quite useful for students, particularly because they are able to generate them independently. As I mentioned earlier, the practice of monitoring comprehension is one aspect that differentiates more successful L2 listeners from their less successful peers (Vandergrift & Goh, 2012). As Schmidt (1990) brought to our attention with his noticing hypothesis, being aware of some aspect of language seems to help us to learn it. If we give learners opportunities and tools to really notice their own patterns of mistakes, these are likely to be more salient to them, and they are likely to be more able to monitor their comprehension for these mistakes as they listen. In addition, the paused transcription activity can provide students with an opportunity to see what they are hearing successfully when they circle correctly transcribed words. This helps transform a challenging task into an opportunity to focus on success.

Here are a range of comments students made when asked how they liked doing paused transcription activities.

- It was very difficult for me and so I didn't like this activity. I'm not good at understand what the speaker says in unclear pronunciation.
- It helps me a lot because I could hear and understand even if it's fast.
- It was a good practice to listen more carefully than usual listening. I want you to continue this practice in the same way.
- I prefer this practice to the blank practice [listening and filling in missing words].
- Doing paused transcription makes me understand how English words are pronounced in daily conversation including reductions.
- I like this because I can perceive how I couldn't understand and listen the phrases. This makes me concentrate all the words.
- I can know what I'm not good at. It helps me listen more carefully.
- I became to be able to more catch the sounds of "*–ed*" and "*–s*" than before. I want to continue this activity.
- It helps me find out the words even if I don't know the meaning of them.
- I can notice how I make mistakes, which helps me reflect myself.

Paused transcription is a promising activity, and I hope you will try it in your class. Although it was not a favorite for all students, many were able to give specific reasons why it helped them. Within a supportive classroom environment that values and appreciates mistakes, I believe this technique can indeed be helpful. It is simple to prepare, takes only 15 minutes of class time, and can help you and your students become more aware of how they hear listening input. It can also contribute to a culture of valuing and celebrating mistakes. Paused transcription is a great way to make listening mistakes visible, giving teachers and students in an error-friendly classroom the opportunity to analyze them.

You can also elicit listening mistakes in many other ways. For intermediate and advanced students, paused transcription has the advantage that it makes visible a target snapshot within normal extended listening processes. However, for beginning students, I like to use dictation and gap-filling. Even for beginners, dictation should be given at a natural speaking speed—adjustments for students' lower L2 proficiency are made through the simplicity of the sentences and their short length, not through unnatural delivery. In gap-fill activities, each gap in the transcript should ideally include several words, because listening is not completed one word at a time. Students write what they hear while listening. Even beginners can and should check their own answers, notice mistakes, and reflect on their progress, but the reflections will probably need to be in their L1. Students of all levels find these activities engaging and beneficial. It is rewarding to see their faces light up when they understand something new.

Regardless of how mistakes are elicited, in an error-friendly classroom they will be explicitly welcomed. Many of us mention the value of mistakes in the first week of class, but we can do much more to convince students that their mistakes are valued and appreciated. One way to do this is to greet each mistake with visible pleasure and a reminder of its value. For example, a teacher can make statements such as, "Wow, that was a really perfect mistake. It will help us so much with . . ." or, "See what a helpful mistake you made there? You noticed it, and it helped you to . . ."

Another important part of valuing student mistakes is really making use of them, and teaching students how to use them. This shows that our appreciation of errors is more than lip service. We can encourage students to analyze their mistakes by posing questions such as, "Why did you think it sounded like that?", "What was going on, to cause this mistake?", or "How did this mistake affect your understanding of the whole passage?" We can ask students to regularly indicate their degree of confidence alongside their answer in listening activities such as comprehension questions and filling in blanks on a transcript. This can help them remember to monitor their comprehension and update their hypotheses when needed, as well as add information to their analysis of errors.

Finally, we can set an example by telling students about mistakes we have made in language learning and how we learned from them. We can invite students to tell stories about misunderstandings they have experienced, and treat those stories with humor and appreciation. In language learning, I believe an error-friendly classroom is a safe and effective classroom.

---

*Thanks to Nancy Elliott for piloting the paused transcription activities in her classes!

References

Cauldwell, R. (2018). *A syllabus for listening: Decoding*. Speech in Action.

Council of Europe. (2001). *Common European framework for reference of languages: Learning, teaching and assessment*. Cambridge University Press.

Cross, J. (2009). Diagnosing the process, text, and intrusion problems responsible for L2 listeners' decoding errors. *Asian ELF Journal, 11*(2), 31–53.

Elkhafaifi, H. (2005). Listening comprehension and anxiety in the Arabic language classroom. *Modern Language Journal, 89*(2), 206–220. https://doi.org/10.1111/j.1540-4781.2005.00275.x

Emadi, M. (2015). Individual dynamic assessment: An analysis of Iranian EFL learners' listening comprehension errors. *Theory and Practice in Language Studies, 5*(12), 2599–2605. https://doi.org/10.17507/tpls.0512.22

Estes, R. L. (2014). *Lexical segmentation in Spanish L2 listening* [Unpublished doctoral dissertation]. University of California at Davis.

Field, J. (2004). An insight into listeners' problems: Too much bottom-up or too much top-down? *System, 32*(3), 363–377. https://doi.org/10.1016/j.system.2004.05.002

Field, J. (2008a). Bricks or mortar: Which parts of the input does a second language listener rely on? *TESOL Quarterly, 42*(2), 411–432. https://doi.org/10.1002/j.1545-7249.2008.tb00139.x

Field, J. (2008b). *Listening in the language classroom*. Cambridge University Press.

Field, J. (2008c). Revising segmentation hypotheses in first and second language listening. *System, 36*(1), 35–51. https://doi.org/10.1016/j.system.2007.10.003

Gao, L. (2014). *An exploration of L2 listening problems and their causes* [Unpublished doctoral dissertation]. University of Nottingham.

Goh, C. (1999). How much do learners know about the factors that influence their listening comprehension? *Hong Kong Journal of Applied Linguistics, 4*(1), 17–40.

Goh, C. (2000). A cognitive perspective on language learners' listening comprehension problems. *System, 28*(1), 55–75. https://doi.org/10.1016/s0346-251x(99)00060-3

Graham, S. (2006). Listening comprehension: The learners' perspective. *System, 34*(2), 165–182. https://doi.org/10.1016/j.system.2005.11.001

Graham, S., Santos, D., & Francis-Brophy, E. (2014). Teacher beliefs about listening in a foreign language. *Teaching and Teacher Education, 40*, 44–60. https://doi.org/10.1016/j.tate.2014.01.007

Kim, J.-H. (2000). Foreign language listening anxiety: A study of Korean students learning English. *English Teaching, 57*(2), 3–34.

Liu, N. F. (2002). *Processing problems in L2 comprehension of university students in Hong Kong* [Unpublished doctoral dissertation]. The Hong Kong Polytechnic University.

Mirzaei, S., Meshgi, K., & Kawahara, T. (2017). *Detecting listening difficulty for second language learners using Automatic Speech Recognition errors.* 7th ISCA Workshop on Speech and Language Technology in Education, Stockholm, Sweden. https://doi.org/10.21437/SLaTE.2017-27

Nation, I., S., P., & Newton, J. (2009). *Teaching ESL/EFL speaking and listening*. Routledge.

Pemberton, R. (1995). Listening to listeners: Methodological issues in an investigation of listening difficulty. In K. Wong & C. Green, (Eds.), *Thinking language* (pp 169–182). Language Centre, The Hong Kong University of Science and Technology.

Richards, J. (2005). Second thoughts on teaching listening. *Regional Language Centre Journal 36*(1), 85–92. https://doi.org/10.1177/0033688205053484

Schmidt, R. (1990). The role of consciousness in second language learning. *Applied Linguistics, 11*, 129–158. https://doi.org/10.1093/applin/11.2.129

Sheppard, B., & Butler, B. (2017). Insights into student listening from paused transcription. *The CATESOL Journal, 29*(2), 81–107.

Siegel, J. (2014). Exploring L2 listening instruction: Examinations of practice. *ELT Journal, 6*(1), 22–30. https://doi.org/10.1093/elt/cct058

Siegel, J., & Siegel, A. (2015). Getting to the bottom of L2 listening instruction: Making a case for bottom-up activities. *Studies in Second Language Learning and Teaching, 5*(4), 637–662. https://doi.org/10.14746/ssllt.2015.5.4.6

Vandergrift, L. (2003). Orchestrating strategy use: Toward a model of the skilled second language listener. *Language Learning, 53*(3), 463–496. https://doi.org/10.1111/1467-9922.00232

Vandergrift, L. (2004). Listening to learn or learning to listen? *Annual Review of Applied Linguistics, 24*(1), 3–25. https://doi.org/10.1017/S0267190504000017

Vandergrift, L. (2007). Recent developments in second and foreign language listening comprehension research. *Language Teaching, 40,* 191–210. https://doi.org/10.1017/s0261444807004338

Vandergrift, L., & Goh, C. (2012). *Teaching and learning second language listening: Metacognition in action*. Routledge.

Van Zeeland, H., & Schmitt, N. (2012). Lexical coverage in L1 and L2 listening comprehension: The same or different from reading comprehension? *Applied Linguistics, 34*(4), 457–479.

Ward, J. (2018). *Second language listening in an academic context: Lexical, perceptual, and contextual cues to word recognition* [Unpublished doctoral dissertation]. University of Reading.

Zeng, Y. (2007). *Metacognitive instruction in listening: A study of Chinese non-English major undergraduates* (PE1128 Zen) [Master's thesis]. National Institute of Education, Nanyang Technological University.

BETH SHEPPARD teaches languages at the University of Oregon and Lane Community College and trains teachers internationally. Beth is interested in instruction and assessment for second language listening, speaking, and pronunciation, as well as classroom techniques in support of language revitalization.

Appendix A: Paused Transcription Handout

Paused Transcription

This is a technique that can give you and your teacher more information about what you are able to understand when you listen. You will hear an extended audio text; just listen as usual. Every now and then, there will be a beep and pause, and you should write down the phrase you heard right before the beep. After a pause, the audio will continue, and then there will be another beep and pause. Write the phrase, and keep listening.

Warm Up: "Same & Different"

Try the activity with this short text. Listen to the audio. When you hear a beep and a pause, write down the last phrase you heard. Only the last four words count, but it's okay if you write more.

1. ______________________________
2. ______________________________
3. ______________________________

Check your answers:
1. in my home country
2. brother likes to travel
3. and we are different

Paused Transcription Activity: "Moral Principles"[1]

Just like the warm-up, listen to the text. When there is a beep, write the last phrase you heard.

1. ______________________________
2. ______________________________
3. ______________________________
4. ______________________________
5. ______________________________
6. ______________________________
7. ______________________________
8. ______________________________
9. ______________________________

[1] From Harvard University. (2009, September 4). Justice: What's the right thing to do? Episode 01 "the moral side of murder" [Video]. YouTube. https://www.youtube.com/watch?v=kBdfcR-8hEY

Now look at the correct answers.

Don't change any of your writing, but circle the correct words that you wrote. Then write the number of words correct (0, 1, 2, 3, or 4) next to each line.

It's still correct if you made a spelling mistake, as long as you understood and wrote the correct word. If you want, you can add notes about your mistakes.

Then, complete the reflection on the back of this paper.

Paused Transcription: Reflection

Today, we're going to consider some of the mistakes in your transcriptions. Please answer the following questions.

1. Which phrase was most difficult for you to transcribe? #_______
2. In your opinion, what made it difficult for you to correctly hear this phrase?

____

____

3. Look at all your other transcriptions from this week, and compare any mistakes to the correct answers. Which one has a mistake that you think is funny or interesting? #________
4. Reflect on your mistake in the phrase you mentioned above. What is interesting about it? What caused the mistake? Is this a common type of mistake for you? Can you think of another time when you made a similar mistake?

____

____

____

Appendix B: Activity Answer Key and Example Corrections to Show to Students

ANSWER KEY

1. the discussions we've had
2. moral thing to do
3. end of the day
4. the thing you do
5. man over the bridge
6. of the act itself
7. each story we considered
8. regardless of the consequences

Example corrections prepared by teacher

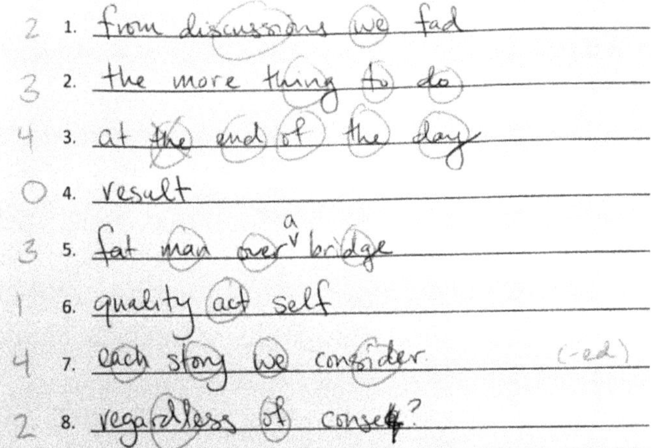
2 1. from discussions we fad
3 2. the more thing to do
4 3. at the end of the day
0 4. result
3 5. fat man over a bridge
1 6. quality act self
4 7. each story we consider (-ed)
2 8. regardless of conseq?

Student corrections

Week 2 Paused Transcription Activity – "Moral Principles"

Just like the warm-up, listen to the text. When there is a beep, write the last phrase you heard.

4 1. from the discussion we've had
3 2. moral thing to do
4 3. the end of the day
2 4. moral the thing you do
4 5. the fat man over the bridge
1 6. morality of the act itself
1 7. each story we consider
1 8. regardless of the something consequences

CONCLUSION

MARNIE REED AND KAREN ROSS

Going Beyond *Listening in the Classroom*: Listening in Messy Speech

The final section of this book addresses the next step: planning classroom listening lessons. Before we address this step, two considerations in addition to those treated in depth in this volume merit our attention, particularly in English as a foreign language (EFL) settings: a heavy test orientation, and listening in the context of English as a global language:

> *The first concern* manifests where high-stakes testing determines the focus of instruction, creating a washback effect. This washback effect—a term used to describe the effects of testing—results in either instructional neglect when listening is not institutionally assessed or test prep emphasis when meeting national or college-entrance listening score requirements dominates teaching and learning activities.
>
> *The second consideration*, global English, ably addressed by Jenkins (2000), concerns the reality that English is the medium of communication most likely to be used by nonnative speaker interlocutors with no language in common. Teachers can refer to the Lingua Franca Core proposed by Jenkins (2002) for guidance on particular pronunciation features that require more, less, or no instructional attention.

In either event—that is, when taking into account either the washback effect or treating English as a global language—it is wise to keep in mind that neither the teacher nor even the students in any given EFL class may know which of those students will one day find themselves in an English-speaking environment, whether for academic, professional, business, or other pursuits. The choice need not be between listening test preparation or listening proficiency preparation. Further, broad access to authentic English language media offers motivating in- and out-of-class opportunities for listening practice.

Therefore, it behooves teachers to provide instruction that will benefit their students in both the short and the potential long term.

Going Beyond *Listening in the Classroom*: Addressing Additional Speech Features

Before you move to the classroom, we'd like to expand upon a key theme that is important to address in your lessons, one that resonates throughout the chapters of this volume: the importance of preparing students for the messiness of naturally occurring, spontaneous speech. As argued in many of the chapters in this collection, it is important that English language instructors make students aware of the range of listening challenges they may encounter, including unexpected and messy, unrehearsed, unedited, colloquial speech both inside and outside of a classroom.

Raising this awareness—of both expected and unexpected challenges—is consistent with a metacognitive approach, requiring students to identify what may be interfering with their own individual listening comprehension. They cannot improve without knowing the real reasons that they are facing listening challenges. For instance, listeners may incorrectly attribute challenges to their own perceived failings, such as the expected and oft-blamed lack of vocabulary, and their own inability to understand native speakers' rapid speech or to decipher different accents. This can lead to frustration and feelings of inadequacy.

Though these expected challenges undoubtedly add to listening struggles, it is important for students to understand that some listening challenges are unexpected and may even be attributable to the speaker using features of speech-in-action. These include fillers, false starts, and other hesitation phenomena (see more below).

Connected speech processes, unless explicitly taught, are also frequently a source of unexpected listening challenges, for example, as described in Brown (2011), how the phrase *assist her* is virtually indistinguishable from *a sister* in naturally occurring speech.

Another great example of a problem with connected speech processes and bottom-up processing can be found in a classroom exchange a former MATESOL student shared recently, which highlights the need to raise both learner and teacher awareness of one of these unexpected listening challenges. It seems the ESL class the student was observing had been engaged in a read aloud activity before taking their midmorning break. When the class returned, a student was selected by name and asked to resume the reading, "Where it says, *It'll*." The student was silent, unable to find what was perceived as "IDL" anywhere on the page. As the instructor repeated her increasingly insistent requests to resume reading, the student turned to a classmate for assistance, further provoking the annoyance of the instructor at the designated reader's seeming intransigence.

This former student, herself a nonnative English speaker, was able to draw upon what she'd learned about connected speech in her MATESOL courses to understand exactly what was happening: The teacher had contracted *it will* to *it'll* (triggering the flapped allophonic variant of /t/, [ɪɾəl]), rendering the contraction unrecognizable in speech. The MATESOL student discreetly met with the instructor after class to illuminate the source of the breakdown in the read aloud task, thus demonstrating that instruction in one of the listening challenges, connected speech processes, is learnable, and therefore teachable. We believe that the chapters in this book provide inspiration and practical suggestions for instructors who wish to teach their students how to listen.

Other listening challenges include figurative, idiomatic, and colloquial uses of vocabulary. For instance, a student who does not know that *make of* can mean *think of* may not know how to answer the question, "What do you make of the assigned reading?"; likewise, a professor asking, "What are the takeaways?" isn't referring to the food you brought home from a restaurant. Similarly, students unfamiliar with article usage may be insensitive to nuances that affect meaning, such as the difference between "Do you have time?" and "Do you have the time?" or be aware that a person taking *the* stand is testifying in court, while a person taking *a* stand is taking a position on an issue (Ross, 2019).

In addition to the bottom-up skill building that helps students master "segmentation of the sound stream into meaningful units to interpret the message" (Vandergrift & Goh, 2012, p. 18), as detailed in Chapters 2 through 8, teachers also need to incorporate instruction and practice that acclimates students to listening to unedited speech-in-action. Whereas writers typically have the luxury of multiple drafts to think through the most precise and efficient way to express their message, speakers often use speech to think aloud, embedding their message in seemingly irrelevant asides, hesitations, false starts, and rambling speech that can be exceptionally difficult for L2 listeners to parse.

In academic settings, students often report that they understand their professors but have more difficulty understanding their fellow students' answers to a professor's questions. Inability to understand peer speech causes frustration and inhibition, and students' class participation may suffer for fear of asking a question already asked and answered or contributing a point already made and acknowledged. Often, this difficulty in understanding can be attributed not to the speaker's pace, but to features of speech-in-action that occur when classmates are "thinking out loud" and formulating their thoughts aloud as they answer a question. Students under pressure to respond on the spot in a classroom environment may include some or even all of the following: "Um, I mean I think that there is, there's I think there's something important about, say, her ability to kind of conclude, again, in contrast to other authors, the point that this like this is um like this is like a novel idea, and she's she's willing to kind of imagine that this was a novel point." instead of delivering a much more concise response, such as, "Yes, the author's point was important and new."

Reed (2000) argues that hesitation phenomena, frequently referred to as disfluencies and ubiquitous in both native and nonnative speech though unpredictable in frequency or occurrence, are actually quality control devices used to buy time and forestall errors. Reed notes, however, that hesitation phenomena "clearly pose perception problems for non-native speakers who show little evidence of recognizing them as such" (Reed, 2000, p. 72).

Unique challenges are posed by the use of actual words as fillers, like *say* and *like* and parentheticals. For example, in a news report of a nurse, a listener hears the nurse say, "I don't like sleep." A student could certainly interpret that the nurse does not enjoy sleeping, but in this context, what the nurse said was, "I don't~~, like,~~ sleep"; *like*, in this case, is a filler that the listener would have to filter out to avoid misunderstanding the speaker's message. Proficient listeners deal with speech-in-action by unconsciously editing as they listen. They edit out the words that aren't necessary and fill in the gaps with inferences. In one sense, we might say that the mechanism available in speaking, namely hesitation phenomena, is comparable to the mechanism afforded in writing—for example, Microsoft Word Track Changes—for editing and refining a message. However, though the use of Track Changes is intentional and results in a proofread "clean copy" of the intended message, hesitation phenomena occur unconsciously and must be bypassed in listening in order to discern the intended message.

Raising awareness that hesitation phenomena are found in all languages is recommended to activate reflection on the actual words or filled pause equivalents learners' own first language uses. Drawing attention to first language skill in deploying hesitation phenomena may facilitate transfer to the L2 context of their skill in editing out these phenomena to access the underlying message. Our students, however, need explicit instruction, exposure to naturally occurring texts, and ample practice for this transfer to take place.

To this end, we'd like to conclude with some practical suggestions for preparing students to effectively manage speech in action.

1. Utilize pre- and postlistening surveys such as those suggested in Chapter 6. To effectively plan, monitor, and improve their listening skills, students must first be able to articulate what real-life listening challenges exist, what their individual challenges are, and what strategies they can use in order to improve. Preinstruction diagnostics provide a baseline for comparison at semester-end assessment.
2. When choosing listening materials, deliberately select those that include examples of the listening challenges described in this book. Short YouTube, podcast, and other widely available materials, including those delivered by nonnative speakers, provide authentic samples with naturally occurring speech-in-action features, including fillers, hesitations, backtracking, and colloquial speech as well as opportunities to extend listening comprehension to highly intelligible, albeit accented speakers, as recommended by Thomson (2018).
3. Postlistening, have students review a transcript of the listening piece and self-evaluate where they may have missed the meaning and why, that is, whether it's a lack of vocabulary or another of the listening challenges.
4. Remind students that while they can control their preparation by building their knowledge of context, language, and the speech signal (Reed, 2019),

impediments may also be attributable to *a speaker's* lack of organization, use of fillers, hesitation phenomena, and backtracking. This is an excellent way of reminding students of their obligations as speakers and giving them opportunities to practice their own speaking skills to guide their listeners.

5. End as you began, with a postlistening survey. Discuss the survey in class and evaluate if individual students recognize their improvement, can identify their individual listening challenges, and have developed strategies for improving.

Given the limited time we have in our courses, it is important to give students tools to continue to build their confidence and skills. Incorporate listening activities that address messy, natural, colloquial speech. Remind students that listening more will not, alone, improve their listening (Vandergrift & Goh, 2012). Encourage them to practice producing words, in combination with other words especially, that they can recognize in writing but that may sound vastly different when spoken. Practicing the speech-in-action features outside of class is good preparation for promoting listening comprehension during class. Using the skills gleaned from the chapters in this volume will benefit not only students' listening but also their speaking in class and interacting with their professors, peers, and conversational interlocutors both in and out of class.

References

Brown, S. (2011). *Listening myths: Applying second language research to classroom teaching.* The University of Michigan Press.

Jenkins, J. (2000). *The phonology of English as an international language.* Oxford University Press.

Jenkins, J. (2002). A sociolinguistically-based, empirically-researched pronunciation syllabus for English as an International Language. *Applied Linguistics, 23*(1), 83–103. https://doi.org/10.1093/applin/23.1.83

Reed, M. (2019). Listening skills instruction: Practical tips for processing aural input. In J. Levis, C. Nagle, & E. Todey (Eds.), *Proceedings of the 10th pronunciation in second language learning and teaching conference* (pp. 401–412). Iowa State University.

Reed, M. (2000). He who hesitates: Hesitation phenomena as quality control in speech production, obstacles in non-native speech perception. *Journal of Education 82*(3), 67–91. https://doi.org/10.1177/002205740018200306

Ross, K. M. (2019). *Essential legal English in context: Understanding the vocabulary of US law and government.* NYU Press.

Thomson, R. (2018). High variability [pronunciation] training (HVPT): A proven technique about which every language teacher and learner ought to know. *Journal of Second Language Pronunciation, 42*(2), 208–231. https://doi.org/10.1075/jslp.17038.tho

Vandergrift, L., & Goh, C. (2012). *Teaching and learning second language listening: Metacognition in action.* Routledge.

MARNIE REED is professor of education and affiliated faculty in the Program in Linguistics at Boston University. She is also director of the graduate program in Teaching English to Speakers of Other Languages (TESOL) in the College of Education, where she teaches courses in linguistics, second language acquisition, and applied phonology.

KAREN ROSS is the director of the Legal English Program and deputy director of the Graduate Lawyering Program at New York University School of Law, where she teaches in the LL.M program. She holds an MA in TESOL and a Juris Doctor degree. Her book, *Essential Legal English in Context: Understanding the Vocabulary of US Law and Government* (NYU Press, 2019) explores legal vocabulary related to the three levels and branches of contemporary U.S. government.

GLOSSARY OF TERMS

Terms in this glossary are defined as they relate to listening and speaking.

A

acoustic cues: Physically observable patterns in the speech signal (e.g., place, manner, and voicing for consonants or duration for vowels).

adjacency pairs: Conversational turn sequences (e.g., request for information/providing information; request for favor/granting or declining the favor; apology/acceptance).

assimilation: A process whereby one sound is affected by its neighboring sounds.

B

bottom-up strategies: Text or sound-driven strategies to improve decoding ability needed to identify word boundaries, segment continuous speech, etc.

C

clause: A speech processing unit containing a verb corresponding to the syntactic clause structure.

cloze test: A gap-fill or fill-in-the blank activity whereby blank lines represent word(s) from a listening passage.

connected speech: The process by which words in continuous speech are reduced (e.g., *here 'n now*), contracted (*I'd, I've*), altered (gonna, wanna), etc.

constituents: Words or groups of words that function as a single grammatical unit within a hierarchical structure.

D

discourse markers: Variously described as fillers (*you know, I mean*) or organizational guides. Types include chronological (*first, second*), contrast (*on the other hand*), enumeration, etc. Also referred to as *cue words, continuers,* or *minimal responses.*

disfluencies/dysfluencies: Words (e.g., *say, like, you know*), filled pauses (e.g., *er, uh, uhm*), false starts, backtracking, etc., that disrupt the continuous flow of speech.

E

elision: A process by which a phoneme is omitted or where words run together in continuous speech. Also referred to as *juncture* or *linking*.

H

hesitations: Hesitation phenomena include silent pauses of 250 milliseconds or greater, filled pauses (*er, uhm*), discourse markers (*well, like, say*), repetitions, repair, and other devices referred to as either dysfluencies or as quality control devices that buy time, for example for word searches. See also *disfluencies*.

M

metacognition: Thinking about one's thinking, facilitating awareness, monitoring and regulating, and evaluation of one's mental processes, including learning.

metacognitive instruction: An approach that promotes learner awareness of their individual learning preferences, the demands of the learning task, and management and evaluation of strategy use in the service of learning.

metalanguage: (Semi)technical terminology used to analyze or describe language.

metalinguistic awareness: Ability to objectify language using relevant terms to think and talk about, not just use, language.

minimal pair: A pair of otherwise identical words that differ in one and only one sound: *cat/bat; cat/cab*.

P

parsing: Segmenting a continuous stream of speech into its component words and syntactic units.

phoneme: Contrastive consonant or vowel speech sounds in a language, denoted within slashes, such as /p/ in *pat* and /b/ in *bat*.

pitch: The rise and fall of the voice determined by the frequency of vocal cord vibration, measured in Hertz.

prosody: The use of pitch, intensity, and duration on syllables and larger units of speech to convey information about the structure and meaning of an utterance. Also referred to as *melody*.

S

schema: Cognitive framework for organizing information.

segmentation: In continuous speech, identifying where one meaningful unit (e.g., word or morpheme) ends and the next begins.

T

thought group: Short grammatically coherent segments or units into which a continuous stream of speech is divided. Also referred to as *tone unit*.

top-down strategies: Knowledge or schema-driven strategies that activate background information, prior knowledge, or world knowledge to facilitate processing orthographic or aural input.

V

voicing: Term used to describe vocal cord vibration in the production of speech sounds. Vowels are produced with vocal cord vibration; consonants can be either voiceless or voiced.

Transcription Key

Consonants

/p/	pie, nap
/b/	baby, lab
/t/	team, cat
/d/	do, sad
/k/	cat, like
/g/	go, big
/tʃ/	chin, touch
/dʒ/	jam, budge
/f/	fill, life
/v/	van, give
/θ/	thin, math
/ð/	then, breathe
/s/	sit, mess
/z/	zoo, buzz
/ʃ/	shoe, wash
/ʒ/	beige
/h/	how, ahead
/m/	me, seem
/n/	new, sun
/ŋ/	ring
/w/	win, away
/hw/	when
/l/	late, fall
/r/	red, car
/y/	yes, royal

Vowels

/iy/	beat, teen
/ɪ/	pin, sit
/ey/	late, pain
/ɛ/	red, bread
/æ/	black, mat
/ɑ/	box, father
/ɔ/	saw, bought
/ow/	so, toe
/ʊ/	good, could
/uw/	boot, blue
/ay/	time, lie
/aw/	how, cloud
/ɔy/	boy, noise
/ʌ/	some, sun
/ɝ/	bird, world

Unstressed Vowels

/ə/	focus, allow
/əʳ/	mother, banker
/i/	city, happy
/ɪ/	music, dancing
/o/	narrow, window
/u/	into, igloo

Transcription Symbols

//	Virgules represent the abstract phonemes, or distinctive sounds, in a language.
[]	Brackets represent how the phonemes are actually articulated.

www.ingramcontent.com/pod-product-compliance
Ingram Content Group UK Ltd.
Pitfield, Milton Keynes, MK11 3LW, UK
UKHW060611180726
13836UKWH00011B/2499